The Making of
Hmong America

The Making of Hmong America

Forty Years after the Secret War

Kou Yang

LEXINGTON BOOKS

Lanham • Boulder • New York • London

Published by Lexington Books
An imprint of The Rowman & Littlefield Publishing Group, Inc.
4501 Forbes Boulevard, Suite 200, Lanham, Maryland 20706
www.rowman.com

Unit A, Whitacre Mews, 26-34 Stannary Street, London SE11 4AB

British Library Cataloguing in Publication Information Available

Library of Congress Cataloging-in-Publication Data

Names: Yang, Kou, author.
Title: The making of Hmong America : forty years after the secret war / Kou Yang.
Description: Lanham, MD : Lexington Books, [2017] | Includes bibliographical
    references and index.
Identifiers: LCCN 2017029848 (print) | LCCN 2017028579 (ebook)
Subjects: LCSH: Hmong Americans—History. | Hmong Americans—Ethnic identity.
    | Hmong Americans—Cultural assimilation. | Hmong Americans—Relocation. |
    Political refugees—United States—History.
Classification: LCC E184.H55 (print) | LCC E184.H55 Y38 2017 (ebook) | DDC
    305.8959/72073—dc23
LC record available at https://lccn.loc.gov/2017029848

ISBN 9781498546454 (cloth)
ISBN 9781498546478 (pbk.)
ISBN 9781498546461 (electronic)

Dedication

I dedicate this book to the loving memory of my father, Say Pao Yang (Nchaiv Pov Yaj), and my uncles, Boua Tong (Npuag Tooj Yaj) Yang and Qiam Yang (Qiam Yaj). The Secret War in Laos hit my family hard: my uncle, Qiam Yang, a military officer, was killed in action at the beginning of 1972. My father, Say Pao Yang, and my uncle, Boua Tong Yang, were both assassinated at the end of 1972 in the month of December. The scars of the war continue to be with my family, to this day. To honor our losses, and prevent it from happening to others, I have committed myself to non-violence and devoted my life to humanitarian work, education, and peace-building. War only brings suffering, hardships, hatred, and sorrow; but peace can bring love, joy, happiness, compassion, prosperity, and most importantly, hope.

Contents

Acknowledgments

After publishing my "40 Years After the Vietnam War: Celebrating the Contributions of Indochinese refugees to the USA," I began to think about drafting a commentary on the Hmong's forty years of becoming American. This thought led me to explore further and do more research on this topic. One research led to another; I found more and more information on the topic. I then began the rough draft. The more I dug deeper, the more information I found, so I kept adding new information to the rough draft. In particular, not only did I want to discuss about the state of Hmong Americans and their success stories, but I wanted to talk about the contentious politics behind their refugee exodus and the United States' initial refusal to admit Hmong refugees following the communist takeover of Laos in 1975. For instance, some newly discovered information revealed that in May of 1975, the United Nations High Commissioner for Refugees did not want to classify Hmong as refugees because, unlike Cambodia and South Vietnam, there was no official taking over of Laos by the Pathet Lao (Lao Patriotic Front or Neo Lao Hak Xat), and the Provisional Government of National Union was still in place in Laos. I became more curious and wanted to include more background knowledge in my draft; I learned of more information after meeting with Lionel Rosen-blatt, a former State Department official, who came to Fresno to present at the symposium on "The History Behind the Hmong Refugee Exodus," which was held at Fresno City College on August 22, 2015. My interview with Yang See and other Hmong who witnessed the challenges of resettling Hmong to the West also encouraged me to add more information to the original draft. The more I spoke to people, the more information I gathered, and I added a bit more here and there to the draft. Eventually, the rough draft became much longer than an article. Therefore, I decided to write it as a book, in hopes that young Hmong will find it useful in learning about their history. In addition, I hope that it will be useful to the general public as well, so that they may have more information about the Hmong, and their resettlement and adaption to life in the United States.

My special thanks go to Pos Moua (Pos Muas), Chao R. Lee (Nyiaj Txos Lis), Gregg E. Umipeg II, and Senda Chang for their proofreading of the manuscript. Senda Chang also helped me with the revision and index of this book. Chee Yang also helped me with background information on the 1975–1976 interviews and the U.S. resettlement process for Hmong refugees. The symposium on "The History Behind the Hmong Refugee Exodus" was also helpful. I am indebted to Lionel Rosenblatt for his generosity in sharing with me his paper, "How The Hmong Came to Be in the U.S." He also provided the foreword for this book. Moreover, as a Hmong person, I am eternally thankful to both Lionel Rosenblatt and Jerry "Hog" Daniels (deceased), a case officer for the Central Intelligence Agency, and to others, including but not limited to Yang See, Lucky Lue Yang, Yang Chee, and MacAllan Thompson, for their passion and tireless advocacy that made it possible for the resettlement of Hmong refugees to the United States. While doing research for this book, Cha Moua drove me from California to Iowa, Minnesota, Montana, and then back to California. Cha Moua also provided me with photos and information about the early years of the Hmong in Missoula, Montana, and beyond. For this, I say "ua tsaug" to Cha Moua from the bottom of my heart. Bruce Bliatout also provided me with a list of Hmong students studying in the United States prior to 1975. My sincere thanks also go to Xia Vue Yang, Master Sergeant Shua P. Yang, Chief Chuepheng Lo, Vungping Yang, and many more individuals, who have assisted me during my gathering of information for this book.

Lastly, without the support and love from my wife Jennifer, this project may not have been possible. Although the year 2015 was a challenging year for her health and work, she did her very best to take charge of family affairs, so that I could travel and work on this book.

Foreword

In early 1975, with a few other and younger State Department Foreign Service officers who served in Vietnam, we began pushing for the evacuation of Vietnamese who had worked with the allied government of South Vietnam, or for the United States. Eventually the Interagency Task Force was formed to coordinate the evacuation of up to 150,000 refugees from Cambodia, Vietnam, and Laos.

In October of 1975, I received authorization from Task Force Director Julia Taft to do a survey of refugees in Thailand, who were from Laos and Cambodia. In the course of that trip, I met the Hmong refugees at Nam Phong Camp in Thailand. I met many Hmong who fought with the United States, and I met Dr. Yang Dao who presented me with a copy of his book about the Hmong. I was struck by the amount of service the Hmong provided to America to support the war, and the fact that despite their vital wartime role, there seemed to be no widespread sense of obligation to resettle them. The U.S. government translated Yang Dao's book into English so that we could educate Americans about the Hmong people. Based in part on my survey report, commencing in January 1976, I was placed in charge of implementing the admission of eleven thousand Indochinese refugees to the United States. Shep Lowman directed the program at the State Department.

The Hmong hoped to stay together, but the only option was to resettle them in the United States or to other countries of resettlement. (Details of this are below).

Kou Yang documents the extraordinary record of success that the Hmong have achieved in the United States—in the professions, academia, the U.S. military, and beyond. Kou Yang himself is a fine example of self-made success in becoming a professor in the California State University system.

One of the most notable Hmong American contributions has been the revival of one of our most respected state capital cities—St. Paul, Minnesota. Those of us who worked so hard to give the Hmong a path to resettlement always predicted they would do well. We have been rewarded beyond our own expectations. Now as their success in the United States grows, there is also the potential of the Hmong American Diaspora to open a new chapter by giving assistance to the Hmong community in Laos. For example, Hmong Americans could provide English as a second language training to young Hmong and others in Laos.

Congratulations to Kou Yang on his fine work.

—Lionel Rosenblatt

Author's note: For additional background on the history of Hmong resettlement in the U.S., please see Lionel Rosenblatt's below paper with inputs from Mac-Allen Thomson. It is a summary of the plight of the Hmong people, their situation during the Secret War in Laos, and their refugee resettlement in the U.S.

We have been asked on many occasions by Hmong American friends to describe how the Hmong came to the United States. We hope this summary provides some useful background.

In early 1975, the U.S.-supported governments in Vietnam, Cambodia, and Laos began to collapse. By early April, prodded by a group of young State Department officers, an Interagency Task Force was formed at the State Department in Washington to evacuate Vietnamese who would be at "high risk" if Cambodia and Vietnam fell. Congressional authority to admit up to 150,000 Indochinese was granted under what was known as "parole authority." A relatively small number of Cambodians were evacuated before Phnom Penh fell to the Khmer Rouge on April 17. On April 30, the government of South Vietnam fell as North Vietnamese troops entered Saigon. A total of more than a hundred thousand Vietnamese were evacuated by air and sea to Guam and the Philippines, and then to the United States. Meanwhile, in Laos, the situation was also deteriorating, somewhat more gradually. In May, some three thousand to thirty-five hundred Hmong were evacuated by air from Long Tieng (Long Cheng) to Nam Phong, a U.S. air base in northeast Thailand. General Vang Pao and his family members were evacuated to Udorn; the general went on to the United States a short time later. The story of the Long Tieng [Long Cheng] air evacuation and the heroic efforts of the U.S. pilots should be described in detail by some of those who have direct knowledge. A key organizing role was played by General Harry C. "Heinie" Aderholt, chief U.S. military officer in Bangkok.

Additional Hmong refugees made their way south from Long Tieng [Long Cheng] and other areas to the Mekong River and crossed into Thailand. Some eight thousand were moved on to Nam Phong, but the latecomers were held up at Nong Khai. Later in the fall of 1975, a refugee camp was opened in Nong Khai to house lowland Lao, Thai Dam, Hmong, and some other highlander refugees from Laos. This camp was operated by the Thai Ministry of Interior with support from the United Nations High Commissioner for Refugees (UNHCR), with funding from the United States and other governments. Hmong and other refugees from Laos were also flowing into a number of smaller camps in the northern Thai provinces of Nan and Chiang Rai. Central Intelligence Agency officer Jerry Daniels and U.S. Agency for International Development staffers Mac Thompson and John Tucker, who all served in Laos during the war, set up a small operation at the U.S. Consulate in Udorn, initially to process Thai Dam refugees, but also to report on the Lao and Hmong refugee situation. Other U.S. officials who had served in Laos and Vietnam set up a small refugee operation in Bangkok under the auspices of the U.S. Embassy. Meanwhile, the evacuees from Vietnam and Cambodia were being resettled under the aegis of the Interagency Task Force using a number of camps located at U.S. military bases. The early wave of Vietnamese and Cambodian refugees was placed in U.S. communities via private U.S. resettlement agencies, then known as voluntary agencies. As this U.S. resettlement process continued, approximately fifteen thousand admission numbers remained under the parole authority granted by Congress in April. In the summer and fall of 1975, about thirty-five hundred refugees from Laos were approved by the U.S. Immigration and Naturalization Service (INS) under this authority. This number included approximately twelve hundred Hmong.

During a late September 1975 visit to Nam Phong by the regional director (based in Hong Kong), Sam Feldman was impressed with meeting Dr. Yang Dao and some Hmong military officers, medics, and nurses in the camp. He then telephoned INS headquarters in Washington and got permission to admit them. There was not, however, any thought of admitting Hmong refugees to the United States after this time. The processing of these refugees was done by the office in Udorn and one that was set up in Bangkok. In August 1975, Lionel Rosenblatt, who was head of the Office of Special Concerns on the Interagency Task Force in Washington, received word that a substantial number of refugees were entering Thailand from Cambodia and Laos. A Cambodian staff member passed along photos of some Cambodian refugees who had been killed in one of the border encampments. Armed with this evidence, Julia Taft, head of the Task Force, authorized Rosenblatt to survey the refugee situation in Thailand and report back to her. In the early autumn of

1975, on a last-minute trip to Nam Phong camp organized by Mac Thompson and Jerry Daniels, Rosenblatt was introduced to the Hmong refugees there, including many who had worked directly for the U.S. government in the war years or in the U.S.-supported Special Guerrilla Unit forces; a significant number were so essential that they had been assigned U.S. government radio call signs. Dr. Yang Dao presented Rosenblatt with a copy of his history of the Hmong, which was translated by the U.S. government from French into English and was very useful in raising awareness about the Hmong within the U.S. government and Congress.

Rosenblatt sent a telegram from Bangkok with his findings to Task Force Chief Julia Taft, who subsequently made the key decision to preserve the unused admission numbers and budgetary funds from 1975 and to admit an additional eleven thousand Indochinese refugees under the April 1975 parole authority. This was a courageous decision, in that there was considerable pressure to end the Indochinese resettlement program when the camps in the United States were emptied and closed in late 1975. Mrs. Taft said that "history would not look kindly on us" if we did not admit refugees in Thailand and elsewhere in southeast Asia who had close associations with the United States.

To implement this decision, Foreign Service Officer Shep Lowman (who had played a major role in the final days of the U.S. Embassy in Saigon in the spring of 1975) agreed to direct the Indochinese refugee effort at the State Department. With Lowman in place in Washington, Rosenblatt was assigned to Thailand as a refugee coordinator to manage the program in Thailand, which came to be known as the Expanded Parole Program. Mac Thompson supervised all U.S. refugee resettlement work on behalf of those fleeing Laos. To implement the program fairly, a point system was used to resettle a family based on its family ties to relatives who were already resettled in the United States and with direct service ties with the U.S. government–supported military in Laos such as the Hmong Special Guerilla Units. Mac Thompson took the lead in designing the point system and Jerry Daniels applied it to the Hmong caseloads. In late 1975, the Hmong from Nam Phong and some other camps were re-located to the newly created Ban Vinai Camp, Pak Chom District in Loei Province. Support for the camp was placed with the UNHCR, as with other refugee camps in Thailand. Most of the Hmong refugee leadership who had escaped from Laos were at Ban Vinai. In early 1976, Rosenblatt and Daniels arranged a pivotal meeting with the Hmong leadership, so that the U.S. side could hear directly from the Hmong about their own wishes for their people's future. The Hmong leaders opened the meeting by asking that the United States thereafter refer to them as Hmong, meaning free men or people, and not Meo with its "savage" connotation as used by others. We readily agreed to this change in nomenclature and this is why the Hmong who were known as Meo during the war years in Laos became known as Hmong in the United States. At the Ban Vinai meeting, Hmong leaders then stated that they would like U.S. government weapons to take and hold Sayaboury Province in Laos, which some Hmong maintained had been promised to the Hmong by the United States in the event that Laos fell to the communists; a list of weapons desired was handed to the U.S. delegation. The U.S. side stated that this was not a viable option. The second choice of the Hmong leaders was for them to be re-grouped in an area of Thailand where they could live on their own. We indicated that Thailand would not likely agree to this. The third choice was to resettle in a third country, all living together. The U.S. side indicated that this would not be feasible, but that we would work toward giving Hmong with close associations to the United States the opportunity to resettle in the United States. We explained that the program was still not finally approved in Washington, but that if and when it was, Hmong would be dispersed around the United States with voluntary agencies finding sponsors for each family, as was done for the Indochinese evacuees and refugees commencing in April 1975. We indicated that Jerry Daniels, with his first-hand familiarity with the Hmong role in Laos, would take the lead in selecting the family heads for resettlement, but that no family would be forced to apply for U.S. resettlement. With some reluctance, the Hmong agreed to these terms. Following this meeting, the race accelerated to develop files on hundreds of Hmong heads of household. Parallel to this, files had to be opened on Iu Mien, Tai Dam, Lao Theung [Kimmu or Khmu], and lowland Lao, as well as on Cambodian and Vietnamese refugees. Final selection would be based on association with the United States based on the point system. All of the eleven thousand refugees had to be selected by the U.S. refugee office and approved by INS prior to June 30, 1976, the end of the U.S. government fiscal year at that time. Each week, the Bangkok refugee office would report on the number of refugees from Laos, Cambodia, and Vietnam being approved. As there were some in Washington who might have raised doubts about the suitability of Hmong and other Highlanders for resettlement in the United States, we did not spotlight that, of the roughly seventy-five hundred approvals for refugees from Laos, about two-thirds were Highlanders. The Bangkok refugee office had trouble obtaining U.S. Embassy and Consulate General Chiang Mai concurrence to interview Hmong and other Highlanders in the camps of northern Thailand until fairly late in the spring of 1976. Rosenblatt and Daniels led the first U.S. team to the north to complete that work in a U.S. military plane provided by General Aderholt, after the Thai Airways flight from Bangkok to Nan departed early, leaving the team and its files stranded in Bangkok. For all Indochinese refugees processed in Thailand in 1976, the bulk of the U.S.

casework was done by American personnel hired by the Intergovernmental Committee for European Migration and seconded to the U.S. refugee offices in Bangkok and Udorn. Initially, all had served in the Peace Corps in Thailand and were able to work six to seven days a week up-country in extreme conditions. There were also large numbers of Thai and Hmong refugee staff. Yang Lue ("Lucky"), Jerry's partner in the war years in Laos, remained with him in the early stages of this work. Opening a file on each refugee family, prioritizing them according to the point system, and presenting them to INS for approval involved a tremendous amount of paperwork initially in the camps, and then in Udorn and Bangkok, and involved transporting trunkloads of files at each stage. After approval, Intergovernmental Committee for European Migration (today known as the International Organization for Migration) handled all of the complex out-processing of refugees, including medical and transport arrangements from the camps to Bangkok and on by air to the United States and other countries of resettlement. The operation was headed by veteran refugee specialist Albert Corcos. Circa 1978, U.S. Vice President Walter Mondale offered the Thai government two million dollars to resettle some of the Hmong in Thailand. The offer inadvertently became public and was rejected flatly by the Royal Thai government. Ultimately, about 105,000 Highlanders from Laos came to the United States. Spurred in large part by the U.S. admission of Hmong, about ten thousand Hmong were also resettled from Thailand to other countries, principally France (including the settlement in French Guiana), which took in a small amount of Hmong starting in 1975, and three thousand to Australia and Canada. Now there are about fifteen thousand Hmong in France and twenty-five hundred in French Guiana. The U.S. Embassy refugee program grew to a staff of several hundred, with most of the Americans, as well as Thai and refugee staff, hired by the International Rescue Committee acting on behalf of all voluntary agencies as the Joint Voluntary Agency. There was some continuing reluctance in the United States, including in the Congress, to resettling large numbers of Hmong on the grounds that they would not assimilate well, that they were "illiterate" (as opposed to pre-literate), and not adaptable to Western living. The State Department held firm and the Hmong proved that they could adapt successfully to the United States in locations across the country. Tens of thousands more Hmong "self-resettled" in Thailand, including some families who chose this rather than going to the United States. A significant number of Hmong who tried to escape to Thailand from Laos were killed by communist forces in Laos or drowned trying to cross the Mekong. Thai authorities generally permitted the Hmong to enter Thailand, though there were exceptions, and most Hmong arriving across the river were stripped of any valuables. U.S. officials played an active role in monitoring and trying to assist the new arrivals. In 1982, Jerry Daniels died in Bangkok while still in service with the U.S. refugee office there. He is still revered by the Hmong and his American colleagues for his work in Laos and in the refugee program. In the early 1990s, a small group of Hmong were repatriated back to Laos under the UNHCR program. Resettlement support for them in Laos was very poor. During that time the remaining Hmong refugees in camps in Thailand were re-grouped at NaPho Camp in Nakhon Phanom Province. From there, subsequent voluntary repatriation to Laos awaited those Hmong who had not opted to resettle abroad (or had been rejected). An informal settlement of tens of thousands of Hmong grew up at Wat Tham Krabok in Saraburi Province in central Thailand. In 2003, about fifteen thousand of this group were offered an option to resettle in the United States. The Thai Abbot of the Wat was very sympathetic to the Hmong and helped protect them, assisted by an American Buddhist monk, Gordon Baltimore. In December 2009, a last group of about forty-five hundred Hmong who were living in Petchabun Province were forced back to Laos, as was a small group in the Thai Immigration detention center in Nong Khai, all of whom had been given refugee status by UNHCR and promised resettlement abroad. There remains a large, but unknown, number of Lao Highlanders living in Thailand. Plus about five hundred thousand Hmong are living in Laos.

After resettlement in the United States, Hmong Americans maintained contact with families and friends and proved to be very flexible in moving away from adverse resettlement areas in search of better opportunity. One such story is the quest of Kue Chaw (U.S. call sign "Bison"), who went from Philadelphia across the country and back to find a new home in North Carolina for himself and many in his group. The Hmong American community should gather such tales to chronicle the history of how Hmong Americans re-grouped throughout the country over the pasty forty years. It is also time to gather profiles of distinguished Hmong Americans and other Lao Highlanders and the contributions that they have made and are making to America. Today Hmong Americans are succeeding in the whole spectrum of professions across the United States, enriching our country as are Hmong in other nations. Hmong Americans visit Laos in large numbers and are building bridges to the Hmong communities of Laos, where their families originated. Lionel Rosenblatt is retired in Washington, District of Columbia, and works to try to assist the Mlabri hill people ("People of the Yellow Leaf") of northern Thailand, many of whose forebears followed the Hmong refugees out to Nan Province in 1976. Mac Thompson is retired in Thailand and visits northeastern Laos two to four times a year to fund construction of schoolrooms and other projects.

Chapter One

Introduction

The year 2015 marks the fortieth anniversary of the presence of Hmong refugees in the United States of America, a milestone to reflect on the progress of the last four decades, assess the present socio-economic situation, and to forge a way forward toward the future. To mark this special anniversary, I want to offer a brief overview of the past and current progress of the Hmong American community. This review focuses more on individual stories of Hmong Americans rather than delving into broader issues and challenges facing the Hmong American community.

The major theme of this book is the state of Hmong Americans in 2015, more so to examine some of their socio-economic and contributions to the United States, their adopted country. From a historical point of view, the present links to the past, and as such, this review provides a historical account of the war experience of the Hmong, their refugee exodus, and the challenges of finding third countries to take Hmong refugees. It includes a brief discussion of their past struggles to adapt to life in the United States as well as their contributions, and other contemporary issues. Unlike other major refugee groups from Indochina, the Hmong, an ethnic minority from the highlands of Laos, were by and large linguistically, culturally, educationally, and technologically unprepared to interface with the cultural shocks of urban life in the United States, a country that is associated with having the largest economy and best developed capitalism among the most industrialized nations in the world. As such, the cultural gap between the Hmong culture and the American culture is profound beyond their understanding, their wisdom, and their coping skills. Like other previous refugees and immigrants who came to the United States before them, the Hmong encountered many acculturation problems and needs during their four decades of transition in America. Despite these challenges, the Hmong have overcome many social and economic obstacles, and it appears that they might thrive in America.

This book describes the Hmong American community as a community of refugees, uprooted from the highlands of the war-torn country of Laos. Their forty years of becoming American has been a narrative of both challenge and success stories. The first fifteen years were preoccupied with acculturation issues as they were in the transitional stage to a better life, where they began to adapt and take control of their problems and needs in the 1990s. At the dawn of the twenty-first century, Hmong Americans began another stage of their adaption, which I call the "Hmong American Era," when the median age of the Hmong population was just about twenty years old, and most of them were born in the United States to first-generation parents. By the year 2000, the Hmong American community appeared to take firm roots in the United States as they have established many small Hmong American institutions, such as the Center for Hmong Studies at Concordia University St. Paul, *Hmong Studies Journal*, Hmong Cultural Center, Hmong Archives, *Hmong Times*, Hmong TV, and other business ventures like the Hmong International Market and the Hmong Village Shopping Center in St. Paul, Minnesota. Many young Hmong have entered diverse professions, including art, computer, corporate America, dentistry, education, engineering, film industries, high-tech, medicine, military, politics, and so on. As such, this book highlights some of the challenges and success stories of Hmong Americans who have overcome many barriers and obstacles as they go through the salad bowl process of becoming American.

Who are the Hmong? This is a common question many readers often ask, especially outsiders who are not familiar with the Hmong; therefore, a brief introduction of the Hmong is necessary. The Hmong, one of the three major groups lumped under the name Miao, is among many Asian ethnic groups found in China, Vietnam, Laos, Myanmar, and Thailand. After the end of the Secret War in Laos in 1975, some Hmong were resettled to Argentina, Australia, Canada, Germany, France (including French Guiana), the Netherlands, and the United States. There are also a few Hmong who work and live in Africa, namely Liberia and Senegal. China, the ancestral homeland of the Hmong, continues to have about three to four million Hmong (known as Western Miao speakers in China); they live mostly in the triangle of Guizhou/ Sichuan and Yunnan, and Quangxi and southern Yunnan.[1] With a population of more than a million,[2] the Hmong is the eighth largest ethnic group in Vietnam, spreading from the border of China to many northern provinces, including Ha Giang, Lao Cai, Lai Cau, Dien Bien Phu, and Son La. Laos has the third largest Hmong population in Asia, estimated to be between 350,000 and 400,000[3]; they migrated from China to Laos more than two hundred years ago and have gradually spread from northern Laos to central Laos. The Hmong in Thailand and Myanmar are the least known; it is estimated that the Hmong population in Thailand is about 150,000 and there is just little over 10,000 for Myanmar.[4] Outside of Asia, the United States has a Hmong population of little more than 300,000[5]; followed by France, 15,000 (including those in French Guiana); Australia, 3,000; and a similar Hmong population in Canada. Germany, the Netherlands, and Argentina each has a Hmong population of less than one hundred.[6] It is also known that one Hmong person is working and living in Liberia, and a Hmong family is working and living in Senegal, Africa.

The Hmong in the United States came to this country as refugees of the Secret War in Laos, so it is essential to make a brief introduction of the Hmong in Laos in their historical context. The history of Hmong of Laos can be traced back to ancient China during and toward the end of the Qing Dynasty (1644 to 1911). Population pressure, economic difficulty, lack of arable lands, tax, rebellions, and civil wars in China during the seventeenth, eighteenth, and nineteenth centuries pushed many Chinese to move southward and into southeast Asian countries. Some of the Hmong in southwest China were also pushed to make a southward migration into Guangxi and southern Yunnan. This migration, however, was not a one-time migration nor in one direction, but occurred in multiple waves and might have gone in many directions, including back and forth. Gradually, some of these Hmong in Guangxi and southern Yunnan were pushed further into Vietnam, then to Laos and Thailand.[7] It is believed that a small number of Hmong migrated into Indochina during the eighteenth century· and it is said that some of them entered Laos between the end of the eighteenth century and early nineteenth century.[8] To keep peace with other ethnic groups, who had already occupied the midland and the fertile lowlands, the Hmong built their houses on the highlands, where they found virgin forests with an abundance of wild animals, and plenty of lands to be used for their slash-and-burn fields. In his "Ethnic Minorities and National Building in Laos: The Hmong in the Lao State," Gary Yia Lee wrote:

> On a fine day in the middle of the dry season, the Lao farmers living in the lowlands nearest to the Hmong looked up to the highlands. They saw nothing but thick smoke burning out of green jungles. This was indeed most unusual, for in all their lives these impenetrable forests had never given up so much grey and black smoke for weeks on end. Perhaps, the evil jungle spirits were angry and were burning up the hills? As quickly as the Lao villagers could run, they reported the strange sighting to their local overlord who sent a few of his best men up the mountains for a closer inspection. Cutting their way through uncharted terrain, they reached where the smoke came from. They discovered

that patches upon patches of virgin forests had been cleared, left to dry and then were burned. Yet no one seemed to be in sight. After much searching, they then found what appeared to be a human settlement perched on a mountain ridge. This was, however, no ordinary Lao village, for all the houses were built on dirt floors instead of on stilts. When the Lao approached the village, all the inhabitants took to the jungle with their children and possessions on the back. These people must be savages, indeed. Otherwise, why would they flee at the sight of other human beings? And look at the spoons and bowls on the kitchen shelves: they were all carved from wood. These foreigners must be really primitive, for no Lao would use wooden kitchen utensils. The country had probably been invaded again, but this time not by the usual Vietnamese from the East who always come with armed troops.[9]

Lee continued to describe that the Lord of Muong Kham (ເມືອງ ຄາ), who controlled the Nong Het area, reported the event to the King of Xieng Khouang or Phuan Kingdom (ອານາຈັກ ພວນ), in whose domain the events took place. The king said to the emissaries from the Lord of Muong Kham, "Return to your master, and tell him not to be alarmed. These forest people are none other than my own subjects. If they prefer living in the highlands, let them be. We will pay them our own visit when the time is appropriate." The king soon sent one of his representatives to see the Hmong and demanded that they pay taxes in return for permission to live in the hills of the northern state.[10] The Hmong have since continued living in the Nong Het region in Xieng Khouang Province and paying tax to the king of the Phuan Kingdom (Xieng Khouang).

By the time the French colonized Laos in 1893, the Hmong might have already migrated to many parts of northern Laos. As France consolidated its colonial administration of the whole Indochina, including Laos, the French masters mandated the Hmong and all subjects to pay their taxes directly to the French. This deprived tax revenues from the local Lao authority, who in turn abused their power to collect their own tax to enrich themselves, creating a burden of double taxes on the Hmong and other subjects. The Hmong felt victimized by these double tax systems, so they rebelled in 1896[11]; this was one of the first rebellions against the French by the people of Laos. Another bigger and bloodier Hmong rebellion against the French occurred from 1918 to 1921, and it was led by Pachay Vue. During this rebellion, Lo Bliayao, who was appointed by the French and held the highest Hmong civilian title, Kiatong (Canton), was able to help the French successfully suppress Pachay's revolt. Pachay was arrested and executed in 1921, along with many Hmong leaders who sided with Pachay. Those who were not leaders had to pay compensation to the French, which is described by Gary Yia Lee as follows:

Altogether, 375 kilograms of silver bars and coins were collected from the Hmong. Many who could not pay had to sell or pawn their children and possessions. The French were not the only ones benefiting financially from the rebellion. Lo Blia Yao [Bliayao], who helped the French put down the revolt in Nong Het also gained incredible wealth acting as collector of these war compensations. The cattle given to him as Kiatong filled a valley which took three hours to walk though, and the money he amassed filled a metal trunk which two strong men could not lift.[12]

The Hmong in Nong Het, thereafter, came under the control of Lo Bliayao, who ruled the area until he died in 1933. His death was succeeded by Song Tou Lobliayao, his eldest son, and Ly Foung, his secretary and son-in-law. Song Tou later resigned his post, and the whole region of Nong Het went to the domination of Ly Foung and the Lee clan. This development became a rival as a result of a family feud which led to two competing factions between the two clans: Lo and Lee. The split between the Lo and Lee clans would eventually set a collision course for the Hmong people of Laos during the Secret War years.

The Japanese began to occupy Indochina in 1940 as Japanese troops swept through the Pacific onto the Far East. However, as World War II was drawing near to an end in favor of the Allied forces in Europe and the Vichy government was ousted, the French Commissar in Xieng Khouang sent two of his right-hand men to see Touby Lyfoung (1917–1979) in Nam Kuang in 1944. Unlike previous Hmong leaders, Touby, who was the son of Ly Foung (Lis Txhiaj Foom) and May Lobliayao, had about a tenth-grade education, which was considered highly educated at the time. May (Mais) was the daughter of Lo Bliayao. Their mission was to ask Touby to help French commandos, who would soon appear in the region.[13] A year later, French commandos arrived and asked Touby and the Hmong to help guide them to safety as well as provide them with information about the movement of Japanese troops. Touby and his Hmong began to help the French in their fight against the Japanese, who soon arrived in the Nong Het area. While helping the French and organizing his own partisans (militia), Touby received an urgent message from King Sisavang Vong (ເຈົ້າມະຫາຊີວິດ ສີສະຫວ່າງວົງ,1885–1959) that the French promised independence to Laos after the war, so he and other leaders must be prepared for the independence of Laos.[14] While Touby was helping the French, Faydang Lobliayao, one of the many sons of Lo Bliayao, became a sympathizer of the Japanese, furthering the division of the Hmong in Laos.

World War II came to an end when the United States dropped atomic bombs on Hiroshima and Nagasaki on August 6 and 8, 1945, respectively. The Japanese surrendered to Allied forces, and in Indochina the Japanese authority also surrendered. Many Japanese troops completed suicide, whereas others returned home. The end of World War II also meant the return of the French colonial administration to Indochina, as one the victors of World War II. Faydang Lobliayao, who escaped to Vietnam after World War II, had joined the Viet Minh (League for the Independence of Vietnam) resistance to fight against the French. Touby continued to help the French in their efforts to suppress the Viet Minh movement, and he was generously rewarded by the French and King Sisavang Vong. In 1946, Touby Lyfoung was appointed the district mayor overseeing all the Hmong people in Xieng Khouang Province in addition to being deputy governor of that province. The king also conferred Touby the title of *Phaya Damrong Ritthikay* (ພະຍາ ດຳລົງ ຣິດທິໄກ), a very prestigious title of the kingdom. All of these occurred before Touby's thirtieth birthday.[15]

In addition to the Royal Lao commendations presented to Touby, the French and the king also appointed Toulia Lyfoung (Tub Liab), a younger half-brother of Touby, as a member of the first National Assembly of Laos (ສະພາ ແຫ່ງຊາດ), which began in 1947, and was charged to draft the first national constitution (ຣັຖະທຳມະນູນ ແຫ່ງຊາດ) of Laos. Toulia argued forcefully to make all people of Laos citizens of the country, and as a result, all people of Laos, regardless of their ethnicity and religion, have been recognized as citizens of the country.[16] In 1948, Tougeu Lyfoung, the most educated among the three Lyfoung brothers, was appointed to the King's Council (ສະພາ ຮາຊະມົນຕຣີ). Tougeu, who was another half-younger brother of Touby and older brother of Toulia, graduated from Lycée de Khaidinh, Vietnam, in 1942, and became the first ethnic minority of Indochina to have a high school education. It should be noted here that at the time, only a small number of the people in Laos had that kind of education or higher. Both Touby and Tougeu Lyfoung went on to play major roles in the post-1954 independence of Laos. In 1951, Tougeu was elected to the National Assembly and served only one term. In 1956, he was appointed as the procurator general of the Court of Appeal of Laos, and a year later, Tougeu was sent to study law at the Ecole National de la France d'Outre Mer in France. He returned to Laos in 1960 and was appointed the general director of the Ministry of Justice, a position he served on and off until he resigned from the post in May of 1975. Tougeu and his family left Laos on July 2, 1975, to become refugees in France.[17]

Touby Lyfoung was elected to the National Assembly in 1959. He went on to serve as vice president of the National Assembly, deputy minister of information in the Royal Lao Government led by Premier Chao Somsanith, minister of justice under Premier Prince Souvanna Phouma's government, minister of human services or social welfare under Premier Prince Boun Oum's counter-coup government, and minister of health in the tri-party government formed after the 1962 Geneva Accords. Touby also served as member of the King's Council (1964–1968),[18] and deputy minister of posts and telegrams (1974–1975) under the Provisional Government of National Unity. Prior to 1975, Touby was the first Hmong and minority to have served as vice president of the National Assembly and held many ministerial posts.

The signing of the 1954 Geneva Accords and granting full independence and neutrality to Laos did not end its civil war. Eventually, the Vietnam War spilled over to Laos in the early 1960s, and the Hmong and other ethnic groups, who lived along the borders of Vietnam and China, were pushed and pulled to become involved in the war. The departure of the French colonial administration at the conclusion of their 1954 military defeat in Dien Bien Phu was only to be replaced slowly by the Americans, the new leader of the non-Communist countries. A second Geneva Accords, which was signed in 1962, reaffirmed the neutrality of Laos, but also failed to bring peace to Laos. Ceasefire broke out in 1963, and the war in Laos began to accelerate in 1964 into a major conflict known generally as the "Secret War." The Hmong and other ethnic groups, who lived along the frontline at the borders of North Vietnam and China, were pushed and coerced to take sides in the Secret War in Laos. The end of the Secret War in 1975 marked the taking over the country by the Lao People's Revolutionary Party (ພັກ ປະຊາຊົນ ປະຕິວັດລາວ) or the Communist Party of Laos. Consequently, the majority of those Hmong, who fought on the opposing side of the Communists, became refugees abroad for fear of persecution, retaliation, oppression, and being sent to post-war reeducation camps. A small number of these Hmong escaped to the jungle, resisting the new Communist government of Laos; among them are those who formed the Chao Fa movement inside Laos. Also, many of the Hmong, who fought under the flag of the Royal Lao government, were sent to re-education camps. Touby Lyfoung, for example, was one of those who was sent to re-education camp; he died in the camp in 1979. About one-half of the Hmong population in Laos have left the country since 1975, and the majority of them were resettled in the United States. These Hmong and their American-born offspring are the main subjects for this book.

This book is divided and organized into six chapters. Chapter 1 is the general introduction of the book, highlighting the Hmong American community and their four decades of struggles in America. In addition, it contains general coverage of the Hmong history in Laos and how Touby Lyfoung led the Hmong from being an impoverished ethnic minority in the highlands of Laos to provincial and national affairs of the country. It also highlights the general outline of this book as well as points of view presented in the book. Chapter 2 briefly reviews historical context, the Secret War in Laos, and how the Hmong, who lived along the border of Vietnam and China, the epic center of the war, were pushed and coerced to fight on both sides of the Secret War. It also highlights the war experience of the Hmong as being heavily impacted by war, perhaps more than any other ethnic groups in Laos. Chapter 3 covers the pre-1975 Hmong students in the United States as part of the foundation of the post-war Hmong American community. Chapter 4 examines the challenges of Hmong Refugee Resettlement in 1975, when the United Nations High Commissioner on Refugees was reluctant to classify Hmong as refugees, and some policymakers in Washington viewed the Hmong as an agrarian people who would not be able to adjust and adapt to American society. It also describes the powerful voices and advocacy efforts of many American individuals who made it possible for the U.S. resettlement of thousands of Hmong refugees. Chapter 5 covers the main theme of the book: the Hmong's forty years of becoming American. This chapter is divided into five sub-topics and they are: 1) Hmong American population, 2) discrimination and prejudice against Hmong, 3) diversity of Hmong Americans (The Hmong Community of Missoula, Montana; The Denver Hmong Community in Colorado; and The Fresno Hmong Community in California), 4) contributions of Hmong Americans, and 5) the passing of the generation who lived through and witnessed the war years. Chapter 6 contains the conclusion and discussion for this book, focusing on the experiences of the Hmong throughout the last forty years and how they overcame challenges and obstacles. The last part of the discussion summarizes the achievements and contributions the Hmong Americans have made to their new homeland. It lists factors that may have made these achievements possible in the United States. The discussion ends by posing some key questions on how the Hmong will change in the next forty years as their culture and linguistics continue to drastically fade away.

NOTES

1. The estimated number of Hmong in China does not include all sub-groups under the lumping name Miao (i.e., Ah Mao, Hmu, and Qho Xiong). Jacques Lemoine estimated the number of Hmong speakers in China to be less than three hundred thousand. See, Jacques Lemoine, "What is the actual number of the (H)mong in the world?" *Hmong Studies Journal*, Volume 6 (2005). Online link: http://hmongstudies.org/LemoineHSJ6.pdf.

2. Minh Phuong Luong and Wolfgang Nieke, "Minority Status and Schooling of the Hmong in Vietnam." *Hmong Studies Journal* 14(2013): 1–37. Online link: http://hmongstudies.org/LuongandNiekeHSJ14.pdf.

3. It should be noted here that some writers estimate the Hmong population of Laos to be about 700,000, whereas others estimate it to be around 450,000. It was generally agreed that the Hmong population in Laos was about 290,000 to 300,000 in 1970, and about half of this population left the country after 1975. As such, the best

estimate of the Hmong population in Laos should be around four hundred thousand, including Hmong Vietnamese, who immigrated to Laos during the last forty years.

4. The Hmong population in Thailand and Myanmar is my educated estimate.

5. Data from the 2014 American Community Survey showed the Hmong American population to be about 301,286.

6. The number of the Hmong population in Argentina, Australia, Canada, France, Germany, and the Netherlands are from my educated estimate, which I base on my conversations with Hmong from these countries. I have visited the Hmong in these countries, except those living in Argentina and the Netherlands.

7. Kou Yang. 2016. *The Hmong and Their Odyssey: A Roots-Searching Journey of an American Professor*, 25. A self-published book.

8. In his *Hmong at the Turning Point*, Yang Dao wrote that the Hmong entered Laos during the early 1800s. See, Yang Dao. 1993. *Hmong at the Turning Point.* Jeanne L. Blake (ed). Minneapolis: WorldBridge Associates, Ltd.

9. Gary Yia Lee. 1985/1986. "Ethnic Minorities and National Building in Laos: The Hmong in the Lao State," 215–32. School of Behavioural Sciences, Macquarie University, North Ryde, Australia. Published in: *Peninsule*, No.11/12. Online link: http://members.ozemail.com.au/~yeulee/History/ethnic%20monirities%20and%20 national%20building%20in%20laos.html.

10. Ibid.

11. Yang Dao. 1993. *Hmong at the Turning Point*, 36. Jeanne L. Blake (ed). Minneapolis: WorldBridge Associates, Ltd.

12. Gary Yia Lee, 1985/86. "Ethnic Minorities and National Building in Laos: The Hmong in the Lao State," 215–32. School of Behavioural Sciences, Macquarie University, North Ryde, Australia. Published in: *Peninsule*, No.11/12.

13. Touxa Lyfounbg. 1996. *Touby Lyfoung: An Authentic Account of the Life of a Hmong Man in the Troubled Land of Laos*, 109. Edina, MN: Burgess Publishing:

14. Ibid, 110.

15. Ibid, 141.

16. Ibid, 143.

17. Tougeu Lyfoung, personal communication. June 22, 1999.

18. Touxa Lyfoung. 1996. *Touby Lyfoung: An Authentic Account of the life of a Hmong Man in the Troubled Land of Laos*, 157–82. Edina, MN: Burgess Publishing.

REFERENCES

American Community Survey. 2014. Data from the 2014 American Community Survey.

Lee, Gary Yia. 1985/1986. "Ethnic Minorities and National Building in Laos: The Hmong in the Lao State," 215–32. School of Behavioral Sciences, Macquarie University, North Ryde, Australia. Published in: Peninsule, No. 11/12. Online link: last modified February 2008. http://members.ozemail.com.au/~yeulee/History/ethnic%20monirities%20and%20national%20building%20in%20laos.html.

Lyfoung, Touxa. 1996. *Touby Lyfoung: An Authentic Account of the Life of a Hmong Man in the Troubled Land of Laos*. Edina, MN: Burgess Publishing.

Vietnam Online. "Hmong People." Last date of access March 21, 2017. https://www.vietnamonline.com/az/hmong-people.html.

Wikipedia. "List of Ethnic Groups in Vietnam." Last modified March 4, 2017. https://en.wikipedia.org/wiki/List_of_ethnic_groups_in_Vietnam.

Yang, Dao. 1993. *Hmong at the Turning Point*. Jeanne L. Blake, ed. Minneapolis: WorldBridge Associates, Ltd.

Yang, Kou. 2016. *The Hmong and Their Odyssey: A Roots-Searching Journey of an American Professor*. A self-published book.

Chapter Two

The Secret War in Laos

The Secret War in Laos was another major military operation as part of the Vietnam War. However, because Laos was a neutral state guaranteed by both the 1954 and 1962 Geneva Accords, U.S. involvement in Laos was kept secret, well kept from the American public throughout the Vietnam War. Yet most nations, including China and the former Soviet Union, knew of the U.S. intervention in Laos. Moreover, North Vietnam, the Soviet Union, and China were also secretly involved in the Secret War. It needs to be noted that the United States, Soviet Union, China, and North Vietnam were signatories of the 1954 and 1962 Geneva Accords, and they did not want to publicly violate their own signatures.

The Vietnam War can be characterized as the second Cold War confrontation between the East and the West, following the stalemate of the Korean War ending in 1953. The Cold War began after World War II over the intention of the *Soviet Union* and its Communist allies to spread Communism to all five continents; therefore, the United States and its Western European allies responded to contain the global spread of Communism. Following the end of the Korean War, Indochina became the target of the Cold War conflict. The French defeat in Dien Bien Phu resulted in the signing of the Geneva Accords in 1954, which granted independence to Cambodia, Laos, and Vietnam. The independence of these countries did little to quell the peace. Instead, the accords partitioned Vietnam into two states—the North and South at the seventeenth parallel. North Vietnam was handed over to the Communist Vietnamese under the leadership of Ho Chi Minh and the famous General Vo Nguyen Giap, whereas South Vietnam became a non-Communist and pro-Western state under the leadership of the former Emperor Bao Dai with Ngo Dinh Diem as Premier, who was a devoted Catholic and pro-Westerner. The Geneva Accords promised that a general election would be held in 1956, in which Ho Chi Minh was projected to win as the new president of Vietnam by uniting both the North and South. Yet the general election scheduled never happened, which angered the North Vietnamese leadership, which then led to the founding of the Viet Minh movement. The failure to unite the two countries was the driving force for the North Vietnamese leadership to reunite with the South as a sovereign country. As the tension increased between the North and South, thousands of refugees streamed toward the South; most of these refugees were those who did not want to stay under the Communists, those who had relatives in the South, and those who were Catholics. After granting independence to the three Indochinese countries in 1954, the French left and the United States stepped in. In Laos, the United States paid for the budget of the Royal Lao Army, which is "the only army in the world completely paid for by the United States."[1] At the time, the United States became the undisputed leader of the non-Communist world. Under the U.S. Navy's Operation Exodus, the United States transported over eight hundred thousand refugees from the North to resettlement in the South.[2] Their humanitarian work eventually became a military involvement in South Vietnam, confronting North Vietnam and the Soviet Union head on.

The major conflict in Laos began when the Royal Lao Army Paratrooper Captain Kong Le led a military coup in August of 1960 that set off a military confrontation between two military factions: the rightists, led by Prince Boun Oum Na Champassack (ບຸນອຸ້ມ ນະ ຈໍາປາສັກ) and Maj. Gen. Phoumi Nosavanh (ພູມີ ນ໌ອະຊາວັນ), and the self-declared neutralists, led by Prince Souvanna Phouma (Premier) and Captain Kong Le. The Communist Viet Minh seized the opportunity to support the leftists and Pro-Lao independence movement called Pathet Lao (Lao Patriotic Front). The conflict between North and South Vietnam was slowly creeping into Laos as the Viet Minh hoped to support the Pathet Lao movement and created a network of Ho Chi Minh trails as the war progressed. The Secret War in Laos had become another theater of major military operations where the Soviet Union and China unleashed military supplies and weapons to support the North Vietnamese Army, the Pathet Lao insurgency, and Viet Congs in South Vietnam. Meanwhile, the United States did the same for the non-Communists.

To better understand the Secret War in Laos, it is essential to offer a brief overview of the modern history of Laos and the significance of its geographical location. Historically and politically, Laos is not a nation-state because it lacks "elements that a nation state requires if it is to function effectively."[3] It also lacks an effective central government, political unity, and other governmental infrastructures that a nation-state usually has. In their chapter on the heritage of Laos, Brown and Zasloff wrote, "There is little foundation for a sense of nationhood and many prejudices and inequalities remain among tribes and social classes."[4] Although this description was made in the 1980s, it remains somewhat true in today's Laos. When the French decided to leave Laos after World War II, they worked with the elites in Laos to patch together many former, poorly governed small states into the modern state of Laos. Specifically, in 1946, the modus vivendi was signed by France and Laos, and the Kingdom of Laos was established; the modern Lao state became finalized. In 1949, the Franco-Lao General Convention granted Laos limited self-government within the French Union; Lao Issara government-in-exile dissolved, and members returned to Laos or they joined the newly formed Pathet Lao in the northeastern provinces of Phongsaly and Houaphanh, which were located near the border of North Vietnam. The newly established Kingdom of Laos was made up of three former and not so friendly kingdoms: Luang Phrabang, Vientiane, and Champassack. Consequently, nation building became a major task, and each region remained under the authority of a different family or group of power holders. The organization of the Royal Lao Army testifies to the regional power holding and the challenges of nation building in Laos. The Royal Lao Army was organized during the war years into five military regions.[5] According to Brig. Gen. Soutchay Vongsavanh,[6] each region was under the domination of a different family or group. Region I, which included four northwest provinces of Laos (Luang Phrabang, Phongsaly, Houa Khong [Luang Namtha], and Sayaboury), was dominated by the Royal Lao family and Lt. Gen. Ouan Rathikul, the former commander in chief of the Royal Lao Army. Military Region II, which included the two northeast provinces of Xieng Khouang and Houa Phanh, was under the domination of Maj. Gen. Vang Pao, the military commander of this region. Military Region III in central Laos, with its headquarter in Savannakhet City, covered the provinces of Khammouane and Savannakhet. It was under the command of Maj. Gen. Nouphet Daohoung, but the real power holder in this region rested in the hands of the Insixiengmay family led by Leuam Insixiengmay, the pre-1975 deputy prime minister and minister of education. Military Region IV, which covered six southern provinces (Saravanh, Attopeu, Champassack, Sedone, Khong Sedone, and Siphandone) was under the command of Maj. Gen. Phasouk S. Rassaphak, and later, Brig. Gen. Soutchay Vongsavanh. The real power holder in this region was the Na Champassack family, led by Prince Boun Oum Na Champassack (1911–1980).[7] Military Region V was commanded by Maj. Gen. Kouprasith Abhay and later, Maj. Gen. Thonglith Chockbengboun. This region covered Borikhane and Vientiane provinces with its headquarters in Vientiane City, the capital of Laos. As a result, the Royal Lao government in Vientiane City was often powerless in keeping Laos under one authority. Reportedly, Prince Souvanna Phouma (ສະເດັດ ເຈົ້າສຸວັນນະພູມາ, 1901–1984), who was the prime minister of Laos several times and a major

Figure 2.1. Map of the five military regions of the Royal Lao Army.
Vungping Yang.

political figure in the early 1950s to 1975, was very proud of his role as peacemaker, and that "there [has] never been official partition of Laos as there had been in Vietnam."[8]

The geographical location of Laos made Laos a buffer zone between North and South Vietnam. Additionally, Laos is bordered with Communist China to the north; Thailand (a pro-American state) to the east; and Cambodia, a fragile neutral country, to the south. Its geographical location made the little, land-locked, and impoverished Laos a strategic location to both the two superpowers of the Cold War: the Soviet Union and the United States. Laos, thus, became the buffer zone between all sides of the Cold War.

The Kong Le (ກອງເລ) coup on August 9, 1960, provided a window of opportunity for both the United States and the Soviet Union to secretly become involved in Laos. Capt. Kong Le (1934–2014), a neutralist and commander of the Paratroop Battalion of the Royal Lao Army, led a successful and bloodless coup d'état while all cabinet members were in Luang Phrabang conferring with the king. As a result, most politicians, including ministers and Touby Ly-foung, were either confined in Vientiane or Luang Phrabang. Touby Lyfoung at the time was the deputy minister of information and justice in the government of rightist Prime Minister Chao Somsanith Vongkoth Rattana, which lasted from April 6, 1960, to August 9, 1960. The coup forced Somsanith and his entire cabinet to resign, and immediately, the king named Prince Souvanna Phouma, a neutralist, as prime minister of the caretaker government. Touby became minister of justice and religious affairs in the caretaker government. Maj. Gen. Phoumi Nosavanh (1920–1985), who was a military leader of the right wing, did not recognize the caretaker government of Prince Souvanna Phouma and fled to Thailand to seek help from Thai Prime Minister Field Marshal Sarit Thanarath (1908–1963) and from the Americans. At the time, the Central Intelligence Agency (CIA) promised "Phoumi that he could count on the United States to meet any reasonable request for financial and logistical support."[9] The leftists, headed by Prince Souphanouvong (ສະເຈົ້າ ເຈົ້າ ສຸພານຸວົງ, 1909–1995) were based in the northeastern parts of Laos, ready to join forces with the neutralists. Consequently, the coup created three factions, who later turned their guns against each other, positioning Laos as a hot spot for the Cold War.

During the commotion of the coup, the United States began to fear that its hesitance to respond to the conflict "might actually promote the disintegration of the anticommunist side."[10] On October 1, 1960, Washington instructed U.S. Ambassador Winthrop Brown in Vientiane to implore the king to "take authority into his own hands and appoint [a] caretaker government under royal decree." Ambassador Brown met the king on October 6, but the king declined to remove Prince Sounna Phouma as caretaker prime minister. The United States had no choice but to agree to work with Prince Souvanna Phouma on one hand, while on the other hand, "unilaterally pay and supply Phoumi's forces in Savannakhet and northerm Laos."[11] To avoid military solution to the conflict in Laos, Washington sent Assistant Secretary of State J. Graham Parsons and Assistant Secretary of Defense John Irwin to Vientiane to press Prince Souvanna Phouma to "bring Kong Le to heel and terminate all overtures to the Soviets." When they did not have firm commitment from Prime Minister Prince Souvanna Phouma, they returned to Thailand. Irwin then "encouraged Phoumi to expect at least secret US support for a march on Vientiane and the seizure of the government."[12] As a result, James William "Bill" Lair (1924–2014), an agent of the CIA and a major in the Thai Border Patrol Police Aerial Resupply Unit (PARU), was dispatched to go from Thailand to Laos in November 1960 to assist Maj. Gen. Phoumi Nosavanh in his attempt to capture Vientiane from Kong Le's forces. During the Kong Le coup, Lt. Col. Vang Pao sided with Maj. Gen. Phoumi Nosavanh while assisting Phoumi Nosavanh's attempt to capture Vientiane. After Phoumi's forces captured Vientiane on December 17, 1960, Kong Le's forces were pushed to Xieng Khouang in the northeast of Laos and that region became the epic center of the fighting between the troops of Phoumi (the rightist), Kong Le (the neutralist), and Prince Souphanouvong (the leftist). Lair and PARU Col. Pranet Ritruechai had intelligence teams all along the border of Laos and North Vietnam, so they knew about Vang Pao, the commander of the military sub-division of Xieng Khouang Province, the frontline of the conflict. "Lair wanted to find Vang Pao, but no one knew of his whereabouts. On the morning of December 21, Lair ran into Ron Sutphin [an Air America Pilot], at the airport. Sutphin told Lair that he had landed the day before at a recently constructed airstrip at Ta Vieng, south of the PDJ [Plain of Jars], and that Vang Pao was there."[13] As a result of this conversation, Lair got permission from his superior to fly to Ta Vieng in Xieng Khouang with Pranet and a PARU team, but they only found an old man near the airstrip, who told them Vang Pao was in the countryside. Lair returned to Vientiane, but Pranet and his team remained behind to search for Vang Pao. The next morning, Lair received a message from Pranet that he found Vang Pao. Lair went back and spoke to Vang Pao, who told Lair, "He had two choices: fight or leave the country. If the [United States] supplied weapons, he would fight. Lair asked [Vang Pao] how many people he could raise. [Vang Pao] said that he could easily raise [ten thousand]. Both Lair and Pranet were impressed with [Vang Pao]."[14] With this discussion, Lair returned to Vientiane to discuss with his superiors and other American officials about his meeting with Vang Pao. The next day, Desmond Fitzgerald, the chief of the Far East Division in the Clandestine Services, asked Lair to provide a writing proposal to be sent to Washington, District of Columbia. He did and was authorized "to arm the first [one thousand] Hmong to see how it would work out."[15] They were armed and trained by the PARU. Thus, the covert operation, known as "Operation Momentum," had begun. At the beginning of Operation Momentum, Warner wrote, "The Hmong wanted to fight to protect their own territory, and Thailand and the [United States] wanted to help keep Laos from falling to the leftists. But Lair also wanted a subtle, low-key operation. In his original plan, the Thai-not Americans-would do all the training in the field," but later CIA case officers became involved in the training.[16] To be a subtle, low-key operation, in addition to the Hmong's skills in guerrilla fighting, Lair created the Special Guerrilla Unit (SGU), which was funded by the CIA and trained by the PARU and CIA case officers. The goal of Operation Momentum was to aid Hmong guerrillas to harass the enemies, gather intelligence, and tie up North Vietnamese troops inside Laos.[17] The Hmong were not the only group who served as SGUs or irregular forces of the Royal Lao Army. In earlier

1962, Washington also authorized new recruitment at Long Cheng, Thakhek in Central Laos, and more importantly, "two new programs aimed at securing territory and people in the far north [Luang Nam Tha's Iu-Mien or Yao ethnic group] and in the southern Panhandle [Khmuic tribes]. Each of these used a local resident whose relationships of trust with tribal leaders furnished access to people even less integrated into Laotian culture than the Hmong."[18] The story below of Major Xiong Doua is a case study of those who served as SGU in the far north, in the province of Luang Namtha (Houa Khong) and under Military Region I.

The tide of Kongle's Coup reached northwestern Laos in August of 1960. Some of the districts of Luang Namtha Province quickly fell into the hands of the Communist Pathet Lao. Hmong leaders of the region were concerned and desperate to find help, so that they could defend their territory. In mid-1961, two sons of Xiong Ka Toua (Xyooj Nkaj Tuam), a prominent Hmong leader in Luang Namtha, were sent to consult with Touby Lyfoung in Vientiane. The older of the two young men was Xiong Chong Ly (Xyooj Ntxoov Lis) and the younger one was Xiong Doua (Xyooj Nruas, later known as Wameng Xiong). To go to Vientiane, they had to travel first to Luang Phrabang, and then to Vientiane by car or airplane. When they reached Luang Phrabang, the two brothers decided to leave the younger brother (Xiong Doua) in Luang Phrabang. Xiong Chong Ly, the older brother, did reach Vientiane, but it was during the turbulent times of the Kongle Coup and counter-coup; therefore, his efforts to meet with Touby Lyfoung and other leaders were fruitless. The younger brother, who stayed behind in Luang Phrabang, went to see an American in Luang Phrabang. He briefed the American about the dire situation in Luang Namtha and was told the information would be passed on to the appropriate American officials in Laos. After many months of traveling, the two brothers returned home in the summer of 1961. When they arrived home, they learned that an American by the name of William (Bill) Young (1934–2011) had already visited the region. Bill Young, who grew up in Thailand, was also known as "Chith" and was fluent in Thai, so he needed no translator. He was in contact with the Hmong and other ethnic groups near the border of Laos and China. As more contacts were made, the Hmong and other ethnic groups in the region agreed to accept the secret involvement of the Americans in their region and used their existing Auto Defense de Choc, which was formed by the French in the 1950s as the foundation of their militia. In January 1962, Xiong Doua and fifteen young Hmong were selected by Bill Young to be sent to a six-month basic military training in Thailand. They were basically prepared to return and train soldiers in their region. After the training, Xiong Doua and the fifteen soldiers were sent to Chiang Khong in Thailand because their villages in Luang Namtha had already been captured by the Pathet Lao and as a result, most of the villagers became displaced else-where in the region. Moreover, Chiang Khong was the base for Bill Young and Thai PARU, whose tasks were to train new soldiers in Luang Namtha.

After a brief stay in Chiang Khong, Xiong Doua and his team were co-vertly sent to the remote areas of Luang Namtha Province. Upon his return, Xiong Doua was appointed second lieutenant and was sent to Na Voua, a remote Hmong village in Luang Namtha. His first task was to build an air-strip with the help of villagers, so that small airplanes and helicopters could land and provide basic needs for soldiers and villagers. Soon after building the airstrip, about three hundred military rifles were dropped by airplane, in addition to food, medicine, and other supplies. Xiong Doua said, at the time, he only had a handful of young men with him, so most of the three hundred rifles were hidden in the forest until more men could be recruited. He wasted no time recruiting young men in the region to join him. Soon, more than three hundred young men from the Hmong, Iu-mien, Khmu, Khoi, Lao, and Tai Lue ethnic groups joined him as guerrilla fighters. Other areas in Luang Namtha also built their own airstrips and recruited young men to serve as guerrilla fighters. Altogether, twelve airstrips were built and twelve militia sites (known as lima sites) were created throughout Luang Namtha Province. Most of the soldiers were trained, and then served as SGUs under Military Region I, which included Luang Phrabang, Luang Namtha (Houa Khong), Phongsaly, and Sayaboury. In the early 1960s, the commander of the military in Luang Namtha was Col. Chao Vannaseng, but later, the military affairs of Luang Phrabang, Luang Namtha (Houa Khong), Phongsaly, and Sayaboury were organized into Military Region I, under the command of Brigadier Gen-eral Chao Sayavong, a half-brother of the king. In March 1963, Moua Sue from Military Region II (commanded by Maj. Gen. Vang Pao) was sent to Luang Namtha to serve as the advisor for the SGUs in Luang Namtha. Bill Young continued to serve in Luang Namtha as the CIA case officer, assisting them on their daily intelligence and military activities.

In 1964, Xiong Doua sent several hundred soldiers from his region to receive military training in Thailand. The military activities in the region increased and expanded very rapidly. In the same year, he assisted the reloca-tion of Chao Mai and Chao La and their followers from Muong Sing, near the border of China, to Nam Teuy. Chao Mai and Chao La were leaders of the Iu-Mien (Yao) in Luang Namtha. In the same year, they moved the Hmong from many villages to Nam Yu. Xiong Doua and his men also relocated to Nam Yu, and were tasked with building a larger airstrip and the town of Nam Yu; they completed these tasks in 1966. Since then, Nam Yu became the largest base for SGUs in Luang Namtha Province. It also became home to a large displaced population. Because Xiong Doua was the son of a prominent leader, had a third-grade education, was one of the first to receive military training in Thailand, and spoke several local languages, including Chinese, he became the troubleshooter for both civilian and military affairs of the whole region and beyond. He was not assigned to a specific commanding post, but all commanders and civilian leaders consulted with him on important matters. Because of his unusual work, he often flew to remote sites and faced many dangerous situations. He recalled that his helicopter was hit twice on two separate occasions; in both events, the pilot managed to land the helicopter on nearby airstrips, and as a result, he survived.

In 1966, Anthony Alexander Posheny (1924–2003) replaced Bill Young as the CIA case officer in Luang Namtha. He was commonly known by the name of Tony Poe and was an outspoken and daring person, paying little attention to proper protocol and channel of communication. In early 1970, Xiong Doua sent one regiment of his men to be trained in Udorn, Thailand. When they were about to complete their training, Tony Poe came to Xiong Doua and informed him that Maj. Gen. Vang Pao wanted the regiment to go to Muong Suey in Military Region II. As a result, those men were sent to Military Region II. Soon afterwards, Tony Poe was pulled out to Thailand.

In March 1972, Nam Yu was captured by the Pathet Lao, and the whole region was in disarray; civilians became refugees to towns and villages near the border of Thailand. Most of the soldiers escaped to Luang Phrabang and many of them were sent to Long Cheng under Military Region II. Xiong Doua, too, went to Long Cheng and served with his men. He was sent to fight in many battles, including some of the conventional battles near the Plain of Jars. On February 21, 1973, a peace agreement was signed in Vientiane between the Royal Lao government and the Pathet Lao; the war soon came to an end.

Xiong Doua and his family were evacuated by air on May 14, 1975, from Long Cheng to Nam Phong in Thailand. They later relocated to Ban Vinai refugee camp and stayed there until May 1979, when they became refugees to France. Before going to France, he changed his name to Wameng Xiong (Vam Meej Xyooj). In France, they made their home in Alsace, Strasbourg, in northeast France. In 1991, the family moved to Merced, California, and has since called California their home. Although the family has lived in Merced since 1991, Wameng Xiong and his second wife, Ntxheb Lis, did not get their Green Cards until 2011; they were undocumented immigrants. They supported their family by doing strawberry farming. Their hard work has paid off; all of their children have either completed college or have attained a graduate education.

Wameng Xiong (Xiong Doua) has three wives. In 1958, after completing a third-grade education, he was asked to marry the widow of an older cousin in accordance with Hmong levirate marriage tradition. The levirate rule allows a younger brother or cousin to marry the widow of an older brother or older cousin, so that he could take on the role of a father to the deceased older brother's children, and the mother can continue to stay in the home for her children. The widow, Mao Yang (Mos Yaj), was very young at the time and had no children. Wameng and Mao Yang have only one daughter. Mao Yang did not come to the United States with the rest of the family. She resides in France with the daughter.

In 1967, Wameng Xiong married Ntxheb Lis, who became his second wife. Wameng and Ntxheb have seven children together: one son and six daughters. The children came with them to California and have done well in school; most of them hold graduate degrees. Wameng Xiong married Kiab Vaj, his third wife, in December 1974. He and his third wife have three sons and they are all college graduates. The three sons and their mother live in Minnesota.

As of 2016, Wameng Xiong and his second wife, Ntxheb Lis, live in Atwater in central California. Their children are all grown and on their own. He will soon turn eighty and appears to be in good health and spirit. He continues to be very active in his daily life; he walks every morning for several miles. He is also actively involved with the affairs of the Hmong communities in Merced, Fresno, and nearby towns.[19]

In January of 1961, the outgoing U.S. President Dwight Eisenhower briefed John F. Kennedy, the incoming president, that Laos was "the key to Southeast Asia. If Laos fell, the United States would have to write off the whole area."[20] In March, President Kennedy announced that the United States would support Laos' sovereignty, and as a result, the U.S. secret involvement in the civil war in Laos was moving one step further. To avoid direct violation of Laos' neutrality guaranteed by the 1954 Geneva Accords, the United States secretly increased military assistance (monetary funds, weapons, military supplies, etc.) to the non-Communist Royal Lao government. The Soviet Union, China, and North Vietnam did the same for the Communist Pathet Lao. In essence, the Vietnam War had spilled into Laos, creating a conflict of three factions: the left, neutral, and right. All of the three fighting factions of the Secret War in Laos claimed not wanting to fight, so another Geneva Accords was signed on July 23, 1962, by fourteen nations, including the Soviet Union, China, North and South Vietnam, and the United States. This agreement reaffirmed Laos' neutrality, requiring all foreign troops to be pulled out. North Vietnam pulled some of its troops home, but kept more than seven thousand of them imbedded with the troops of the Communist Pathet Lao. The United States pulled its military personnel and advisors to Thailand, but did not totally cease their secret involvement in Laos; their clandestine involvement continued.[21] Consequently, fingers were pointing at each other as violators of the 1962 Geneva Agreement; the fighting resumed in 1963, and the so-called SGUs were further expanded.[22] Conversely, the 1962 Geneva Agreement and the forming of a new government in Vientiane did not bring peace to Laos, so the conflict continued, and the Secret War in Laos further escalated from 1964 to 1975. The conflict in Laos had become another major battle as a part of the Vietnam War and the Cold War.

On the diplomatic front, it should be noted here that William Harriman, assistant secretary of state for east Asian and Pacific affairs, and his deputy, William H. Sullivan, had arrived at "an informal understanding with Soviet deputy foreign minister Georgi M. Pushkin to the effect that as long as the United States did not technically violate the Geneva Protocol the Soviet Union would not feel compelled, out of consideration of its ally in Hanoi, to respond to United States activities in Laos."[23]

The SGUs (also known as irregular forces) had gradually been increasing since 1964 and expanded to four (I, II, III, and IV) of the five Military Regions of the Royal Lao Army. The mission of the SGUs in Military Region III was to operate along the Ho Chi Minh Trails, and the mission of the SGUs in Military Region IV was to interdict the Ho Chi Minh Trails.[24] It needs to be noted here that the building of the Ho Chi Minh Trails, which includes many previously smaller trails, began on May 19, 1959, the sixty-ninth birthday of Ho Chi Minh.[25] The trails are a network of sixteen thousand kilometers (9,940 miles) of a web of tracks, roads, and waterways, passing through southern Laos. The trails branched out to South Vietnam and Cambodia (in Cambodia, it was called Sihanook Trail). This network of trails was used by North Vietnam to transport supplies, such as weapons, ammunitions, and others, to the Viet Cong in South Vietnam.[26] The overall revised goal of the SGUs (in 1964) from the U.S. point of view was to exclude U.S. ground troops in Laos. "U.S. ground troops in Laos would allow the [United States] to strike a heavy blow at North Vietnam without provoking full Chinese or Soviet entrance into the war. The division of the effort—with the Lao supplying the ground troops and the [United States] carrying out air strikes. A second objective of our [U.S.] operation in Laos was for the friendly Lao forces to occupy as much territory as possible to enhance their negotiating position should political solution to the Laotian conflict be found."[27]

By mid-1964, the ceasefire totally broke out; the civil war in Laos had escalated into a major war.[28] William H. Sullivan (1934–2013), who was the U.S. ambassador to Laos from 1964 to 1969, "Imposed two conditions upon his subordinates. First, the thin fiction of the Geneva Accords had to be maintained to avoid possible embarrassment to the Lao and the Soviet Governments; military operations, therefore, had to be carried out in relative secrecy. Second, no regular U.S. ground troops were to become involved."[29]

The Secret War in Laos had since expanded to the whole country. By mid-1964, it appeared that forces of the Royal Lao Army "held the numerical advantage, with some [fifty thousand] regulars and [twenty-three thousand] CIA-supported irregulars [SGU] facing perhaps [eleven thousand] NVA [North Vietnamese Army] troops and about [twenty thousand] Pathet Lao [soldiers]."[30] The numerical advantage did not last long as the eleven thousand North Vietnamese troops increased to seventy thousand by the end of the 1960s.[31] In March of 1965, the United States had decided to escalate the war in Laos and Vietnam. Their "Rolling Thunder" program was implemented to bomb North Vietnam; "one of their main military target was the Ho Chi Minh Trails."[32] In his "Interdiction, 1960–1968," Van Staaveren wrote:

> When manpower and supply infiltration through southern Laos failed to diminish in 1964, the United States secured the Lao government's approval to expand the anti-infiltration effort. It launched in December of that year a limited Air Force and Navy interdiction campaign against fixed targets and infiltration routes throughout Laos. The principal purpose of these strikes was to signal the Hanoi government [that] greater military pressure was to come, unless Hanoi ceased supporting the insurgencies in Laos and South Vietnam. When the signal was not heeded, the United States in April of 1965, inaugurated a day-and-night Air Force and Navy interdiction campaign in southern Laos while continuing a separate program in the north.[33]

One of those who served as SGU officers in southern Laos is Col. Khao Insixiengmay. In his *Khao Insixiengmay War Experience*, he wrote that he began his military career at the age of eighteen in 1962 and received a number of military trainings, including military training in Laos, France, and the United States. In the United States, he went through the English Advanced Class to learn U.S. military terminology at Lackland Air Force Base in Texas. At the U.S. Army Armor School in Fort Knox, Kentucky, he went through the Special Leadership Course, which was similar to the Officer Basic Training. He stated that his Infantry Officer Advanced Course at Fort Benning, Georgia, helped him to become a strong unit commander, and later, he went on to serve as SGU colonel and commander of SGU Groupement Mobile (GM) 33, a regimental-sized unit trained, supported, and directed by CIA case officers in Laos. Col. Khao Insixiengmay stated that due to his special skills and capacities, he was recruited on March 18, 1968, by SGU Headquarters from the Royal Lao Army to serve with the SGU, supported by the CIA. During his seven years working with CIA case officers, he had been involved with many events, including rescuing an American helicopter pilot and a crew of five men, and witnessing the killing in action of Lt. Col. Wayne McNulty. Col. Khao himself was wounded by a hand grenade in 1968 while leading one

Military Region III SGU battalion and another Military Region II SGU battalion in cutting the North Vietnamese Army line of communication in the Plain of Jars. During the March 1972 operation to retake the Plain of Jars, 251 men of his GM33 continued to operate in the area occupied by one North Vietnamese Army Division despite the retreat of eight other SGU GMs (four GM of Military Region II, two GM of Military Region III, one GM of Military Region IV, and one GM of Military Region I). He was also involved in the June 1972 battle to retake Khongsedone, and the battle in late 1972 and early 1973 in southern Laos, where his GM33 destroyed five and damaged three North Vietnamese tanks, blew up several ammunition trucks, and captured three thirty-seven millimeter anti-aircraft guns used against U.S. Air Force fighter jets. He also wrote that on November 6, 1972, his men rescued four Air America crew members of a C-123 cargo plane shot down at Paksong, in Military Region IV—southern Laos—while dropping supplies to Thai troops.

As the war in Laos drew to a close in 1974, his SGU GM33 was turned over to the Royal Lao Army and he was transferred to the Seventh Airborne Brigade. The ceremony of turning over his SGU GM33 to the Royal Lao Army was witnessed by the CIA Station Chief Hugh Tovar and Military Region III Commander Maj. Gen. Nouphet Daoheuang. As of 2015, Col. Khao Insixiengmay is a resident of Brooking Park, Minnesota, and is actively involved with activities related to SGU veterans.[34]

During the peak of the Secret War in Laos around 1968, "North Vietnam deployed approximately [seventy thousand] troops in Laos"[35] and China had sent more than three hundred thousand troops to help North Vietnam during the Vietnam War[36]; many of these Chinese soldiers and advisors were sent to Laos. In 2008, I met a Hmong Chinese in Wenshan, Yunnan, who proudly showed me his photo with the uniform of the troops of the Pathet Lao (Lao People's Liberation Army). Because of his language skills in Hmong, this Chinese advisor was sent to northern Laos to advise Pathet Lao soldiers of Hmong descent. The number of Pathet Lao troops is not known, but the Pathet Lao relied heavily on ethnic minorities to shoulder this and other tasks of the revolution. It is estimated that more than 60 percent of the forces of the Pathet Lao were ethnic Khmu,[37] and members of the Pachay Battalion, for example, were all Hmong. The Royal Lao Army had about fifty-eight thousand regular troops and about thirty-eight thousand irregular forces or SGUs; the exact number of SGUs was never known to the Royal Lao Army.[38] Colonel Moua Sue, who was chief of staff and then later an SGU brigade commander in Military Region II during the early 1970s, related that the "ghost soldiers" of SGUs were larger in number than the real actual human soldiers. On paper, he said, for example, a GM had twelve hundred soldiers on paper, but the real body count indicated that it only had three hundred soldiers. According to Col. Moua Sue, Military Region II had seven GMs of SGU and several battalions of regular forces of the Royal Lao Army.[39] If the account of Col. Moua Sue is accurate, then seven GMs would mean twenty-one hundred actual body counts of SGU soldiers in Military Region II, and sixty-three hundred ghost SGU soldiers. Casualties had reduced SGU soldiers of Military Region II to the point of being ineffective in defending their territory; as such, SGU soldiers from Military Region III and Military Region IV, as mentioned above, were sent to help Military Region II in the late 1960s, when North Vietnam sent more of its troops to northern Laos, and the war expanded beyond guerrilla warfare. Moreover, since 1969 Thai soldiers were sent to Laos and played a major role in the defense of northern Laos. By 1973, for example, there were twenty-seven infantry and three artillery battalions (about seven thousand) Thai soldiers serving in Laos.[40]

The Hmong and other ethnic groups who lived along the foothills of the Annamite Mountain Ranges and the border between Laos and Vietnam, and the border of Laos and China, were at the crossfire. Also, those who lived along road 6 and 7 in the northeast and the Ho Chi Minh Trails in southern Laos were heavily impacted by U.S. bombing. The U.S. legacy in Laos, for example, states that the:

> U.S. bombing of Laos was unprecedented. The U.S. Air Force carried out 580,000 missions against the country. That breaks down to about one planeload of bombs dropped every eight minutes, [twenty-four] hours a day, for nine years. According to the experts, the [United States] dropped over [two] million tons of bombs in Laos, more than all of the bombs dropped during the World War II. . . . The United States dropped [eighty] million cluster bomblets on Laos. Ten percent to 30 percent did not explode.[41]

As mentioned above, the people of Laos, even family members, were forced and split to take sides in the Secret War where both sides were decimated.[42] During the war years, the Hmong of Laos, for example, paid a heavy price to fight on both opposing sides of the conflict. About one-half of the Hmong in Laos fought under the Royal Lao government, which received humanitarian and secret military assistance from the U.S. government. And nearly half of the Hmong of Laos fought under the flag of the Communist Pathet Lao (the Lao Patriotic Front), who received secret military assistance from North Vietnam, China, and the Soviet Union. A small number of Hmong were neutral, but were impacted by the war as much as the left and the right. More importantly, the war left no room for anyone to safely be in neutral; neutral villagers were subjected to abuse by both sides.

These developments expanded the U.S. involvement in Laos in multiplicity, scope, and size. To contain Communist advances in Laos, the United

States began to secretly provide military aids to the pro-Western faction in Laos, including some Hmong, who lived along the borders of China and North Vietnam. Unlike the U.S. intervention in South Vietnam, which was made known to Congress and the American public, the U.S. effort in Laos was kept in the dark from the American public. The 1954 and 1962 Geneva Agreements guaranteed Laos as a neutral state, prohibiting the deployment of foreign forces inside the territory of Laos. It was obvious that the signatories of those peace agreements only chose to fight the war in Laos by proxies. The Soviet *Union*, China, and North Vietnam supported the Communist revolutionaries (Pathet Lao or Lao Patriotic Front), whereas the United States supported the Royalists and pro-Western Royal Lao government.

As the war in Laos raged on, the relationships between the American military advisers in Laos and the Hmong and the Royal Lao government grew closer and stronger. The United States needed reliable and competent guerrilla fighters in Laos. At the first contact in the late 1960s, Col. Bill Lair found the Hmong and other ethnic guerrilla fighters to be fierce and determined warriors. Especially Lt. Col. Vang Pao, a commission officer of the Royal Lao Army, at the time appeared to be quite an effective and experienced guerrilla commander. The soldiers of Hmong and other ethnic descent in the region were excellent and willing guerrilla fighters. With the full backing of the United States, providing money, military supplies, and training, members of the Military Region II, who were mostly Hmong, expanded quickly while Lt. Col. Vang Pao was on the fast track to become a commanding general of Military Region II, which comprised of Xieng Khouang and Houa Phanh Provinces. How he became the commanding general of Military Region II is another fascinating and a very "lucky" story. From August 1964 to January 1965, Maj. Gen. Phoumi Nosavanh, and Siho Lamphouthakoul (1934–1966), the head of the police forces, led another unsuccessful coup d'état. Before the coup, Maj. Gen. Phoumi Nosavanh, the rightist general of the Royal Lao Army and former minister of defense, had secretly requested then Brigadier General Vang Pao, the sub-division commander of Xieng Khouang Province, and Maj. Gen. Khamkhong Bouthavong, the commander of Military Region II, to send soldiers to help Phoumi's upcoming military coup. Touby Lyfoung at the time distanced himself from the rightist leader of this coup and heard that Phoumi had made such a request, so he promptly advised Vang Pao not to send any soldiers as this coup was doomed to fail. Touby reasoned that the coup was nothing more than fighting for political offices and personal power. Maj. Gen. Khamkhong Bouthavong, on the other hand, sent two companies as requested by Maj. Gen. Phoumi Nosavanh. The coup failed and Phoumi exiled himself to Thailand. Consequently, Maj. Gen. Khamkhong Bouthavong resigned his commission as commander of Military Region II, was later arrested,[43] and spent a year in jail. The top post of Military Region II became vacant. Touby was on the winning side of this coup, and he continued to play a major role in the political affairs of Laos. When the Royal Lao Army brought up the vacancy of the top post of Military Region II to the government, Touby recommended Vang Pao to the post, reasoning that Vang Pao, who had already served under Military Region II as Brig. General and did not join Maj. Gen. Phoumi's coup, should be the man for the job.[44] As a result, Brig. Gen. Vang Pao officially became commander of Military Region II on February 28, 1965,[45] and later got a promotion to Major General. The headquarters of Military Region II was soon moved from Park Song to Long Cheng, and the operation of the SGUs became more secretive and was firmly controlled by Vang Pao because Long Cheng was far from Vientiane and too remote from the eyes and ears of the diplomats and foreign media.

Military Region II was located on the western border of North Vietnam, strategically sandwiched between the Pathet Lao and other forces of the Royal Lao government. Further, Military Region II covered roads 6 and 7, the two major arteries linking North Vietnam to Laos, making it a major strategic location for both North Vietnam and the United States as far as logistical military operations were concerned. Furthermore, the Plain of Jars, an ancient holy site filled with thousand-year-old stone jars, was located within the territory of Military Region II. The Plain of Jars area became an important strategic location for all parties involved in this war. Thus, beyond countering the Pathet Lao, which made Houa Phanh its home base, Military Region II also provided the United States with an option to track the movement of North Vietnamese forces from entering Laos as well as using the territory of Laos bypass to South Vietnam and Cambodia. Military Region II experienced the most heavily fought zone from the air and on the ground as the main battlegrounds throughout the conflict in Laos.

The Secret War magnified the split among the Hmong of Laos. The conflict brought modern warfare to Laos, and heavy casualties were inflicted on all sides of the war. It caused unprecedented displacement and disruption in the lives of the people. As North Vietnam deployed large numbers of ground troops into Laos, the United States responded with heavy carpet-bombing in Military Region II and along the Ho Chi Minh Trails, which passes through the territory of Military Regions III and IV in the southern parts of Laos. In his *Terms of Refuge*, Robinson wrote that "Hmong losses during the war were catastrophic. Between 18,000 and 20,000 were killed in combat, and as many as 50,000 civilians were dead or wounded, and by 1973, 120,000 Hmong—nearly half of the entire population—were refugees in their own land."[46] While everyone agrees that Hmong losses during the war years were catastrophic, they do not share the same statistics. In his *No Place to Run*,

White estimated that 10 percent or approximately thirty thousand of the estimated three hundred thousand Hmong of Laos died as a result of the war,[47] whereas some 30 percent were displaced. To describe the refugee movement of the Hmong during the war, Nicholas Tapp wrote:

> As the Pathet Lao advanced, entire populations were evacuated in case they fall prey to the communists. While many were airlifted, hundreds died on forced evacuation marches, particularly the children and elderly, and a major refugee problem within Laos resulted. The evacuees were resettled in the most strategically important zones as buffet-hostages between the opposing forces. Those who refused to be evacuated were automatically treated as enemies and subjected to indiscriminate bombing. Before 1967, over 88,000 Hmong refugees were being supported by [U.S. Agency for International Development] funds in Xieng Khouang; by 1974, there were more than 120,000. For example, the number of Hmong refugees in Xieng Khouang Province alone grew rapidly from 88,000 in the middle of the 1960s to more than 120,000 in 1974.[48]

While the war caused heavy casualties and tremendous upheaval to the Hmong, it did raise the profiles of the Hmong people by elevating Hmong status and promoting awareness of the Hmong people to the outside world where they were virtually unknown to the outsiders prior to the Secret War in Laos. With funding support from the United States, the war brought education to Hmong children and introduced them to modernization. Most importantly, it inspired Hmong to pursue socio-political participation in Laos.[49] Touby Lyfoung became the first Hmong and ethnic minority to hold a few ministerial positions in the Royal Lao government. Vang Pao was the first Hmong and ethnic minority to achieve a top military post of being a major general and regional commander in the Royal Lao Army. In top academia, Yang Dao was the first Hmong ethnic minority to earn a doctorate degree in social sciences from Sorbonne University-Paris in France in 1972, and later returned to Laos to serve in the Ministry of Planning before he was appointed to serve in the new coalition government as a member of the National Political Consultative Council (NPCC) in 1974. It was partially Yang Dao's doctorate dissertation in addition to Jacques Lemoine's research that changed Westerners' view of the Hmong of Laos and their identity. In his dissertation, Yang Dao used the name "Hmong" and wrote that the Hmong call themselves Hmong, not Miao or Meo—the name imposed on them by outsiders with negative connotation. Since then, the Hmong of Laos have been universally known and referred to as Hmong.[50]

By mid-1975, the Hmong of Laos had one deputy minister, one chief procurator of the Lao Supreme Court, one general, two members of the NPCC, two directors general of two different ministries, one person with a

PhD, and more than thirty students attending universities abroad. This seems like a small achievement, but no other minority of Laos had ever reached such levels of achievement. It must be noted that Laos is one of the poorest countries in Asia, and having more than thirty students studying abroad was a major milestone for Hmong during that period.

As the Vietnam War was winding down and the Secret War in Laos slowly came to a standstill, pressures from key supporters of the conflict finally took effect. On January 27, 1973, North Vietnam and its backers along with the United States and South Vietnam had agreed to make plans for peace after a decade of conflict. Specifically, the United States was leaving the conflict behind and had pressured the Royal Lao government to sign a peace deal with its foes. The Pathet Lao leaders and Prime Minister Prince Souvanna Phouma from the Royal Lao government signed a Peace and National Reconciliation Agreement on February 21, 1973. This agreement called for a ceasefire; it replaced the Royal Lao government and National Assembly with a Provisional Government of National Union (PGNU) and an NPCC. Overall, it was an agreement for peace and national reconciliation. Following the provisions of the agreement, a PGNU was established on May 4, 1974, with Prince Souvanna Phouma as prime minister. His half-brother, Prince Souphanouvong, was given the presidency of the NPCC (a provisional legislative body). Touby Lyfoung was appointed deputy minister of posts and telecommunications in PGNU. Two Hmong were appointed to serve on the NPCC: Yang Dao, on the Royal Lao government side, and Lo Fong, on the Pathet Lao side. The agreement called for the total cessation of hostilities between the parties and the demobilization of forces. A line of control was drawn. The parties were committed to work toward peace and national reconciliation. In reality, sporadic fighting continued.

In March 1975, fighting erupted several times between forces of Military Region II, under Maj. Gen. Vang Pao and those of the Pathet Lao in the area known as Sala Phoukhoun, located on road 13, between Vientiane and Luang Phrabang. Witness accounts indicated that the Pathet Lao forces were moving their demarcation markers in the line of their control into the territorial jurisdiction controlled by forces under Maj. Gen. Vang Pao. After unsuccessful attempts to persuade the Pathet Lao forces to remove the markers, Maj. Gen. Vang Pao ordered an aerial bombing. The fighting threatened the ceasefire agreement.[51]

On May 6, Vang Pao met with Prince Souvanna Phouma, the prime minister of the PGNU, to explain his military response to the removal of the markers by forces of the Pathet Lao. The prime minister advised Vang Pao not to fight. Vang Pao was furious and threatened to resign his commission.[52] The prime minister also threatened Vang Pao with dismissal for insubordination. The latter reportedly defended his action on the basis of self-defense. Despite the verbal threat, Souvanna Phouma did not discharge the general at the meeting.[53] Vang Pao returned to his headquarters in Long Cheng. There was a real possibility that he would be dismissed. More pressingly, though, he was anxious about the likely invasion from the Pathet Lao forces. They were already deployed to striking positions around Long Cheng. After signing the peace agreement in 1973, the United States started restricting military aids to Vang Pao and his forces, and all of the Royal Lao Army. More importantly, the treaty between the Royal Lao government and the United States, which was signed in Vientiane on June 28, 1973, stipulated that "All SGU units are to be deactivated by June 30, 1974."[54] Most of the forces of Military Region II were deactivated and the soldiers returned to their villages. The inexhaustible supply of weapons and ammunition during the war had dwindled to small quantities at the depot in Long Cheng. Moreover, "the Royal Lao Air Force T-28s, on which Maj. Gen. Vang Pao had often relied, had been pulled back to Vientiane on orders from Souvanna Phouma."[55] Therefore, the military option for Vang Pao at this point was precarious. On May 8, Vang Pao planned an air force rally at Wattay Airport in Vientiane.[56] Witness accounts suggest that Vang Pao also wanted to bomb the Nam Ngeum Hydro Power Dam and initiate a coup d'état to bring down the PGNU.[57] Vang Pao was not the first general to think about a coup to take down the PGNU of Prime Minister Prince Souvanna Phouma. On August 20, 1973, the Brig. Gen. Thao Ma Sengsavangsay, who was in exile in Thailand, led an unsuccessful coup to bring down the Royal Lao government headed by Prince Souvanna Phouma in order to derail the 1973 Peace and National Reconciliation Agreement, and then establish a new rightist government. In his "Roots of Souphanouvong/ ຫາກ ສຸພານຸວົງ," Mothana Vilaysith provided a long, fictional-sounding account of this coup.[58] The following is my own summary of the account as well as a paraphrased and translated version of his account from Lao into English. The rightwing members of the Royal Lao government were not pleased with the Peace and National Reconciliation Agreement signed on February 21, 1973. One day in May of 1973, Sisouk Na Champassack, the deputy prime minister and minister of defense called for a secret meeting of the rightwing group. The meeting, which took place in Sisouk's house in Vientiane, included many generals and some politicians. Among the generals were Oudone Sananikone, Sourith Donsasorith, Phasouk Rassaphak, Aetam Sinvongsa, Kouprasith Abhay, Bounma Vongphrachanh, Chao Sinh Saysana, Khamhou Boussarath, Bouathong, Silack Pathammavong, Bounleuth Sanichanh, and other military officers. Politicians attending this meeting included Souvannarath Chindavong, Dr. Tem Teso, and so on. Police Lt. Col. Praveth, who was a personal body guard of Prince Souvanna Phouma, was also present at this meeting. Everyone spoke in one voice in their displeasure with the 1973 Peace and Reconciliation Agreement, but no one wanted to be the leader of any military coup to bring down the government. Also, no one volunteered to serve as prime minister, if the coup was successful. In the end, all agreed to offer the post of prime minister to Maj. Gen. Phoumi Nosavanh, who was, at the time, in exile in Thailand. They designated Maj. Gen. Aetam to go to Thailand to contact Phoumi. He did contact Phoumi, who was willing to serve as prime minister, if the coup was successful. About three months later, Maj. Gen. Phoumi along with Brig. Gen. Thao Ma and several exiled military officers came to Udorn, the Thai side of the Mekong River, preparing to enter Vientiane. Sisouk Na Champassack sent Phasouk, Aetam, Souvannarath, and Police Lt. Col. Praveth to meet with Maj. Gen. Phoumi in Udorn to discuss details of the upcoming military coup. On August 19, 1973, some rightwing generals met in the office of Maj. Gen. Sourith Donsasorith at the headquarters of the air force. Prior to this meeting, Sisouk had sent his men to bring Brig. Gen. Thao Ma and some of his men to Vientiane, leaving Maj. Gen. Phoumi in Udorn, Thailand. During the August 19 meeting, no one volunteered to lead the coup, so Brig. Gen. Thao Ma volunteered himself for the job with a condition that he be named the commander in chief of the army, if the coup was successful. Everyone agreed to his condition. The details were that the coup was to take place in the morning of August 20, 1973; Col. Prany Phonthipsavath was to take over the National Radio at 5:00 o'clock in the morning; Col. Bounleuth Saycosy and his commando team were to take over the Command Center of the Royal Lao Army in Phonh Kheng at 5:00 o'clock in the morning; and Police Lt. Col. Praveth and Mr. Souvannarath were to arrest Prime Minister Prince Souvanna Phouma in his residence before the coup started, and then take him to the Command Center in Chinaimo. Unknown to the rest of the coup team, Maj. Gen. Kouprasith Abhay[59] secretly went to see Prince Souvanna Phouma during the night before the coup. Soon after that secret meeting, a jeep from the French Embassy in Vientiane came to the residence of Prince Souvanna Phouma and took him away.

The coup was carried out as planned, and when Police Lt. Col. Pravet and Mr. Souvannarath arrived at the residence of Prince Souvanna Phouma in the early morning of August 20, they learned that the prince had already been taken away by the French Embassy. Without Prince Souvanna Phouma in their control, the coup was doomed to fail. When Brig. Gen. Thao Ma learned of the disappearance of Prince Souvanna Phouma, in addition to the information that Maj. Gen. Kouprasith did not order his troop to help the coup as planned, he knew right away that it was the work of Kouprasith Abhay. He was very furious and directed his anger toward Kouprasith; he took a T-28 at Wattay Airport and flew it into the sky. He bombed the home of Maj. Gen.

Kouprasit, but missed. He then flew to Chinaimo, the office of Maj. Gen. Kouprasith and dropped a bomb there, killing Lt. Col. Thongkham Abhay, who was the nephew of Kouprasith. Instead of flying to Thailand, Thao Ma landed his T-28 at the Wattay Airport in Vientiane.⁶⁰ When Thao Ma landed his T-28 at Wattay, CIA agents radioed him and told him to take a Cessna at the Wattay Airport and fly to Thailand, but he did not want to go to Thailand. He wanted to confront Kouprasith, which was a bad and fatal decision. Soon, Kouprasith's forces surrounded the airport and captured Thao Ma. They tied him up and took him to Chinaimo, where Kouprasith was waiting for him. As soon as the soldiers dropped Thao Ma from their truck onto the ground in Chinaimo, Kouprasith came forward and used one of his feet to step on the face of Thao Ma and said, "You killed my nephew and you must die." Thao Ma responded, "Fat Kouprasith. You tricked me into the coup and then broke my back behind me. I am also a general, so why do you treat me in this manner?" They exchanged a few angry words, and Kouprasith ordered his assassin to finish Thao Ma off, and the coup ended there.

On May 10, Prime Minister Prince Souvanna Phouma announced Maj. Gen. Vang Pao's replacement⁶¹ as commander of Military Region II.⁶² Vang Pao began to send members of his family to Thailand. However, he was prepared to defend Long Cheng and confront the Pathet Lao forces.⁶³ In Vang Pao's judgment, Souvanna Phouma had capitulated to the Pathet Lao. On this same day, Dr. Yang Dao, who was in Vientiane, received a message from a close Lao friend that shook his very existence. The friend told him, "I have heard some very bad news," that the "Pathet Lao and North Vietnamese troops are surrounding Long Cheng and they will attack at any moment."⁶⁴

On May 11, Yang Dao went to meet with Prime Minister Prince Souvanna Phouma in Vientiane to request the prime minister convince the Pathet Lao to not attack Long Cheng. Yang Dao was very concerned with the above message that the Pathet Lao had deployed forces surrounding Long Cheng and could attack at any moment. Upon hearing Yang Dao's request, the prime minister picked up the telephone on his desk to call Phoumi Vongvichit (ພູມີ ວົງວິຈິດ), the deputy prime minister on the Pathet Lao side, but his phone was out of order. The prime minister then instructed Yang Dao to go see Phoumi Vongvichit. Yang Dao met with Phoumi Vongvichit (1909–1994), who was very angry and said, "If Vang Pao wants war, we will give him war. We will fight with him as long as it takes; we will fight for [five or ten] years, if that is what it takes." In the end, Phoumi calmed down and agreed not to attack Long Cheng. Many years later, Yang Dao brought the incident on May 11 to Prince Souvanna Phouma's son, Chao Mangkhala. He asked Mangkhala about the unimaginable out of order telephone on Prime Minister Prince Souvanna Phouma's desk. Mangkhala told Yang Dao that on May 11, the Pathet Lao had cut off all telephone lines of ministers on the side of the non-Pathet Lao, including the telephone of Prime Minsiter Prince Souvanna Phouma. Mangkhala added that the Pathet Lao had taken control of the government of Laos since that day on.[65]

On May 12, Yang Dao, a member of the NPCC and a confidante of Vang Pao at the time, met with Vang Pao in Long Cheng. Reportedly, Vang Pao had ordered Colonel Shoua Yang to organize the defense of Long Cheng, but it was operationally not possible. The demobilization had severely depleted the forces. There were simply not enough forces for an effective defense. Yang Dao advised Maj. Gen. Vang Pao to reconsider his decision to engage with the Pathet Lao by military means and his plan to bomb Nam Ngeum Dam and Wattay Airport in an effort to bring down the PGNU. After a lengthy discussion, Yang Dao was able to convince Vang Pao to abandon his plan to bring down the PGNU of Prime Minister Prince Souvanna. They also discussed that Vang Pao's only option was to find passage out of Laos.[66]

On May 13, Prince Souvanna Phouma sent his son, Chao Mangkhala Souvanna Phouma, and two foreign diplomats to Long Cheng to appeal to Vang Pao not to provoke the Pathet Lao. For Souvanna Phouma, the implementation of the 1973 Peace and National Reconciliation Agreement was the only option for peace.[67] Before Mangkhala left Long Cheng, Vang Pao asked him to personally deliver Vang Pao's official resignation as commander of Military Region II to his father, the prime minister.[68] On this same day, an emissary from the U.S. Embassy in Thailand visited Long Cheng to impress upon Vang Pao to leave the country.[69] A few days earlier, Vang Pao had given a list of twenty-five hundred people to the Americans. These were his high-ranking military officers and their families as people to be evacuated from Long Cheng to Thailand; many on this list were evacuated on May 13 from Long Cheng to Nam Phong, Thailand. Among those who were evacuated on May 13 was Colonel Moua Sue, his four wives, and their children.

Moua Sue is the son of Colonel Cher Pao Moua, the famous colonel of Bouam Long, who has never fallen into the hands of the Pathet Lao. He had an eighth-grade education and was the bodyguard of Touby Lyfoung when Touby was the vice president of the National Assembly of Laos in the late 1950s. His first wife, Mo Nao Lyfoung, was the half-sister of Touby and sister of Tougeu and Toulia. She was also the widow of Vang Pao's older brother. After marrying Touby's half-sister, Touby sent him to work for the National Radio of Laos as the Hmong radio announcer and was in this position for about a year. Then in early 1960, he returned to his village in Xieng Khouang to help his father, who was a military officer of the Royal Lao Army and was in charge of the military base at Bouam Long. He later volunteered to serve in the SGU under then Lt. Col. Vang Pao, and was sent to get special

Figure 2.2.   Evacuation of Hmong from Long Cheng, May 1975.
Bertrand Moua.

military training in Vientiane. Soon after the completion of his training, he returned to Xieng Khouang, was promoted to first lieutenant, and became a company commander. In 1965, he was promoted to captain and became battalion commander. Since then, he has been on a fast track to higher military ranks; he was promoted to major in 1966, lieutenant colonel in 1968, and then full colonel in 1972. During his tenure with Military Region II, he had held many important posts, including SGU liaison officer to Houa Khong (Luang Namtha) Province, chief of staff of Military Region II, GM commander, and from 1974 to 1975, he was a brigade commander. In short, he was one of the most well-known military officers of Military Region II. With the first wife, he has four children; the second wife, three; the third wife, one child; the fourth wife (a Lao Chinese), two children. His four wives and their children were evacuated from Long Cheng by a C-130 and flew directly to Nam Phong, Thailand. While in the refugee camp in Thailand, he divorced all of his four wives and later married another young woman by the name of Ia Xiong. He and his young wife were resettled in Providence, Rhode Island, in 1979. They lived there for three years before moving to other places, such as Petersburg, Pennsylvania; Salk Lake City, Utah; Santa Ana, California; Sheboygan, Wisconsin; and North Carolina. With his fifth wife, he has one child, but they divorced before he returned to Thailand in 1986. He has lived in Thailand for more than twenty years, and while living in Thailand, he married his sixth wife, Kanapha Lee, and they have one son, who was nineteen years old in 2015. In February 2015, he came back to the United States and was in his seventies. He plans to bring his sixth wife and their son to the United States, to spend the rest of his life in America.[70]

On May 14, 1975, Maj. Gen. Vang Pao, former commander of Military Region II of Laos, made an historic exit from Laos to Nam Phong, Thailand. Two pilots landed their planes in Long Cheng airport; one with a helicopter and another with a Cessna. They went to the residence of Maj. Gen. Vang Pao to discuss their next rendezvous. After the two pilots agreed on their next meeting point, they left Vang Pao's house. Vang Pao then took the helicopter from Long Cheng to Muong Cha, and then got on a Cessna plane to fly to Nam Phong, Thailand. Vang Pao and his family stayed in Nam Phong, Thailand, where many thousands of other Hmong refugees were staying; most of these Hmong refugees were his former officers and their families. Shortly after his arrival in Thailand, the Government of Thailand asked Vang Pao to leave Thailand for fear that his stay would complicate Thailand's relations with Laos.[71] In June 1975, Vang Pao and his youngest wife Chong and their son Chu Long left Thailand for the United States with a brief stop in France. They came to the state of Montana in the United States of America.

Touby Lyfoung, who was the political leader of the Hmong in the Royal Lao government and the first Hmong of Laos to hold a cabinet post, came to see Vang Pao twice in Thailand, but to no avail. Maj. Gen. Vang Pao refused to meet with Touby in person while in Thailand, and he had privately told Yang Dao that he did not want to see Touby because Touby bad mouthed him while meeting with the Hmong in Ban Sone. According to Yang Dao, a week after Vang Pao arrived in Thailand, he sent a voice cassette tape to Prime Minister Prince Souvanna Phouma. Apparently, the cassette tape was in Hmong, so the prime minister asked Touby to translate it for him. In the tape, Vang Pao had said that no country had yet agreed to take Hmong refugees, so the Hmong should stay put in Laos. Upon hearing this, the prime minister asked Touby to tell the Hmong not to escape out of the country. Touby went to Ban Sone and told the Hmong there that Vang Pao and Yang Dao left Laos because of political reasons. The ordinary Hmong do not have political problems, so they should not escape Laos to Thailand in large groups. Touby also told the Hmong there that they should learn from history of how the Hmong escaped from China to Laos. He said, back then the Hmong did not escape in large groups, but "Qev kauv txhais"—loosely translated as "follow the gazelle," or using the forest to escape. Many Hmong did not understand Touby; they assumed that Touby tried to prevent them from escaping. After some of them escaped to Thailand, they told Vang Pao that Touby had told them not to escape and bad mouthed Vang Pao (meaning that Vang Pao escaped out of Laos because of his political problem).[72] Touby did not leave Laos and was sent to re-education camp by the end of 1975. He reportedly died in detention in 1979. His half-brother, Tougeu Lyfoung, the director general of the Ministry of Justice and procurator of the Supreme Court, fled Laos on July 2, 1975, to Thailand and then to France. Toulia, another half-brother of Touby, also left Laos to France.

Although Yang Dao, who was a member of the NPCC, had worked well with both the left and the right during his tenure in the NPCC, he was surprised to see a Pathet Lao newspaper continue to denounce the Hmong on the Royal Lao government side after the peace agreement had been signed and both sides were supposedly working toward national reconciliation. One day in mid-May 1975, Chansamone Voravong, a senior official of the Royal Lao government, came to see his friend, Yang Dao, with a Pathet Lao newspaper in hand. The headline read, "ເສິກແລ້ວ ແມ້ວຕາຍ," meaning "War ends, Meo Die." The term "Meo" had been used during the war by the Pathet Lao to refer to those Hmong who opposed them. This was a total contradiction to the letter and spirit of the Peace and National Reconciliation Agreement. With this and other developments, which portended great danger for the Hmong, Yang Dao and other educated Hmong decided to leave Laos. Yang Dao left Laos for Thailand by the middle of May 1975. He later resettled in France and then immigrated to the United States in early 1983.

By the end of 1975, most of the Hmong leaders and civil servants of the Royal Lao government had fled the country, except Lyteck Lynhiavu (1940–1978), the pre-1975 director general of the Ministry of Interior. In his *The Liver and The Tongue*, Lynhiavu wrote that Lyteck was arrested on November 30, 1975, and sent to re-education camp number 6 in Houa Phanh Province, where he was executed in December 1978. Trusting Col. Ly Nou, who knew the terrains of Houa Phanh Province well, Lyteck and Lt. Cols. Blong Thao, Moua Pao, and Yang Yi escaped from the re-education camp as planned with Ly Nou. Apparently, Ly Nou changed his mind; he did not escape as planned and went to inform the camp authorities about the escape of his colleagues. The authority went after the escapees and captured them. They then executed Lyteck, Moua Pao, and Yang Yi.[73]

By November 1975, most of the rightist generals and politicians were either sent to re-education camp or left the country to become refugees abroad. The Pathet Lao had total control of Laos. As indicated in my writing elsewhere, the next major move was to rotate all ministerial meetings in both the major cities controlled by the Royal Lao government and the Pathet Lao. The first few meetings went as planned. The meeting in late November 1975 took place in Sam Neua Town, a town controlled by the Pathet Lao. All ministers were told to have their personal drivers transport them there by car. It was reported that the first day went well and was productive; however, the agenda included more work than they could finish in one or two days. The organizers told the ministers to instruct their personal drivers to return home first, as the work might require them to stay behind for a few more days. The ministers took the advice, and their drivers returned to Vientiane. Several days later, the November 28 demonstration took place in Vientiane and elsewhere—demanding the abolition of the monarchy institution, the PGNU, and the NPCC. The Pathet Lao officials politely apologized for the inconvenience, but said the people are now the lords of the land and were just exercising their right to demand a government that was more representative of the wishes of the people—from the people, by the people, and for the people. The ministers had no choice but to submit their resignations. The moment in which this happened, the ministers were told that they were no longer officials and would have to support themselves as did the rest of the country's people.[74]

Touby Lyfoung was among these ministers. He was then sent to re-education camp and reportedly died in 1979. Many of his colleagues suffered similar a fate. There are a few inconsistent accounts of Touby Lyfoung's death. An account from Touby's family indicates that Touby along with many ministers from the non-Pathet Lao side were chained and deprived of food and other basic needs, and as a result, all of them died of malnutrition, but Touby Lyfoung died of a single bullet from a guard. This account also indicates Touby was deprived of food and basic needs, therefore, he lost a lot of weight and might have been delusional; he may have used strong words with the guard who shot him.[75] Another account says:

> In August and September of 1977, a group of twenty-six "reactionary" high-ranking officials and military officers in Camp 05 were accused of plotting a coup and arrested. These persons were taken away to Camp 01. They included Pheng Phongsavan, the minister who had signed the [1973]Vientiane Agreement; Touby Lyfoung, the Hmong leader; Soukhan Vilaysan, another of Souvanna Phouma's ministers who had been with him in the Lao Issara and had risen to become secretary general of the Neutralists; and Generals Bounphone Maekthepharak and Ouan Ratikoun. All died in Camp 01.[76]

On November 28, 1975, as mentioned above, demonstrations took place in Vientiane and elsewhere, denouncing the monarchy and demanding the dissolution of the PGNU and NPCC. "The next day, the NPCC president, Souphanouvong flew to the royal capital [Luang Phrabang], where he, Souvanna, and Phoumi Vongvichit informed the king's letter of abdication and 'voluntary' renunciation of the royal wealth.".[77] Below is King Sisavang Vatthana's (ເຈົ້າມະຫາຊີວິດ ສີສະຫວ່າງວັດທະນາ) abdication speech, which was his last speech:

> Laos is a peaceful nation, but has never seen peace. We have never invaded our neighbors, but have long been kept under subjugation. When Laos was not being attacked by foreign powers, we fought amongst ourselves. Our great nation has been ravaged by enemies from outsides, as well as within. For more than thirty years, we have been fighting. If my abdication shall bring peace, a mere citizen is what I shall become.[78]

On December 2, 1975, shortly after King Sisavang Vatthana (1907–1978?) was forced to abdicate from the throne, the Lao People's Democratic Republic (LPDR) was proclaimed by the Lao People's Revolutionary Party (the Communist Party of Laos) under the leadership of Kaysone Phomvihane (ໄກສອນ ພົມວິຫານ, 1920–1992). A Communist government was instituted, and the Lao People's Revolutionary Party[79] became the only ruling party of the new government. The government of the LPDR included Faydang Lobliayao as one of its vice presidents; Nhiavue Lobliayao, another son of Lo Bliayao and a half-brother of Faydang, as a high-ranking member of the Lao People's Revolutionary Party and chairman of minority affairs[80]; Vongphet XaykeuYachongtoua as the governor of Luang Phrabang; and Yongyia Ya as the governor of Xieng Khouang Province. Col. Paseuth Fong Ya, the sub-division commander of the Pathet Lao Army in Xieng Khouang, took charge of the region of Long Cheng (after Vang Pao left on May 14, 1975). He was assassinated in October 1975 and did not have the opportunity to take an active role in post-1975 Laos. Col. Paseuth Fong Ya was the nephew and successor of Col. Ya Thotou, the legendary founder of the Pachay Battalion, and commander of Battalion 2 of the Pathet Lao forces. Ya Thotou died in January 1961 from a single car accident, and Paseuth Fong Ya took over his commanding post of the Pachay Battalion and other leadership roles. Overall, the Hmong of Laos on both sides suffered heavy casualties during the Secret War. More than 10 percent of their estimated three hundred thousand population perished, and more than half of them became refugees abroad after the war. Arthur Dommen Jr., a senior scholar of Laos, made the following summary about the impact of the war on the Hmong. "Among the sorriest of the exiles were the Hmong, who were virtually destroyed as a significant ethnic group as a result of the years of warfare, dislocation, and, finally, a determined extermination campaign mounted against them."[81]

Four decades have passed, and the Hmong have slowly emerged from the rubble of the war. In today's Laos, many Hmong have served in the LPDR government, and many have been promoted to hold important posts in the new LPDR government. As of 2016, Pany Yathotou is the third member of the Politburo and president of the National Assembly, and Chaleun Yiapao-heu is minister in the prime minister's office, and had previously served as the minister of justice. Additionally, two vice ministers and three brigadier generals are Hmong. The uprooted Hmong American community has also survived the turbulence of their adaptation to the United States and has become a community of a very young and active population. The following chapters highlight the unique stories of Hmong Americans and their contributions to the United States, their adopted country, and Laos, their former homeland.

NOTES

1. Christopher Robbins. 1987. *The Ravens*. New York, NY: Crown Publishers, p. 99.
2. Jeremy Heine. 1995. *From Vietnam, Laos and Cambodia*. Twayne Publisher, p. 11.
3. MacAllister Brown and Joseph J. Zasloff. 1986. *Apprentice Revolutionaries: The Communist Movement in Laos, 1930–1985*. Hoover Institution Press, p. 1.
4. Ibid, 208.
5. Only Military Region V did not have Special Guerrilla Units in their forces. Although Military Regions I, II, III, and IV had Special Guerrilla Units in their rank and file, Military Region II had more Special Guerrilla Units or irregular soldiers than regular forces.
6. Soutchay Vongsavanh. 1981. *RLG Military Operation and Activities in the Laotion Panhandle*. Virginia: Dally Book Service.
7. Members of the Na Champassack family are the descendants of the rulers of the former Champassack Kingdom (in today's southern Laos).
8. MacAlister Brown and Joseph J. Zasloff. 1986. *Apprentice Revolutionaries: The Communist Movement in Laos, 1930–1985*. Hoover Institution Press, p. 154).
9. Thomas L. Ahern Jr. 2006. *Undercover Armies*. Center for the Studies of Intelligence, p. 14). Declassified on February 19, 2009. http://nsarchive.gwu.edu/NSAEBB/NSAEBB284/6-UNDERCOVER_ARMIES.pdf.
10. Ibid, 14.
11. Ibid, 15.
12. Ibid, 19.
13. University of Texas at Dallas. 1993. Interview with James W. (Bill) Lair and Lloyd (Pat) Landry. Bangkok, p. 2). https://www.utdallas.edu/library/specialcollections/hac/cataam/notebooks/sepcop65.pdf.
14. Ibid, 2.
15. Ibid, 2.
16. Roger Warner. 1990. *Out of Laos: A Story of War and Exodus, Told in Photographs*. Rancho Cordova, CA: Southeast Asia Community Resource Center.
17. James Lilley with Jeremy Lilley. 2004. *China Hands*. New York: Public Affairs, p. 117.

18. Thomas L. Ahern Jr. 2006. *Undercover Armies*. Center for the Studies of Intelligence, p. 127. Declassified on February 19, 2009. http://nsarchive.gwu.edu/NSAEBB/NSAEBB284/6-UNDERCOVER_ARMIES.pdf.

19. Wameng Xiong, personal communication. August 15, 2016.

20. Christopher Robbins. 1987. *The Ravens*. New York, NY: Crown Publishers, p. 102.

21. Andrea Matles Savada. 1994. *A Country Study: Laos*. Federal Division, Library of Congress, p. 57. https://archive.org/stream/laoscountrystudy00sava_0/laoscountrystudy00sava_0_djvu.txt.

22. Douglas S. Blaufarb. 1977. *The Counterinsurgency Era: U.S. Doctrine and Performance, 1950 to the Present*. New York: The Free Press, p. 2.

23. Andrea Matles Savada (Ed.). 1994. *Laos (Laos Index): A Country Study*. Federal Research Division, Library of Congress, p. 59. https://cdn.loc.gov/master/frd/frdcstdy/la/laoscountrystudy00sava_0/laoscountrystudy00sava_0.pdf.

24. Oudone Sananikone (Major General). 1984. *The Royal Lao Army and U.S. Army Advice and Support* (Indochina monographs), p. 138.

25. Kenneth Conboy. 1995. *Shadow War: The CIA's Secret War in Laos*. Paladin Press, p. 115.

26. To read more about the Ho Chi Minh Trail, see Ho Chi Minh Trail. United States History. http://www.u-s-history.com/pages/h1875.html.

27. James Lilley with Jeremy Lilley. 2004. *China Hands*. New York: Public Affairs, p. 118.

28. Douglas S. Blaufarb. 1977. *The Counterinsurgency Era: U.S. Doctrine and Performance, 1950 to the Present*. New York: The Free Press, p. 2.

29. Sullivan's War (listed in the website of the T-28 Trojan Foundation). file:///K:/Books%20and%20Proposals/SGU%20Book/Secret%20War.html.

30. Thomas L. Ahern Jr. 2006. *Undercover Armies*. Center for the Studies of Intelligence, p. 210. Declassified on February 19, 2009. http://nsarchive.gwu.edu/NSAEBB/NSAEBB284/6-UNDERCOVER_ARMIES.pdf.

31. James Lilley with Jeremy Lilley. 2004. *China Hands*. New York: Public Affairs, p. 130.

32. Ibid, 115.

33. Jacob Van Staaveren. 1993. *Interdiction, 1960–1968*. Washington, DC: Air Force History, p. IV. http://www.afhso.af.mil/shared/media/document/AFD-100927-078.pdf.

34. The military story of Col. Khao Insixiengmay is a paraphrase summary of his biography, which he shared with me. I also had a telephone conversation with Col. Khao Insixignmay about his past service and his view on Special Guerilla Unites in Laos. Khao Insixiengmay, personal communication. April 28, 2015.

35. James Lilley with Jeremy Lilley. 2004. *China Hands*. New York: Public Affairs, p. 130.

36. Deseret News. May 16, 1989. "China Admits It Sent Troops to Fight the U.S. during the Vietnam War." http://www.deseretnews.com/article/46743/CHINA-ADMITS-IT-SENT-TROOPS-TO-FIGHT-THE-US-IN-VIETNAM.html?pg=all.

37. MacAllister Brown and Joseph J. Zasloff. 1986. *Apprentice Revolutionaries: The Communist Movement in Laos, 1930–1985*. Hoover Institution Press, p. 277.

38. Oudone Sananikone (Major General). 1984. *The Royal Lao Army and U.S. Army Advice and Support* (Indochina monographs), p. 139.

39. Sue Moua, Col., personal communication. September 25, 2015.

40. Timothy N. Castle. 1995. *At War in the Shadow of Vietnam: U.S. Military Aid to the Royal Lao Government–1955–1975*. https://books.google.com/books?isbn=023107977X.

41. See USA Legacy in Laos, http://www.savannanet.com/uslegacy.htm. Also see Arthur Dommen Jr. 1985. *Laos: Keystone of Indochina*. Boulder, CO: Westview Press, p. 90. According to Dommen, by the time the bombing in Laos halted in 1973, the U.S. aircraft had dropped 2,092,900 tons (1,898,260 metric tons) of bombs on Laos, approximately the total tonnage dropped by the U.S. air forces during all of World War II in both European and Pacific theatres.

42. For more discussion on Hmong history and their involvement during the war years, see Roger Warner. 1995 *Backfire*. Simon and Schuster; and Paul Hillmer. 2010. *A People's History of The Hmong*. Minnesota Historical Society Press. Also see Kou Yang. 2003. "Hmong Diaspora of the Post-War Period." *Asian Pacific Migration Journal*, 12(3):271–300.

43. According to a declassified cable from the U.S. Embassy in Vientiane, General Phoumi had ordered General Thao Ma to bomb the fifth zone camp at Chinaimo (Military Central Command), and Gen. Khamkhong to attack Chinaimo from the east (the cable is dated February 2, 1965). Also see Kenneth Conboy. 1995. *The CIA's Secret War in Laos*. Paladin Press.

44. Ly Fu, personal communication. December 18, 2014.

45. Kenneth Conboy. 1995. *The CIA's Secret War in Laos*. Paladin Press, p. 125.

46. W. Courtland Robinson. 1998. *Terms of Refuge*. New York: Zed Books Ltd., p. 13.

47. W.E. Garrett. 1974. "No Place to Run: The Hmong of Laos." *National Geographic*, 145(1):78–111.

48. Nicholas Tapp. 1986. *The Hmong of Thailand: Opium People of the Golden Triangle*. Cambridge, MA: Anti-Slavery Society, p. 31, 43.

49. Yang Dao. 1993. "Hmong at The Turning Point." In *Hmong at The Turning Point*, Jean L. Blake (ed.). Minneapolis: WorldBridge Associates.

50. Jacques Lemoine, another scholar on the Hmong, also made a similar statement in his studies of the Hmong in northern Laos. See, for example, Jacques Lemoine. 1972. "Un Village Hmong Vert du Haut Laos." *Editions du Centre National de la Recherche Scientifique*. http://www.renincorp.org/bookshelf/un-village-hmong_lemoine.pdf.

51. Yang Dao, telephone interview. May 6, 2003.

52. Gary Yia Lee. 1982. "Minority Policies and the Hmong in Laos." In *Contemporary Laos: Studies in the Politics and Society of the Lao People's Democratic Republic*, Martin Stuart-Fox (ed.). St. Lucia: Queensland University Press, p. 199–219. http://members.ozemail.com.au/~yeulee/History/minority%20policies%20and%20the%20hmong%20in%20laos.html.

53. Keith Quincy (2000:361) notes that Souvanna Phouma had offered Vang Pao a desk position in Vientiane, if he would relinquish his commission as commander of Military Region II, but Vang Pao responded with outrage: he ripped the stars off his shirt and threw them on Souvanna Phouma's desk, telling Souvanna Phouma that he was resigning. Chan (1994:44) also states that Souvanna Phouma relieved Vang Pao from his post as commander of Military Region II. Yang Dao, who has a copy of Vang Pao's resignation and was a confidante of Vang Pao at the time, disputes the notion that Vang Pao resigned on May 6 when he met with Souvanna Phouma. Yang Dao stated that Vang Pao gave his resignation to Chao Mangkhala Souvanna Phouma on May 13 to take to Souvanna Phouma. Lyblong Lynhiavu includes in his book, *The Liver and The Tongue*, a copy of the order of Prime Minister Prince Souvanna Phouma to send Chao Mankhala to accompany two diplomats to go to Long Cheng. The order was signed on May 12. See Lyblong Lynhiavu. 2015. *The Liver and The Tongue*. Self-published, p. 244.

54. See "Treaties. Equipment and guerrilla unit forces, special, Laos." 1978. In *United States Treaties and Other International Agreements*. https://books.google .com/books?id=Tr4BdNUkwpUC.

55. Andrea Matles Savada (Ed.). 1994. *Laos (Laos Index): A Country Study*. Federal Research Division, Library of Congress, p. 59. https://cdn.loc.gov/master/frd/ frdcstdy/la/laoscountrystudy00sava_0/laoscountrystudy00sava_0.pdf.

56. Macalister Brown and Joseph J. Zasloff. 1986. *Apprentice Revolutionaries: The Communist Movement in Laos, 1930–1985*. Hoover Institution Press, p. 321.

57. Yang Dao, telephone interview. May 6, 2003.

58. Mothana Vilaysack. 2011. *Roots of Souphanouvong* (ຕົ້ນ ຕໍຂອງ ສຸພານຸວົງ). p. 450. Vilaysith passed away in 2012. As a result, this author is unable to get his permission released letter. Translation from Lao to English is made by this author.

59. At the time, Kouprasith Abhay (1932–2011) was deputy commander in chief of the Royal Lao Army. He resigned his commission on May 11, 1975, and later became a refugee in France. He died in France in 2011 (some literature said he died in 1999).

60. Another account by Kenneth Conboy indicates that a soldier of the Royal Lao Army fired a truck-mounted machine gun and hit Thao Ma's orbiting T-28. Streaming smoke, the general crash-landed at Wattay. Wounded but still alive, he was lifted from the cockpit, thrown in the back of a truck, and driven to Chinaimo. See Kenneth Conboy. 1995. *Shadow War: The CIA's Secret War in Laos*. Boulder, CO: Paladin Press, p. 409.

61. Witness account provided by Yang Dao indicated that Vang Pao did not officially resign his post as commander of Military Region II until May 13, the day before he left Laos.

62. Macalister Brown and Joseph J. Zasloff. 1986. *Apprentice Revolutionaries: The Communist Movement in Laos, 1930–1985*. Hoover Institution Press, p. 321.

63. This account is from Lt. Col. Chou Peter Vang, who was with the family of Maj. Gen. Vang Pao during this crisis. Peter Chou Vang, personal communication. February 6, 2003.

64. Wameng Moua. April 13, 2008. "The Scholar Hero: The Untold Story of How Dr. Yang Dao Negotiated the Fate of the Hmong in Laos in 1975." *Hmong Today.* http://www.tcdailyplanet.net/scholar-hero-untold-story-how-dr-yang-dao-negotiated -fate/.

65. Yang Dao, personal communication. April 30, 2015.

66. Yang Dao, telephone interview. February 6, 2003. Also see Wameng Moua. April 13, 2008. "The Scholar Hero: The Untold Story of How Dr. Yang Dao Negotiated the Fate of the Hmong in Laos in 1975." *Hmong Today.* http://www.tcdaily planet.net/scholar-hero-untold-story-how-dr-yang-dao-negotiated-fate/.

67. The history of Laos maintained by Vientianetimes.net, and available from http://www.vientianetimes.net/history/may75.html, indicates that Prince Souvanna Phouma summoned Vang Pao to see him in Vientiane to persuade him to leave.

68. Yang Dao, telephone interview. February 6, 2003.

69. Sucheng Chan. 1994. *Hmong Means Free.* Philadelphia: Temple University Press, p. 45.

70. Col. Moua Sue, personal communication. September 25, 2015.

71. Lt. Col. Chou Peter Vang, personal communication. February 6, 2003. Quincy (2000:443) stated that Vang Pao left Thailand because the Thai government wanted him to go and the U.S. Embassy in Thailand had persuaded Washington to bend immigration rules to allow Vang Pao and his family to enter the United States. See Keith Quincy. 2000. *Harvesting Pa Chay's Wheat.* Eastern Washington University Press.

72. Yang Dao, personal communication. April 30, 2015.

73. Lyblong Lynhiavu. 2015. *The Liver and Tongue: Memoir of Lyblong Lynhiavu.* Self-published, p. 90.

74. See, for example, Kou Yang. 2013. *Laos and Its Expatriates in the United States.* PublishAmerica, p. 61.

75. Anonymous person, personal communication. January 23, 2010.

76. Andrea Matles Savada (Ed.). 1994. Laos (Laos Index): A Country Study. Federal Research Division, Library of Congress, p. 69. https://cdn.loc.gov/master/frd/ frdcstdy/la/laoscountrystudy00sava_0/laoscountrystudy00sava_0.pdf.

77. MacAllister Brown and Joseph J. Zasloff. 1986. *Apprentice Revolutionaries: The Communist Movement in Laos, 1930–1985.* Hoover Institution Press, p. 119.

78. Constitutional Monarchy and Laos in the 21st Century (June 2000). http:// freelao.tripod.com/id69.htm.

79. The Lao People's Revolutionary Party or Communist Party of Laos was founded in 1955, but operated in secrecy. During the war years, the public only knew New Lao Haksat (ແນວລາວ ຮັກຊາດ) or Pathet Lao (ປະເທດລາວ), which traced its roots back to 1950, when its name was publicly used by Prince Souphanouvong and his followers.

80. To read more about Nhiavue Lobliayao, see Kou Yang. 2000. "The Passing of a Hmong Pioneer: Nhiavu Lobliayao (Nyiaj Vws Lauj Npliaj Yob), 1915–1999." *Hmong Studies Journal,* 3. http://hmongstudies.com/HSJv3_Yang.pdf.

81. Arthur Dommen Jr. *Laos: Keystone of Indochina.* Boulder, CO: Westview Press, p. 114.

REFERENCES

Ahern Jr., Thomas L. 2006. *Undercover Armies: CIA and Surrogate Warfare in Laos 1961–1973.* Center for the Studies of Intelligence. Washington, DC: Central Intelligence Agency. Declassified on February 19, 2009. http://nsarchive.gwu.edu/NSAEBB/NSAEBB284/6-UNDERCOVER_ARMIES.pdf.

Blaufarb, Douglas S. 1997. *The Counterinsurgency Era: U.S. Doctrine and Performance, 1950 to the Present.* New York: The Free Press.

Brown, MacAllister, and Joseph J. Zasloff. 1986. *Apprentice Revolutionaries: The Communist Movement in Laos, 1930–1985.* Hoover Institution Press.

Castle, Timothy N. 1995. *At War in the Shadow of Vietnam: U.S. Military Aid to the Royal Lao Government 1955–1975.* New York: Columbia University Press.

Chan, Sucheng. 1994. *Hmong Means Free.* Philadelphia: Temple University Press.

Conboy, Kenneth. 1995. *Shadow War: The CIA's Secret War in Laos.* Boulder, CO: Paladin Press.

Deseret News. China Admits It Sent Troops to Fight the U.S. during the Vietnam War. Deseret Digital Media. May 16, 1989. Copyright 2017. http://www.deseretnews.com/article/46743/CHINA-ADMITS-IT-SENT-TROOPS-TO-FIGHT-THE-US-IN-VIETNAM.html?pg=all.

Dommen Jr., Arthur. 1986. *Laos: Keystone of Indochina.* Boulder, CO: Westview Press.

Garret, W.E. 1974. No Place to Run: The Hmong of Laos. *National Geographic,* 145(1), 78–111.

Insixiengmay, Khao, personal communication. April 28, 2015.

Heine, Jeremy. 1995. *From Vietnam, Laos, and Cambodia: A Refugee Experience in the United States.* Twayne Publisher.

Hillmer, Paul. 2010. *A People's History of The Hmong.* Minnesota Historical Society Press.

Lee, Gary Yia. 1982. "Minority Policies and the Hmong in Laos." Martin Stuart-Fox, ed. *Contemporary Laos: Studies in the Politics and Society of the Lao People's Democratic Republic,* 199–219. St. Lucia: Queensland University Press.

Lemoine, Jacques. 1972. *Un Village Hmong Vert du Haut Laos.* Editions du Centre National de la Recherche Scientifique.

Lilley, James, and Jeremy Lilley. 2004. *China Hands.* New York: Public Affairs.

Lynhiavu, Lyblong. 2015. *The Liver and the Tongue.* Self-published.

Quincy, Keith. 2000. *Harvesting Pa Chay's Wheat.* Eastern Washington University Press.

Robbins, Christopher. 1987. *The Ravens.* New York: Crown Publishers.

Robinson, W. Courtland. 1988. *Terms of Refuge.* New York: Zed Books Ltd.

Sananikone, Oudone (Major General). 1984. *The Royal Lao Army and U.S. Army Advice and Support* (Indochina monographs).

Savada, Andreas Matles, ed. July 1994. *Laos: A Country Study.* Washington, DC: Federal Research Division, Library of Congress. https://archive.org/stream/laoscountrystudy00sava_0/laoscountrystudy00sava_0_djvu.txt.

Sullivan's War (listed on the website of the T-28 Trojan Foundation). file:///K:/
Books%20and%20Proposals/SGU%20Book/Secret%20War.html.

Tapp, Nicholas. 1986. *The Hmong of Thailand: Opium People of the Golden Triangle*. Cambridge, MA: Anti-Slavery Society.

United States Treaties and Other International Agreements. 1978. "Laos. Special
Guerilla Unit Forces and Equipment. Memorandum of Understanding: Signed June
23, 1973." Washington: U.S. Government Printing Office. https://books.google
.com/books?id=Tr4BdNUkwpUC.

Van Staaveren, Jacob. 1993. *Interdiction in Southern Laos, 1960–1968*. Center for
Air Force History (IV). Washington, DC: Library of Congress. https://media
.defense.gov/2010/Sep/27/2001329814/-1/-1/0/AFD-100927–078.pdf.

Vilaysack, Mothana. 2011. *Roots of Souphanouvong (תית ‏ສພ‌າ‏ຍຈ‏ອ‌ງ)*. Self-published.

Wameng Moua. "The Scholar Hero: The Untold Story of How Dr. Yang Dao
Negotiated the Fate of By." *Hmong Today: Twin Cities Daily Planet*. April 14,
2008. http://www.tcdailyplanet.net/scholar-hero-untold-story-how-dr-yang-dao
-negotiated-fate/.

Warner, Roger. 1996. *Out of Laos: A Story of War and Exodus, Told in Photographs*.
Rancho Cordova, CA: Southeast Asia Community Resource Center.

Yang, Dao. 1993. *Hmong at the Turning Point*. Jean L. Blake, ed. Minneapolis, MN:
WorldBridge Associates Ltd.

Yang, Kou. 2013. *Laos and Its Expatriates in the United States*. Maryland: PublishAmerica.

———. 2000. The Passing of a Hmong Pioneer: Nhiavu Lobliayao (Nyiaj Vws Lauj
Npliaj Yob), 1915–1999. *Hmong Studies Journal*, 3. http://hmongstudies.com/
HSJv3_Yang.pdf.

Chapter Three

The Pre-1975 Hmong Students in the United States

There were only a few Hmong students studying in the United States prior to the arrival of the first wave of Hmong refugees to the United States in 1975. Among these students was Bruce T. Bliatout, who was a graduate student at Tulane University in New Orleans. Bliatout provided a list of Hmong students that included Tou Fue Vang and Shur Vang, who already graduated from college and returned to Laos prior to 1975. The list also included Lytong Lytsongtseng, Vang Xiong, Chao (Co) Xiong, Vang Chong, Anthony K. Vang, Jerry Bliatout, Vang Chue, Vang Cheng, and Moua Chong. Vang Chue, Vang Cheng, and Moua Chong were high school students.[1] Some of these students went on to be the voices and community leaders of the Hmong refugee community in the United States. In my "The American Experience of the Hmong," I wrote that Bruce Bliatout and Anthony K. Vang later became major players in helping Hmong refugees adapt to their new life in the United States. They are also co-founders of the Hmong National Development, Inc., the only Hmong American national organization with headquarters in Washington, DC.[2] I also added that "Having been the first Hmong to earn his doctorate in the United States, Bruce Bliatout took on many roles and responsibilities to help the Hmong adjust to their new life in the United States. He was the Director and Coordinator of several refugee and community-based organizations, including: Refugees of Indochina Culture Education in Honolulu (1978–81), Southeast Asian Refugee Federation in Portland (1981–82), and Refugee Coordinator-Community Relations for the City of Portland (1982–90)."[3] He retired from his work as the director of the Tuberculosis Prevention and Treatment Center in Portland, Oregon. Anthony K. Vang was the executive director of Lao Family of Fresno in the 1980s and early 1990s. He founded the Fresno Center for New Americans, and then began teaching in higher learning institutions. As of 2015, he is an associate professor of

education and coordinator of the Multilingual Program at California State
University, Fresno. He previously served on the Board of Trustees for Fresno
Unified School District.

Not included in Bliatout's list is Cha Moua, who was an undergraduate
student at the University of Montana, Missoula, in 1975. There were also
several children of Maj. Gen. Vang Pao and other military families, who were
sent to study in Missoula, Montana, prior to 1975. According to Cha Moua,
three of these children were Sisouk, Cha, and Chai, who were Vang Pao's
children; they stayed with Wallie and Dixie Mace in Missoula. The other two
children were Saykham (son of Col. Cher Pao Moua) and Khamseng (son of
Col. Lee Teng), who stayed with the Stowald family in Missoula.[4] Although
Cha Moua was one of the few Hmong students studying in the United States
prior to the arrival of Hmong refugees, his life story and war experience was
very unique; it is, however, representative of the experiences of many Hmong
who lived through the war years.

Cha Moua was born to Say Shoua Moua and Ying Thao in 1948. At the
time of his birth, his family lived in Pak Kha Village in Sam Neau District
(ເມືອງ ຊຳເໜືອ), Houa Phanh (ແຂວງ ຫົວພັນ) Province, Laos. Houa Phanh
Province is in northeastern Laos and bordered by Dien Bien Phu, Vietnam.
It needs to be noted here that the Geneva Agreement in 1954 stipulated that
Houa Phanh and Phongsaly, the two northeastern provinces of Laos, be des-
ignated as a safe haven for the Pathet Lao revolutionaries until political settle-
ment could be made. Specifically, the Viengxay Caves, a small town in Houa
Phanh, became the headquarters of the Communist Pathet Lao (ປະເທດລາວ),
Lao Patriotic Front, or Neo Lao Hak Xat[5] during the war years.

He recalled seeing French soldiers retreat from the 1954 Dien Bien Phu
Battle, which took place from March 13 to May 7, 1954. The French forces
were defeated by the Viet Minh (League for the Independence of Vietnam).
Many French soldiers used road number 6 to escape from Dien Bien Phu to
Laos, and they passed through his village; road number 6 is the major artery
linking Dien Bien Phu to Laos. The defeat of the French by the Viet Minh
in Dien Bien Phu led to the signing of the 1954 Geneva Agreement, which
granted total and full independence to the three Indochinese countries: Vietnam, Laos, and Cambodia. However, the French's granting of independence
to Laos in 1954 was only the beginning of the civil war in Laos where the
young Cha Moua would later grow up to witness one of the most horrific
and violent destructions of the second Indochina war. His older brother and
father were recruited to join the armed forces in Military Region II, which
covered Xieng Khouang and Houa Phanh Provinces. Unfortunately, his father was killed in action in 1964, leaving the family to fend for themselves.
His schooling itself is another fascinating, interesting, and unique story. As

the older child at home and the second oldest child of the family, his parents wanted to keep him home to help them with work in the fields, but he wanted to attend school, so he persuaded his parents to let him go to school. In 1963, a year before the death of his father, his father took him to Hong Nong (Lima Site 86) and registered him at the village school there. While attending school in Hong Nong, he was drafted to join the Special Guerrilla Units (SGUs). Basically, he was a student in the classroom and a soldier outside of the classroom. He was given an M-14 rifle, which was too long and too heavy for him. He recalled that when he put the sling on his shoulder and let the rifle down to the ground, the other end of the barrel was dragging on the ground. He had to find his own way to carry his M-14 rifle. Fortunately, he received a pay of four hundred kip (Lao currency) per month (about eighty-five cents in U.S. dollars) in those days, and used this money to buy his civilian clothes, notebooks, and pencils. He was in school from 1963 to 1965, and thus, he acquired basic literacy skills. Due to the heavy fighting in 1965, his family became displaced. He went to Phou Phathi (Lima Site 85) and found himself alone. One day in July 1965, he saw the mayor of Sam Neua Town, which is the capital of Houa Phanh Province. He approached the mayor and asked the mayor to take him along so that he could go to school. Previously, he had helped the mayor while the mayor was running away from his enemies, therefore the mayor recognized him and agreed to take him to his home in Vientiane. On the way to Vientiane, the mayor was found carrying opium with him. The opium was confiscated and the mayor had no other choice but to stay behind and deal with his legal issue. The mayor told Cha Moua to go ahead of him, and Cha Moua did. He went to the military air strip in Na Khang and saw an American packing ammunition at the air strip. By that time, the young Cha Moua had already learned a few words of English. He approached the American, who just happened to be Jerry "Hog" Daniels, the Central Intelligence Agency (CIA) case officer assigned to work as the liaison between the CIA and Maj. Gen. Vang Pao. Cha Moua was taken to Long Cheng and later to Vientiane. By then, the mayor had already returned home from Na Khang. Soon after Cha Moua's arrival in Vientiane in 1965, the wife of the mayor registered him to one of the local elementary schools. He also studied English at night at one of the nearby Buddhist temples. He did well and completed sixth grade in the summer of 1967. That same year, his cousin Moua Sue was elected to the National Assembly, so Cha Moua moved into his house in Vientiane and became his personal driver. While staying in Moua Sue's house, Cha Moua continued to attend a private junior high school. A few years later, he completed ninth grade, then took a civil service examination at the Ministry of Justice. He passed the examination and took an entry-level job as an investigator. His salary, however, was very low and was not enough to support the cost of living in Vientiane, the capital of Laos. He began thinking about getting a new and better paying job. Two months later, he met a Hmong military officer, who came to Vientiane to attend Special Military Leadership Training. Cha Moua learned from this officer that there were only two major requirements to receive this Special Military Leadership Training, something that Cha Moua might be able to do. These two requirements were that 1) the candidate had to be an officer in the Royal Lao Army, and 2) the candidate must pass a vigorous examination. Cha Moua wanted to get into this Special Military Leadership School, so he wrote a memo to the director of his department, requesting the director to send him to the army as an officer. The director denied his request, but Cha Moua did not give up. He went to see Phaya Inpeng Souriyathai, the minister of justice. After his formal salutation, Cha Moua told the minister his reasons to see him and gave him the memo. The minister read his memo and smiled. He turned his eyes turned to Cha Moua and said, "Son, I am pleased and proud that you are very patriotic and want to defend the country as well as to rescue your parents from the territory occupied by the Communist Pathet Lao. I will send you to the army as a second lieutenant." The minister approved the request and sent Cha Moua to the army. With his approval from the minister of justice, Cha Moua rushed to the army's Special Military Leadership School. He met with the acting director of the school, who checked the roster for the next examination and found one name missing, so he filled Cha Moua's name in the roster. Cha Moua was sent to the headquarters of the Royal Lao Army for detailed information of the examination; there, he was told that he would be called when the time and date for the next examination were set.

While waiting for the date and time of the next examination, Cha Moua went to Long Cheng, the headquarters of Military Region II, and signed up as second lieutenant in the SGUs. Because of his ability to speak some English, he was assigned to work as a Forward Air Guide, guiding pilots for bombing missions. After less than a month on this job, Cha Moua received a telegram message directing him to return to Vientiane. He went to Vientiane to take the military examination, and fortunately, he was one of the five candidates who passed it. He got himself into the Special Military Leadership School in 1969, and he did well. He graduated from this school in 1971, and he was among the twenty-five officers who were selected to go to Kentucky in the United States to get Special Officer Leadership Training. He arrived in Kentucky on January 1, 1972, and completed the intensive six-month training program on June 30, 1972. He was then sent home to serve in the Royal Lao Army.

Upon his arrival in Vientiane, he was assigned to train soldiers of Hmong descent in Kilometer Six near Vientiane. He soon found out that the job did not suit him well. He asked his older brother, Wa Chou, to talk to Col.

Chao Monivong Kindavong (the second in command of Military Region II) about a request to transfer him to work under Military Region II. Col. Chao Monivong accepted the request, and soon Cha Moua got himself to Long Cheng. In Long Cheng, he met with Jerry Daniels, who took him in to work as a Forward Air Guide. Cha Moua took the code name "Spider." He was soon promoted to captain and was sent to Bouam Long, assigned to be the person responsible for directing air force pilots to bomb enemy sites on the frontlines. On January 27, 1973, the United States and North Vietnam signed the Paris Peace Agreement to end the Vietnam War. A month later, on February 21, 1973, the Royal Lao government and the Communist Pathet Lao signed a Peace and National Reconciliation Agreement to end the Secret War in Laos. Cha Moua followed these agreements very carefully, so he knew that the war was coming to an end; he had to ponder about the post-war development of Laos. There were many questions in his mind: What is the priority for Laos? What do the Hmong and Lao need in the aftermath of the Secret War? He figured out that education was the most important for the Hmong and Lao. And as such, he wanted to come to the United States for an education. In June 1973, he informally approached Jerry Daniels about his idea to go to the United States for his education. Daniels looked at Cha Moua and said, "Are you serious?" Cha Moua told Jerry Daniels that he was serious about it and that the Hmong will need people with education after the war. Daniels was pleased to hear his reasons and said to Cha Moua, "You are the first Hmong person, who has come to me with a desire to get an education in the United States." About a month later, Jerry Daniels came to visit Cha Moua in Bouam Long; they chatted for a while and he asked Cha Moua, "Did you say you wanted to go to America to study?" Cha Moua reconfirmed his desire to study in the United States. Jerry Daniels looked at him in the eyes and said to him, "I think you can go, but you need to talk to the U.S. ambassador in Vientiane as soon as possible. Call Porter now to take you from Lima Site 32 [Bouam Long] to Vientiane." The next day, Cha Moua arrived in Vientiane and went directly to the U.S. Embassy. At the U.S. Embassy, he told the secretary at the front desk that Jerry Daniels sent him to see the U.S. ambassador about going to America. He soon met with the U.S. ambassador to Laos, and he was told to get an I-20. Cha Moua related the need to have an I-20 to Jerry Daniels, who then called his mother in Montana and asked her to talk to the principal of Hell Gate High School in Missoula to write a letter of acceptance for Cha Moua, to this school, so that an I-20 could be issued. She did and within a month, Cha Moua got his I-20. He took it to the U.S. Embassy in Vientiane, and all was set to go. Jerry Daniels asked Zack, another CIA agent and friend, to make all the arrangements for Cha Moua to leave for the United States. Cha Moua had saved most of his per diem while attending military training in Kentucky, totaling a thousand dollars. Cha Moua used half of this money to buy his airplane ticket from Bangkok to Montana in the United States. The other half was used for his needs during the first few months in the United States until he could get part-time job to support himself.

On August 31, 1973, Cha Moua left Vientiane and two days later, arrived in Missoula, Montana. Jerry Daniels' mother took Cha Moua to stay with her temporarily. She enrolled him in Hell Gate High School in Missoula on September 3, 1973, to refresh his general academic skills, in addition to his English. Soon, he found a part-time job and moved into a small studio to live on his own. He earned his high school diploma from Hell Gate High School on June 19, 1974, and went on to the University of Montana, Missoula, that fall, majoring in political science.

He graduated with a bachelor's degree in political science in the summer of 1982; his schooling slowed down due to incoming Hmong refugees to Missoula after the end of the Secret War in 1975. For example, in June 1975, Maj. Gen. Vang Pao, the former commander of Military Region II of the Royal Lao Army and his youngest wife and son, and Chu Long, arrived in Missoula. In August 1975, Cha Moua's wife, May, and their son arrived; he married his wife in 1973 just before he left Laos to travel to the United States. Additionally, a few of the first wave of Hmong refugees arrived in Missoula before the end of 1975. Consequently, Cha Moua became a liaison and spokesman for these refugees, spending much of his time helping them. Initially, he volunteered to help them as much as he could and as his time allowed.

In 1977, they formed the Lao Family Community of Missoula, and Cha Moua became its director. The Lao Family Community of Missoula was a non-profit organization formed to specifically help the refugee community in Missoula. Moreover, he had to support his young family. In 1982, Cha Moua resigned from his job as the director of Lao Family Community in Missoula to become the executive director of a newly formed Hmong Economic Development in Billings, Montana. While he held this position, he also served on the Montana Governor's Advisory Board. He held the mentioned position until 1986, when he moved his family from Billings to Chico, California.

In 1988, he became the coordinator of the Secondary Resettlement Program, and later moved to Texas to coordinate the movement of Hmong refugees to areas where they could find work and become self-sufficient. The program ended in 1989, and his family moved back to California. In early 1991, he began working for the Sacramento Department of Social Services as an eligibility worker. It was a temporary job, so he stayed at this job for less than three years. In 1994, he accepted an offer to become a social worker for Butte County Department of Social Services in California. In this position, he was assigned to link Hmong refugees to employment and related services.

He resigned from this position in 1996 to move his family to Sacramento and take an offer for a social worker position with the Sacramento County Department of Social Services. This job was also to help refugees become employed and self-sufficient. He retired from this job in 2012 at the age of sixty-two. After retirement, Cha Moua continued to be involved in the Hmong community, and on November 6, 2011, he formed the United States Special Guerrilla Units Vietnam War Veterans, Inc. He devotes much of his retirement time to this organization, trying to bring recognition to the SGU veterans who have been mostly forgotten after the war.

On a personal note, Cha Moua and his first wife, May, divorced in 1996. After the divorce, May went to Wisconsin and Cha Moua continued to stay in California. In this union, they have six children: Fong, Pa Ying, Kongfeng (died in 1992), Longtoua, Charlie Jr., and Olivia.

In 1997, Sheng Xiong and Cha Moua moved in together and continued to live together until 2009, when they decided to part. In this union, they had only one son, named Paoze, who stayed with Cha Moua. In 2011, Cha Moua married Manila Vang, whom he has known since her teenage years in Laos. She, too is a divorcee. The marriage lasted less than one year; they filed for divorce and finalized it in August 2012. They had no children. On February 8, 2014, Cha Moua and Rosie Yang, also a divorcee, held a Hmong customary marriage ceremony. She is a teacher and her children are all grown and on their own. So far, she and Cha Moua appear to be compatible and share many common values and lifestyle. They often travel places together. Since 2014, Cha Moua has been living with Rosie Yang in Merced, California.[6] In addition to his volunteer work for the SGU Vietnam War veterans, Cha Moua occupies himself with community services. As of 2016, he is the president of the California Branch of Moua International Council.

In addition to his active civic engagements in the State of California, he often travels to other states to visit Hmong American communities. Cha Moua is also a Hmong cultural specialist; he spent his youth among Hmong villagers and has learned much of the Hmong culture, religion, and the Qeej. He is an expert of most aspects of Hmong culture and their way of life; therefore, he is often asked to guide the younger generation in the mentioned aspects of Hmong culture. To learn and broaden his knowledge of Hmong history and culture, Cha Moua has visited the Hmong in China many times and has sponsored and hosted the visits of many Hmong scholars and officials from China.

Cha Moua is also a gardener, converting his large backyard, in the suburb of Merced City, into a lovely garden with varieties of fruits and plants. He also grows vegetables and raises dozens of chickens. He, Rosie, and his son Paoze formed a small family unit that survives almost entirely on the food they grow and the chickens they raise. He says, they try to go green and live more naturally and simply, just as the Hmong have done in their villages in northern Laos.

The story of Cha Moua is compelling: a young man who grew up during the war years, and who later found himself taking part in the conflict. He and his family were devastated when his father was killed in action. His service in the military during the war and his luck helped him to gain a solid education in Laos, which allowed him to enhance his formal studying in the United States prior to 1975. His career brought him from a community service provider to a county social worker, and now he dedicates his golden years to assist in Hmong SGU veteran services. His personal life represents the tragedy of the war and the stress from the challenges of the adaptation of Hmong Americans to the United States. Despite being divorced many times over the years, he continues to be a great father, a role model, and a community leader; he continues to communicate with all his ex-wives as they are friends. He says he sleeps like baby and is active like a teenager, and he is happy with his life. Overall, Cha Moua represents many of the Hmong who served during the war years, then came to study in the United States prior to 1975, and then served the Hmong during their first stage of their adapting to the United States. He also represents the generation between the older, traditional leaders and those who are younger, American-educated Hmong American leaders. His personal life represents the struggles of Hmong men, who experience countless hardships in their journey to adapt to life in the United States.

NOTES

1. Bruce Bliatout, personal communication. October 5, 2015.
2. Kou Yang. 2013. "The American Experience of the Hmong: A Historical Review." In Mark Pfeifer, Monica Chiu, and Kou Yang (eds.). *Diversity within Diaspora: Hmong Americans in the Twenty-First Century.* University of Hawaii Press.
3. Ibid.
4. Cha Moua, personal communication. November 3, 2015.
5. The Lao Issara or Free Lao was renamed in 1950 as Pathet Lao or Lao Patriotic Front, under the leadership of Prince Souphanouvong.
6. Cha Moua, personal communication. February 19, 2015.

REFERENCE

Yang, Kou. 2013. "The American Experience of the Hmong: A Historical Review." In Mark Pfeifer, Monica Chiu, and Kou Yang (eds.). *Diversity within Diaspora: Hmong Americans in the Twenty-First Century.* University of Hawaii Press.

Chapter Four

The Challenges of
Hmong Refugee Resettlement

The story of Hmong refugee resettlement to the United States is an epic of unprecedented migration of thousands of people crossing the Pacific Ocean over ten thousand miles from Indochina to North America, only second to the mass land migration of Hmong people fleeing from China during the seventeenth and eighteenth centuries into Indochina as an oppressed ethnic minority for thousands of years. This epic is all about wars, tragedies, devastations, struggles, resilience, and triumphs. After the Secret War ended in 1975, the Hmong, who were on the side of the Royal Lao government, became the targets for the Communist Lao People's Revolutionary Party. These Hmong had no choice but to flee persecution again. As pointed out earlier in chapter 1, policymakers in Washington and many others in the U.S. government were reluctant to accept the resettlement of Hmong refugees in the United States. Edgar Pop Buell, an American farmer from the State of Indiana who had worked for the U.S. Agency for International Development in Laos during the war summed it up this way, "The end of the war means we can't use you no more. Goodbye. We finished with you."[1]

Since day one of the Hmong refugees' arrival in Thailand, the United Nations High Commissioner for Refugees did not recognize Hmong and other refugees from Laos as refugees, and the United States turned their ears and eyes away from this population. In his speech to the Tenth Hmong National Conference, Yang Dao stated that he met in Bangkok in June of 1975 with "Dr. Berta, the Representative of the United Nations High Commissioner for Refugees (UNHCR) in Thailand. . . . and [Dr. Berta] courteously replied that the UNHCR did not recognize [classify] as refugees the Laotian people who had left Laos, because there was still a government of coalition in Vientiane who worked, he said, for national reconciliation and peace. He added that these Laotian people were not like the Cambodian and the Vietnamese

53

refugees who lost their countries after being militarily defeated by the communists."[2] Moreover, the Hmong and other highlanders from Laos were considered by the U.S. government and its Congress as "not suitable for U.S. resettlement."[3] The opponents argued that the Hmong are a hill tribe people who would not be able to adapt and adjust to American society for survival. Jerry Daniels and other Americans, who were helping Hmong refugees in Thailand, were frustrated with the reluctance of the United States to accept Hmong refugees. Nonetheless, the American advocates were able to close an early case for Yang See and his wife and child for resettlement to the United States on November 22, 1975. In his early days of resettlement in the United States, Yang See was among those early Hmong advocates in the United States to lobby U.S. policymakers to accept the Hmong because of his fluency in English and educational background, in addition to his unusually tall and calm personality; it was their hope that he would represent the positive side of Hmong refugees. Below is Yang See's brief biography and his account of the challenges of early refugee resettlement to the United States.

Yang See was born in 1946 in a Hmong village in the highlands of Luang Phrabang Province, Laos. He completed junior high school at a private Catholic junior high school in 1964 in Paksane, Laos. He then went to Vientiane to attend Lycée de Vientiane, the most prestigious high school in Laos. In the middle of 1966, Yang See went to Long Cheng and signed up to join the five thousand-meter run. He took first place, and Bruce Thowpow Bliatout came in second. He was proud of this competition but had to return to school. Shortly after this game, he came back to Vientiane to look for work so that he could continue his education, but there were no jobs. He heard that there were jobs in Savannakhet, the second largest city in Laos. He packed his belongings and took his motorbike to the Wattay Airport, where he boarded a U.S. Agency for International Development airplane to Savannakhet. There, he found a few jobs that required field work and travel, but he declined them, and took a second shift job as a security guard so that he could attend school during the day. He registered for class again in Lycée de Savannakhet and graduated with the French's Baccalaureate or diploma for the completion of twelfth grade. At the time, those who held French's Baccalaureate were considered well educated as the country had only a few high schools. He returned to Vientiane to apply for scholarships to attend universities abroad, but he was too late as all available scholarships had already been awarded. He had no choice but to study English at a junior high school in Vientiane and waited for an opportunity to study abroad. In 1968, he took the examination to study in the United States and was one of the top ten candidates who were destined to come to the United States. Unfortunately, his name was later replaced by a son of a high-ranking military officer who had strong ties to the

U.S. Embassy. He was not happy with the results; he dropped out of school and went to Samthong, a town in Military Region II. As an English speaker, it was easier for him to find jobs in a town where few people spoke English. Soon after his arrival on January 1, 1970, he was hired by Frank Albert to replace Bounlieng, the station chief, who had just resigned. His job was to disseminate information in the form of printing materials and newsreel to the local people. Additionally, he was assigned to write some articles in Lao and English for the Psychological Warfare Department (USSIS) magazine called the *HORIZON*. Unfortunately, a few months after he started working, the Communist Pathet Lao attacked and took over Samthong on March 18, 1970. His office and their staff moved to Ban Sone; to get to Ban Sone, he followed some students and their school principal, Tou Fue Vang, and his deputy, Yee Vang, by walking on foot for a whole day to Muong Phone. Yang See stayed there for about ten days before going to Ban Sone. A few months later, on July 19, 1970, Yang See became very ill and was sent to a hospital in Vientiane, where he stayed for ten days. After he recuperated, Yang See was transferred to work for the U.S. Military Attaché Lt. Col. John Miley, who worked closely with the USSIS at Phon Kheng in Vientiane. Yang See was assigned to fly from the Udorn U.S. Air Force Base in southeast Thailand to southern Laos; he did this for more than a year from the summer of 1970 to December 1971. He resigned from USSIS and went to Long Cheng, hoping to get job there, so he could stay closer to the Hmong people. He began to work temporarily for SKY (a Central Intelligence Agency [CIA] secret operation) in Long Cheng, the headquarters of Military Region II. After a week in Long Cheng, Col. Shoua Yang took him to see Jerry Daniels, the CIA operations manager of Military Region II. Yang See spoke to Jerry Daniels and turned over two letters of recommendations from his previous bosses: one from Lt. Col. John Miley, and the other one from the deputy director of USSIS. He also turned over his resume. Jerry Daniels hired Yang See on the spot to work in the Joint Operation Center (JOC). With Yang See's documents in hand, Jerry Daniels immediately drove Yang See to the Joint Operation Control Center, where Yang See worked for the next two months. Two months later, Jerry Daniels' brother passed away in Montana, so he returned home to the United States. During his absence, another CIA case officer by the name of Mr. Clean assigned Yang See to work for Forward Air Guide (FAG), the unit that guided pilots for bombing missions on enemy targets. This new assignment occurred on the same day that FAG, and the field liaison officer met with Maj. Gen. Vang Pao. At his new post, Yang See was assigned as the top assistant to Moua Chou, the commander of FAG as Yang See was the most educated and was better trained in the Lao and English language. He handled paperwork and daily management of the command center of FAG.

In mid-1972, Jerry Daniels came back to Long Cheng. After Kia Tou Lee, the chief of JOC, moved to Bouam Long to become a field liaison officer, Yang See was assigned to lead JOC and take on the leadership of the field liaison officers. Since then, Yang See, Jerry Daniels, and an American finance director by the name of Dennis had jointly made the decision to automatically increase the salary of their staff by about one thousand kip every six months. In addition to his job as leader of both JOC and field liaison officers, Yang See helped Jerry Daniels and other Americans with translation and consultation. Yang See stayed with this job until December of 1973, when Special Guerrilla Unit troops were integrated into the Royal Lao Army and the Americans began to pull back their assistance. From this point on, Yang See was assigned to do post-war economic development programs. In this new job, he was in charge of buying animals, such as chickens, pigs, cows, buffalos, and so forth, from the people and take them to market. He was also helping people grow coffee and other cash crops. By early 1975, Jerry Daniels had a plan for Yang See to come to the United States for more education, though the departure date had not yet been determined. In March of 1975, Yang See took a vacation to Bangkok, Thailand, to get an operation done on a hernia in his abdomen. Soon after his operation, he received a telephone call from Jerry Daniels asking him to return to Long Cheng immediately. He did and was told by Jerry Daniels that Long Cheng was in a dire situation, therefore he must stay in Long Cheng for the time being. In early May of 1975, Yang See learned that Maj. Gen. Vang Pao had already given to the Americans a list of twenty-five hundred persons (or 120 families) of higher-ranking military officers and their families to be evacuated from Long Cheng to Udorn, Thailand. It is worthy to note here that each flight from Long Cheng to Udorn, Thailand, was designated for each colonel and his family members. Both Yang See and Jerry Daniels were concerned about the welfare and safety of the lower-ranking officers, soldiers, their families, and the rest of the Hmong and other ethnic populations. They knew that in April of 1975 Maj. Gen. Vang Pao had visited Mae Hongsone in northern Thailand and would like for the Hmong to settle there. In the middle of May, when the 120 high-ranking military officers and their families were evacuated to Thailand, Yang See told Jerry Daniels that justice was not served to all the Hmong and other ethnic groups, who were also involved in the war. Yang See could just do as Maj. Gen. Vang Pao wanted, but he is a Hmong and his heart and mind were with his people. He could not just watch and wait for his people to perish. On May 10, he decided to break away from both Jerry Daniels and Maj. Gen. Vang Pao, so that he could do what he thought was the right thing to do to help the Hmong, Iu-Mien (Yao), Khmu, and other ethnic groups to safely escape out of Laos. He asked Jerry Daniels to take care of his wife and son; Jerry

Daniels agreed to take charge of their well-being and to safely evacuate them to Thailand. Jerry Daniels said to Yang See that a porter airplane would soon arrive with Pat McHugh, who would bring some money to pay construction workers, who were building a large structure in Nam Yen Village for hog farming. Jerry Daniels told Yang See, "You should drive and deliver the cash before you can go with that porter airplane to Vientiane." He did his assignment before 11:00 o'clock in the morning and was about to get out of Jerry Daniels's office to fly to Vientiane, when Dr. Yang Dao came in to speak to Jerry Daniels. Dr. Yang Dao complained to Jerry Daniels about who would help to evacuate his family. Nodding his head, Jerry Daniels told Yang Dao, "Ask Yang See. He is going down to Vientiane for this purpose." Yang See took the porter airplane and went to Vientiane as planned. While he was in Vientiane trying to help the Hmong escape from Laos to Thailand, his wife and son were safely evacuated from Long Cheng to Thailand. In Vientiane, Yang See urged his uncle Yong Sei Yang (Zoov Ntxheb Yaj) in Simuong Village to leave for Thailand. Thus, his uncle's family became one of those first groups of Hmong refugees to temporarily reside in the Wat Samakkhee Buddhist Temple in Nongkhai, Thailand. Yang See went to Dr. Yang Dao's house in Vientiane to help his extended family prepare to flee to Thailand. He helped them, totaling thirty-seven people, to escape from Laos to Thailand; he paid from his own pocket for taxi and boat fares. He also rented three hotel rooms for them to temporarily stay while in Nongkhai. Yang See also assisted many Hmong families in the same manner, so that they could safely escape by crossing the Mekong River from Laos to Thailand

While in Thailand, more refugees poured in every day. Yang See contacted his Thai friends. Together, they were able to establish the Nongkhai Refugee Camp on May 13, 1975. He did not contact his American friends for help because Jerry Daniels told him earlier not to involve any Americans, including Jerry Daniels. However, Jerry Daniels would help in the case Yang See got into trouble or was being mistreated in Thailand.

At the time, the status of Hmong refugees had not yet been determined by the United Nations High Commissioner for Refugees; therefore, self-help was the first step for Hmong refugees to take. Soon, the refugee population swelled in Nongkhai Refugee Camp, therefore requiring larger spaces to accommodate the overflow of refugees from Laos. Jerry Daniels arrived in Thailand by the middle of May 1975 and asked Yang See to plan for the relocation of Hmong refugees to Nam Phong Camp, which had already been populated by the abovementioned twenty-five hundred people who were evacuated directly from Long Cheng to Nam Phong in Thailand. But before any action could take place, Jerry Daniels had to request for permission and needed funds from Washington. His persistence payed off; Jerry Daniels had successfully obtained permission and the needed funds to help and relocate the mentioned refugees to Nam Phong Camp. Part of the funds was used to provide basic needs for the refugees. The rest of the funds were for Yang See and Jerry Daniels to relocate Hmong refugees from Nongkhai Camp to Nam Phong Camp. Each day, they transported about two thousand people, and this went on for many days until Nam Phong Camp became full.

A month after the transfer of Hmong refugees from Nongkhai Camp to Nam Phong Camp, the Thai government wanted to use Nam Phong Camp for military training; therefore, the Hmong refugees residing there had to be moved to a new camp that was not yet determined. The Thai government provided a helicopter to fly Hmong camp leaders twice to find a suitable camp, but to no avail; those leaders could not decide from the air which site was the most suitable. At the end of September 1975, the Thai government held a final meeting in Charoen Hotel, where Yang See was staying at the time. Many Nam Phong Camp leaders attended the meeting, and so did Yang See, Jerry Daniels, and Thai Col. Saen, who was deputy of the Regional Military Intelligence and acted as the liaison between Jerry Daniels and the Thai government. The Thai government basically said they had flown camp leaders to select a new camp site, but no decisions were made yet by Hmong refugee camp leaders. Therefore, the Thai government would have to select the new camp on their own and asked the Hmong camp leaders to accept the decision and cooperate. After the meeting, Yang See took Jerry Daniels aside and told him to talk to Col. Saen to postpone the Thai government's decision, so that Col. Saen, Jerry Daniels, and Yang See could select the new camp site. Jerry Daniels heeded Yang See's advice; he talked to Col. Saen to convey his message to the Thai government. As a result, the Thai government agreed to postpone their decision and to help them select a new camp site. The next day, the Thai government provided a helicopter for the three of them to look for a new camp site. Yang See also brought his wife, Pia, to go along with them. With a map of Nongkhai, Udorn, and Loei Provinces in hand, they circulated over a site between Chiang Khan and Pak Chom. Yang See pointed to a site to Col. Saen and said that it should be a good site. They then landed at Loei Airport, where a car was there to take Jerry Daniels and Col. Saen to meet with the provincial authorities of that town to discuss the possibility of selecting that site as a new refugee camp. Yang See and his wife waited for them at the airport. About an hour later, Jerry Daniels and Col. Saen returned to the airport. Col. Saen turned to Yang See and said, "You can go ahead with your preference and plan. I think that place is good." After they returned to the CIA headquarters in Udorn, Jerry Daniels told Yang See, "Go down to Namphong and get some people to go and clear the selected site." The next day, Yang See went down to Nam Phong with Boraphoth, the van driver. He told Namphong Camp leaders to look for two hundred persons to go and clear the new camp site. Yang See brought some cash given to him by Jerry Daniels and rented four buses from Khonekhaene to take the two hundred people to the new selected site. The next day, the four buses came to Nam Phong and picked up Col. Saidang Xiong and 180 more persons, heading toward the selected site near Pak Chom and Chiang Khan. They cleared the site and prepared it for a refugee camp, later known as Ban Vinai Camp.[4]

In those early days, Nam Phong Refugee Camp was under the jurisdiction of Jerry Daniels and the Thai government. It was prohibited for anyone to get in and out of the camp and to have contact with outsiders. Yang See recalled one incident involving Dr. Yang Dao and Vang Shur going out and getting caught. Apparently, they wanted to go to Bangkok, but got caught in Khonekhaene and were detained. Yang See and a Thai major of Thai intelligence had to go to Khonekhaene to take them out and bring them back to Nam Phong Camp. As for Nongkhai Refugee Camp, it was under Yang See's jurisdiction and the governor of Nongkhai. The governor of Nongkhai told Yang See, "Do not allow journalists, newspaper or television to know about anything inside the camp. Do not allow anyone to be interviewed by any journalist. If anything goes wrong, I will be blamed for it, understand. Also, do not let any new refugees get inside Nongkhai Camp." Yang See heeded the words of the governor and made sure that all of the people in the camp knew the rules.

From day one of their arrival in Thailand, Yang See and Jerry Daniels learned that the Hmong and other highlanders from Laos were considered unsuitable for U.S. resettlement. Moreover, the Thai government did not want Maj. Gen. Vang Pao to stay in Thailand for political reasons; the Thai government wanted to be on good terms with the government of Laos. On Tuesday June 19, 1975, Maj. Gen. Vang Pao, his youngest wife, and their son were sent to the United States with a brief stop in France. Jerry Daniels was hoping that Vang Pao would request the U.S. government to include Hmong refugees in their U.S. Resettlement Program, but he heard nothing from Vang Pao. Jerry Daniels used to mumble to himself, "Maybe he forgot all about what we talked to him about after lunch at his house, and in his bedroom on Saturday June 14, 1975." One day, Jerry Daniels turned to Yang See and told him to go to Washington, District of Columbia. But first, Jerry Daniels and Yang See had to select five Hmong refugee families and allow MacAllan Thompson and John Tucker to select five Lao families to be sent to Washington, District of Columbia. These families would be models representing all refugees from Laos. They did, and one week later, they were told that all ten families had failed the interview for U.S. refugee resettlement. Jerry Daniels told Yang See to get someone in Nam Phong who wanted to go. Yang See went to

Nam Phong and selected Dr. Yang Dao. He explained to Dr. Yang Dao that he would go to Washington, District of Columbia, to be a model for Hmong refugees, and to lobby for the United States to include Hmong refugees in their Refugee Resettlement Program. Yang See then dropped Dr. Yang Dao off at the CIA headquarters in Udorn, where Jerry Daniels would provide him with needed information and give him ten thousand baht. Jerry Daniels instructed him to go to the U.S. Embassy in Bangkok and apply for a visa to go the United States. Dr. Yang Dao did, but he carried a Lao diplomatic passport, which was issued to him when he was a member of the National Political Consultative Council. He did not get a U.S. visa, so he called Jerry Daniels from Udorn. Jerry Daniels told Yang See to go to Nam Phong and get another person to go to the United States. He did, and got Moua Lia to agree to go; Moua Lia successfully got his U.S. visa. He went to the United States and stayed there for about a month before returning to Thailand without any good news from Maj. Gen. Vang Pao. In the end, Jerry Daniels turned to Yang See and said, "You must go and prove to the U.S. Government that there are many educated Hmong people and that the Hmong could survive in the [United States]." With a height of five feet, eight inches, and a calming personality, Yang See was not only educated and an English speaker, but could serve as a positive image for Hmong refugees. As a result, Yang See, his wife Pia, and their son Asahi were sent directly to Washington, District of Columbia; they arrived there on November 23, 1975.

They were taken to the home of Peter Kneck, a member of the Interagency Task Force at the State Department in Washington, District of Columbia. Three days after their arrival, Yang See was taken to meet with Robert Ingersoll, the number two deputy of Henry Kissinger, the U.S. Secretary of State at the time. It took Yang See three times before he could meet with and talk to the deputy. Yang See briefed Ingersoll of the Hmong and their past involvement with the Secret War, and asked that the United States open its doors for Hmong refugee resettlement. Robert Ingersoll took notes and then told Yang See that the timing was not good as it was Christmas season, so all members of the U.S. Congress were out of Washington, District of Columbia. He said that after Christmas he would work with members of the U.S. Congress on Yang See's request. Robert Ingersoll also told Yang See that if there was no positive news within the next few weeks or month, he will arrange for Yang See to meet face to face with Dr. Henry Kissinger, the U.S. secretary of state.

About a month later, Ingersoll's office called and told Yang See that the United States had opened its doors to refugees from Laos, including Hmong, Iu-Mien (Yao), Khmu, and Lao refugees.[5] As a result, there would be no need for Yang See to meet with the U.S. Secretary of State Henry Kissinger. Peter

Kneck and others who were involved with the case of the Hmong Refugee Resettlement were very pleased upon hearing the positive news. Yang See and his wife also agreed to stay in the United States as refugees.[6]

Forty-five days after Yang See and his family arrived in Washington, District of Columbia, Maj. Gen. Vang Pao and his nephew Paul Vang came to visit Yang See. Yang See's wife Pia recalled that Maj. Gen. Vang Pao spent two hours scolding Yang See for coming to the United States without his permission. Vang Pao told Yang See that he would return to Thailand in early 1976 to take down the government of Laos, so that he and the Hmong could return to Laos. He forbade Yang See to lobby for U.S. resettlement of Hmong refugees who were living in the Thai camps. Yang See politely replied that his mission in the United States was to lobby for the resettlement of Hmong refugees to the United States and that he would carry out his mission. At one point during their heated exchanges, Yang See told Vang Pao that he may keep the twenty-five hundred people on his list—to be evacuated from Long Cheng to Thailand—but not the rest of the Hmong refugees in Thailand. Pia recalled that it was a heated debate, but after two hours, Paul Vang told his uncle to stop the scolding, and the heated argument ended.[7]

At the end of 1977, Jerry Daniels came to visit Yang See and Pia in Washington, District of Columbia, and said he needed Yang See to help him in Thailand. Yang See immediately responded that he wanted to return to Thailand to help Hmong refugees. His wife, Pia, protested and said she did not want Yang See to return to Thailand. In the end, Yang See decided to stay put in the United States. After five years in Washington, District of Columbia, Yang See and his family moved to Chicago where they could find work for other members of his extended family, whom they had sponsored to be reunited with them in Washington, District of Columbia. In 1986, the family moved again, this time to St. Paul, Minnesota, where a large Hmong community had already settled. They have since then called St. Paul their home. The family has grown from one child when they first arrived in the United States in November of 1975, to seven more American-born children. One each was born in Washington, District of Columbia, and Chicago; the rest were born in St. Paul, Minnesota.

There was also a small list of Hmong who arrived before the end of 1975. The list also includes, but is not limited to, the families of Dang Her in Minnesota, Vang Nhia in southern California, and Jou Yee Xiong in Santa Barbara, California. Dang Her arrived in Minnesota on December 2, 1975, just in time to experience the extreme cold weather of Minnesota. Vang Nhia also arrived in southern California at the end of 1975 and started his new life in the metropolitan area of Orange County. Most of the few Hmong refugee families who arrived in 1975 were those who worked directly with

Americans or American agencies, such as the U.S. International Development. The story of Jou Yee Xiong and his group stood out as a unique and memorable one among those who came to the United States in 1975. Jou Yee Xiong and many of his relatives, who departed Thailand on December 29, 1975, also arrived in the United States on December 29, 1975 (this occurred because they crossed the international dateline). Jou Yee Xiong and his followers, who were devoted members of the Christian Mission Alliance, resettled in Santa Barbara, California.[8] The above account is a small sample of Hmong refugees who arrived in the United States before the end of 1975. The list of those who came in 1976 is much longer, so I will only list a few of them, such as Sam Bliatout and his extended family members who came to Hawaii, Chee Yang and his family who came to Colorado, and myself and a few other Hmong families were sent to New Orleans, Louisiana. A sample of the list of those who came to California include, but are not limited to, Touxia Thaoxaochay, Dang Moua, Cha Mao, Peter Vang, and so on. Other Hmong families were sent to Minnesota, Florida, New Mexico, Oregon, and other places in the Midwest and the eastern region of the United States.

The 1975 Indochinese Refugee Act did not include refugees from Laos, reflecting the U.S. government's failure to publicly and fully recognize their covert involvement in the Secret War in Laos from the early 1960s to 1975. Additionally, the Hmong and other minorities from Laos were determined by the United States as unsuitable for the U.S. Refugee Resettlement Program. In essence, there was no urgency or justification for the United States to take the refugees from Laos. Complicating the matter, Laos was still considered as a neutral country, guaranteed by both the 1954 and 1962 Geneva Agreements where the U.S. government simply rebuffed the humanitarian crisis in Laos. Although the Nixon administration acknowledged in 1971 that the United States was involved in the Secret War in Laos,[9] the Secret War was mostly not known to the American people. There was also no desire or interest on the part of the U.S. government to take Hmong refugees, who were deemed unsuitable for U.S. resettlement. The United States and the Congress argued that the Hmong people would not acculturate well in American society as they were largely pre-literate in their country of Laos.[10] As a result, only a small number of Hmong refugees were accepted for resettlement to the United States by the end of 1975, and as mentioned above, these refugees were mostly employees of the American agencies in Laos. In *Harvesting Pa Chay's Wheat*, Keith Quincy estimated that Hmong American population by the end of 1975 was about five hundred.[11] Although an amendment was added in 1976 to the Indochinese Refugee Act to include refugees from Laos,[12] the number of Hmong refugees resettled in the United States continues to be small. According to Lionel Rosenblatt, thirty-five hundred refugees from Laos, including twelve hundred Hmong refugees, were approved by the U.S. Immigration and Naturalization Service under the parole authority. It is speculated that many of these arrived in the United States in early 1976.

In addition to sending Yang See to Washington, District of Columbia, the lobby of many Americans, such as Jerry Daniels and Lionel Rosenblatt, made it possible for the United States to include Hmong refugees in their refugee resettlement program by early 1976.

Although the U.S. resettlement program might have been opened to Hmong refugees, it did not mean that the screening for resettlement was free of problems. Yang Chee, one of the principal tri-language interpreters/translators, said, one day in the early spring of 1976, a group of high-level U.S. officials came to lay out eligibility criteria and interview screening process at the Nongkhai Refugee Camp. At that time, there were three categories that would determine the eligibilities of refugees/applicants who would be approved for resettlement to the United States. The three categories were: CAT I—family reunification (for refugees who already had family member[s] in the United States); CAT II—past employment with the U.S. government (for refugees who worked with/for and were paid by the U.S. government); and CAT III—high risk (for former military personnel, namely members of the Special Guerrilla Units or irregular forces, operating from bases in Laos in support of the United States during the Secret War [closely linked to the Vietnam War]). It should be noted that CAT IV was later added to the program as a gesture of pure goodwill to include those (especially the Hmong) who one way or the other had played critical roles in connections with the Secret War in Laos during the Vietnam War era. Jerry "Hog" Daniels was not happy with the large number of well-qualified Hmong refugees being interviewed, who were ironically "disapproved" to come to the United States by the non-Hmong interpreter and an American official in Thailand. Jerry Daniels, then, adamantly told his Hmong staff to not go to lunch that day. Instead, he ordered the Hmong staff to reprocess and re-interview those cases that had been marked "REJECTED" by an American official and his Lao staff. The Hmong staff followed Daniels' instructions. They thoroughly re-interviewed and "APPROVED" most of those cases that were previously being "REJECTED." Although this historic act to right the wrong had led to a major verbal disagreement and confrontation between Jerry Daniels and the mentioned American official, many Hmong families were approved and resettled in the United States in 1976 and 1977.[13] It should be noted that Xuwicha (Noi) Hirampruek, who worked very closely with Jerry Daniels and other Hmong staffers, confirmed this story during his remarks at the Symposium on "The History Behind The Hmong Refugee Exodus," which was held at Fresno City College on August 22, 2015. As a result of these efforts, more Hmong refugees were resettled in the United States in 1976, but a larger number had to wait until after the passing of the 1980 Refugee Act, which allowed large numbers of refugees to come to the United States. Consequently, about twenty-seven thousand Hmong refugees entered the United States in the 1980s, marking the peak of Hmong refugee resettlement in the United States.[14] The flow of Hmong refugees to the United States since 1980 has been growing steadily; the Hmong population has rapidly increased from more than 5,204 in 1980 to 94,439 by 1990, an increase of 1,714 percent in just one decade. More discussions on the Hmong population is made in the next chapter, which also highlights the adaptation of Hmong Americans and the roots of the Hmong American community, which relies on the best of Hmong heritage and builds upon the knowledge and the know-hows of their adopted country, the United States of America.

NOTES

1. Hmong: Our Secret Army. CBS 60 MINUTES. https://www.youtube.com/watch?v=iFRgOjG-gvU&ab_channel=YawmSaub.
2. Dao, Yang. April 8, 2005. "The Hmong Odyssey from Laos to America." A speech at the Tenth Hmong National Conference. Fresno, CA.
3. See, Rosenblatt, Lionel. "How the Hmong Came to be in the U.S." A paper to be published in final form by the Center for Hmong Studies, Concordia University St. Paul. Also, MacAlan Thompson mentioned this in his remarks at the symposium on "The History Behind the Hmong Refugee Exodus." Fresno City College. August 22, 2015.
4. In an Internet discussion on October 22, 2016, about the history of Ban Vinai Camp, Lee Pao Xiong provided a different version of the history of this camp. He wrote that, "Colonel Bill Laid flew on the helicopter to scout out the location. According to a document we have from the Jerry Daniels files at the Center for Hmong Studies, Jerry Daniels sent Noi Xuwicha and Yang Lue to assess the camp. The camp was named after General Vinai, according to Colonel Song Leng Xiong. The reason why the camp was located so close to the border was because the Thai wanted to use the Hmong to intimidate the Lao in case Lao Communists decided to cross the border into Thailand. In such case the Thai would just arm the Hmong and send them across into Laos (according to Noi Xuwicha). Other colonels didn't want to go to Ban Vinai because it was built over cemetery grounds and was too close to Laos. That is why the first [one hundred] families to be transferred from Nam Phong Camp into Ban Vinai Camp were Hmong Christians (according Xeev Nruag Xyooj who worked as the Assistant to Col. Xay Dang Xiong)." Another account provided by Bertrand Moua says this refugee camp is named after "Vinai," the name of the director of refugees from the Thai minister of interior, who officially opened this camp. He also confirmed that

Col. Xai Dang Xiong and one hundred Hmong refugee families (3,003 persons) were transferred to Ban Vinai on November 16, 1975, and they were the first to move into this camp.

5. According to Lionel Rosenblatt, the basic decision to allocate numbers left over from the April 1975 evacuation to refugees in Thailand was made in October 1975, to be implemented starting in January 1976. Personal communication. November 22, 2016.

6. See Yang and Pia Lee, personal communication. September 26, 2015.

7. Lee, Pia, personal communication. September 3, 2015.

8. See Chan, Suecheng. 1994. *Hmong Means Free*, 72. Philadelphia: Temple University Press.

9. It is documented in *This Day in History* that the Nixon administration acknowledged in 1971 that the United States was secretly involved in the war in Laos and has supported an irregular force of thirty thousand. http://www.history.com/this-day-in-history/nixon-administration-acknowledges-secret-army-in-laos.

10. See Rosenblatt, Lionel, "How the Hmong Came to be in the U.S." A paper to be published in its final form by the Center for Hmong Studies, Concordia University St. Paul.

11. See Quincy, Keith. 2000. 2000. *Harvesting Pa Chay's Wheat*, 446. Eastern Washington University Press. This number might have been liberally estimated as there were a small number of Hmong families who entered the United States prior to 1975. Also, this number might have included Hmong students, who studied in the United States prior to 1975.

12. See Immigration in America. Indochina Migration and Refugee Assistance Act of 1975. http://immigrationinamerica.org/607-indochina-migration-and-refugee-assistance-act-of-1975.html. The 1976 inclusion of refugees from Laos to the 1975 Refugee Act might have been the result of the efforts of many individuals, such as Sisouk Na Champassack, the pre-1975 deputy prime minister and minister of defense of Laos, and several Hmong individuals, who lobbied the U.S. Embassy in Bangkok to include refugees from Laos in the U.S. resettlement of refugees from Indochina. In the United States, Bruce T. Bliatout and his American-born wife, Hollis Yap, strongly advocated for the inclusion of Hmong refugees to the 1975 Indochinese Refugee Act. More important than anyone else is the passion and tireless work of Lionel Rosenblatt, an official of the U.S. Department of State, who lobbied heavily, but quietly for the United States to include Hmong refugees in their Indochinese refugee resettlement program.

On July 3, 1975, the U.S. Embassy in Bangkok sent a cable to the commander in chief of the U.S. Pacific Command/Department of State/France Paris/Secretary of State. The cable says in part as follows, "*Sisouk called me after his return from Paris and I met with him yesterday. He is very concerned over the plight of the Lao refugees in Thailand and I urged him to make contact with the UNHCR and the PRO-NUNCIO noting that this mission could play the role in refugee relief which we had earlier played in Laos and Vietnam.*" https://www.wikileaks.org/plusd/cables/1975BANGKO13131_b.html.

13. Chee, Yang, personal communication. September 7, 2015.
14. Bulk, Jac. February 1996. "Hmong on the Move: Understanding Secondary Migration." *Ethnic Studies Review* 19(1):7–28.

REFERENCES

Bulk, Jac. February 1996. "Hmong on the Move: Understanding Secondary Migration." *Ethnic Studies Review* 19(1):7–28.
Chan, Sucheng. 1994. *Hmong Means Free*. Philadelphia: Temple University Press.
Quincy, Keith. 2000. *Harvesting Pa Chay's Wheat*. Washington: Eastern Washington University Press.

Chapter Five

The Hmong's Forty Years of Becoming American

There was no permanent Hmong American community in the United States until the arrival of Hmong refugees to the United States in late 1975. Maj. Gen. Vang Pao, his young wife, and their child, Chu Long, arrived in Missoula, Montana, in June 1975 with tourist visas with their Lao passport.[1] In his book, *Harvesting Pachay's Wheat*, Quincy stated that the U.S. Embassy in Thailand had persuaded Washington to bend immigration rules to allow Vang Pao and his family to enter the United States.[2] Although they did not come as refugees, their arrival in June 1975, and subsequent arrival of Hmong refugees, helped pave the way for the beginning of the Hmong refugee resettlement program in the United States. It was also the beginning of the forming of the Hmong American community. Shortly after his arrival in Thailand, a Thai general, who knew Vang Pao well, came to meet with Vang Pao in Nam Phong Refugee Camp. He urged Vang Pao to leave Thailand as soon as possible. He told Vang Pao that his stay in Thailand might complicate Thailand's relations with Laos, so he needed to leave Thailand for the time being.[3] Pressure for Vang Pao to leave continued into the first part of June 1975. On June 19, 1975, Maj. Gen. Vang Pao, the former commander of Military Region II of the pre-1975 Royal Lao Army, hesitantly left Thailand for the United States with his youngest wife (Chong) and their young son. They made a brief visit to France and then flew to Missoula, Montana. It should be noted here that Maj. Gen. Vang Pao had married eight times to eight different women. May Lo, the first wife, died young; she and Vang Pao had only three children. The second wife ended up in a divorce with no children; she is the sister of Col. Shong Leng Xiong. Vang Pao's third wife was Xia Thao (Ntxhiav Thoj); the Hmong called her *Niam Loj* or Elder Mother, and she was the most well-known among all his eight wives. She died in Glendale, Arizona, on March 5, 2007. Her funeral was held in Fresno, and she was buried in southern California.[4] The fourth wife was Tru Ly (Rws Lis), the sister of Col. Ly Tou Pao; she did not have any children with Vang Pao. His fifth wife was Mei Lor (Me Lauj), the younger sister of his first wife. Vang Pao married her so that she could help raise the three children of her older sister. As of 2015, she is the only one still alive and lives in Sacramento, California. The sixth wife was Chia Moua (Txiab Muas) and was one of the two of his eight wives who continued to live with Vang Pao until her passing on August 22, 2009, in southern California. The seventh wife was Mae La or Sivay, who is a Lao, and had divorced Vang Pao soon after they arrived in the United States. The eighth and youngest wife was known as Mother Song (Niam Ntxhoo), who accompanied Vang Pao on his exile to Missoula in June 1975. She died from cancer on August 5, 2013, in southern California. Five of Vang Pao's six wives joined him and his youngest wife in Missoula, Montana, in 1976. They came to the United States as refugees.

Lt. Col. Tou Fue Vang was the only military officer who came to visit Vang Pao in Missoula in July of 1975. Tou Fue Vang received his college education in the United States prior to 1975, so he was an English speaker. About one month after Vang Pao arrived in Missoula, Moua Lia, the former superintendent of Xieng Khouang Public Schools, was dispatched by Jerry Daniels in the refugee camp in Thailand to follow up with Vang Pao in Montana. His mission was to learn about Vang Pao's well-being and his advocacy for the United States to include Hmong in their Indochinese refugee resettlement program. After about four weeks, Moua Lia returned to the refugee camp in Thailand without any positive news about Maj. Gen. Vang Pao's advocacy for Hmong refugees to the United States.[5] However, a small number of Hmong families were approved for resettlement and they began to depart for the United States toward the end of 1975. Some of them arrived in the United States before the end of the year; others arrived right after 1975. Among those who arrived in the United States before the end of 1975 was the wife, children, and one sister of Lt. Col. Tou Fue Vang. Tou Fue Vang and his family later moved to Des Moines, Iowa. In August 1975, Moua Sue Bliaya and his wife Bao (Vang Pao's niece) also came to Missoula. It should be noted here that Moua Sue Bliaya is a graduate of the University of Montana in Missoula prior to 1975 and returned to Laos before the end of the war in 1975. In the same month, the wife (May Ly) and son (Fong) of Cha Moua, who was studying at the University of Montana at the time,[6] also came to Missoula. As mentioned in chapter 4, a few Hmong families also arrived in California and elsewhere before the end of 1975. Gradually, the uprooted Hmong American community began to form in Missoula and other cities across the United States. As indicated in my writing elsewhere, I described the Hmong American community as not a geographical or ecological system community, but rather, an ethnic and cultural community without a geographical boundary. It is a community undergoing the process of bicultural and bilingual socialization. Hmong Americans brought with them their unique cultural, historical, and oppressed minority experiences that have no exact parallel with any prior ethnic immigrant group. They have a long history of being a minority within Asia and do not exactly resemble the early or the post-1965 Asian immigrants to America.[7]

During the past forty years, the Hmong American community has gone through many stages of adaption to life in the United States. In my "The Experience of Hmong American: Three Decades in Retrospect Review," I wrote that the Hmong went through at least three distinctive adaptation stages. I list them as the "Refugee Years," from 1975 to 1991, the "Transitional Period," from 1992 to 1999, and the "Hmong American Era," from 2000 to the present day.[8] I described the Refugee Years as the most challenging stage for Hmong refugees. Hmong refugees were an ethnic minority from the highlands of Laos, and they were unprepared educationally, vocationally, and technologically to start their new lives in the United States. They had to start their lives in the United States from scratch. As such, they were faced with a variety of acculturation problems and needs, including the high rate of reliance on public assistance, high unemployment, poverty, youth gangs, and language and cultural barriers. They are named so because they came to the United States as refugees: they perceived themselves as refugees and the U.S. public also identified them as refugees.[9] Also, the Hmong came from the rural highlands of Laos, so they not only had to adapt to the fast pace and technologically oriented life in the United States, but also to an urban/metropolitan life. The second stage, or the "Transitional Period," was their period of going through the transition from being refugees to becoming new Americans. This stage is marked by the election victory of Choua Lee, a twenty-two-year-old Hmong woman, to the Board of Education of St. Paul Public Schools in 1991. Choua Lee's election victory made her not only the first former Hmong refugee, but the first former refugee from Indochina to hold an elected office in the United States. Following her footsteps, many young Hmong were inspired by her success and began to run for political office years later. Many young Hmong professionals began to identify themselves as new Americans as they attempted to address the broader community's needs and issues facing the new Americans. Also, these young Hmong Americans began to address the Hmong's needs and problems as American problems that require the response from multiple American agencies. By the end of the 1990s, most Hmong students, in a study to explore Hmong students' self-perception of their identity, had identified themselves as Hmong Americans, and they also expressed a strong desire to be Hmong.[10] This and other improvements during the past years prepared Hmong Americans to enter another phase of their journey to become American: the Hmong American Era, which is from the year 2000 to the present day. Some of the trends of this era include Hmong's very young population with the median age in 2000 at only twenty; most of them were born outside of Laos, mostly in the United States. By the year 2000, young Hmong had entered many professions, including high-tech, journalism, engineering, teaching, military, medicine, and other areas of employment. By 2010, the Hmong American population had spread to all fifty states plus Washington, District of Columbia, and Puerto Rico. Lastly and most importantly, the Hmong appear to have preserved the best of their heritage while adopting the most from American culture and scientific know-how; thus, they have established many institutions, such as the Center for Hmong Studies, Hmong Cultural Center, the Center for Hmong Art and Talents, *Hmong Studies Journal*, *Hmong Times*, *Hmong Today*, various Hmong radio and television stations, and so forth. Overall, the Hmong American community is a distinct community of an American ethnic group that is made up of a population from many parts of the country that share a common history, culture, language and most importantly, ethnicity.

HMONG AMERICAN POPULATION

The Hmong population in the United States did not proliferate significantly until after the passing of the 1980 Refugee Act, which enabled the U.S. government to generously take large numbers of Indochinese refugees from southeast Asian countries into the United States. According to the 2000 U.S. Census, there were 102,773 foreign-born Hmong in the United States,[11] and it is estimated that nearly 130,000 Hmong refugees were admitted to the United States since 1975. Since 1980, the Hmong American population has continued to increase due to incoming refugees and high birth rates, as they have enjoyed better living standards combined with better access to healthcare needs and medical care. The number of refugee-born children nearly quadrupled over the past forty years. Today, the Hmong American population is estimated approximately at 315,000 by year-end 2015. The 2014 American Community Survey (ACS) estimated the Hmong population to be about 301,286. By 2015 this number might have increased to about 315,000, after children born between 2014 and 2015 have been added, including the addition of undocumented Hmong immigrants from Europe and Asia, especially those from Laos; many of them have overstayed the duration of their U.S. visas. The following table illustrates the increased number of the Hmong American population during the last forty years.

Table 5.1. Hmong Population Increase: 1980 to 2014

	1980 Census	1990 Census	1980–1990 Population Increase	2000 Census	1990–2000 Population Increase	2010 Census	2000–2010 Population Increase	2014	2010–2014 Population Increase
Hmong	5,204*	94,439	1,714%	186,310	97%	260,076	40%	301,286	16%

Sources: S0201: Selected Population Profile in the United States Population Group: Hmong alone or in any combination. U.S. Census Bureau (2000, 2010). Also, based on files compiled by Mark Pfeifer (2011, 2014).

*Although data from the 1980 U.S. Census revealed that the Hmong population was 5,204, the actual number might have been higher as many Hmong might have identified themselves as Laotian. Many Hmong might have checked the box for Laotian as the Laotian population in 1980 was unusually large at 47,683 persons. Also, from the account of Lionel Rosenblatt, the number of Hmong refugees being resettled in the United States by 1980 might have been more than 5,204 persons. In "Hmong on the Move: Understanding Secondary Migration," Jack Bulk (1996) wrote that the peak year of Hmong refugee resettlement in the United States was 1980, when more than twenty-seven thousand Hmong refugees were resettled in the United States. See Jack Bulk, "Hmong on the Move: Understanding Secondary Migration." *Ethnic Studies Review* 19(1):7.

As indicated in Table 5.1, the Hmong population in 1980 was only a little over five thousand, but it increased dramatically from 1980 to 1990, and then began to dwindle from 1990 to 2000. The decade between 1990 and 2000 marks a new trend of Hmong population increase. That is, it increased only by 97 percent from 1990 to 2000, and then by 40 percent for the first decade of the twenty-first century. Careful estimation puts the Hmong population increase at only 16 percent from 2010 to 2014. The slowing of population growth during the last fifteen years reflects the common belief that the flow of Hmong refugees to the United States almost completely halted by 2010, and the number of Hmong immigrants to the United States during the last fifteen years has been very small. Another important factor here is that the preference for a large family is no longer the norm among younger Hmong, who have become the majority of Hmong Americans during the last fifteen years.

In effect, the Hmong American population continues to be very young, with the median age being just a little over 22.8 years old in 2014 compared to 37.7 for the general U.S. population. In 2000, the median age of the Hmong American population was about twenty years old, the youngest ethnic group in the United States. The 2013 ACS data shows that the Hmong American household size was about 5.09 persons compared to that of 2.65 for the general U.S. population. The 2014 Hmong American average household size of 4.93 indicates that it has slightly decreased when compared to 5.65 persons in 2010 and 6.51 in 2000.

DISCRIMINATION AND PREJUDICE AGAINST HMONG

Unlike European immigrants and post-1965 Asian immigrants, Hmong refugees came to the United States from a war-torn country and were from a pre-literate highland ethnic group of Laos. Throughout history, the Hmong had no written language of their own as they were constantly being pushed and pulled to move from north to south, east to west, and from the fertile lowlands of central China to the inhospitable highlands of southwest China and then to the mountains of southeast Asia. Those who settled in Laos had little education and no written language until the 1950s, when the Romanized Phonetic Alphabet and other Hmong written languages were developed for them. Prior to the Secret War in Laos in the early 1960s, the Hmong in Laos were mostly farmers concentrated on high hills, mountaintops, and remote areas dominated by slash-and-burn agriculture. As such, the Hmong, as a group, were considered one of the least culturally, linguistically, educationally, and vocationally prepared Indochinese refugee groups to come to the Unites States post-1975. As a result, they faced many problems and had many needs during their years adapting to the United States, which is the most developed country in the world. They have had to start their new lives in the United States from the very bottom up, overcoming many obstacles. Because the gap between Hmong and American culture is very wide, it has been more difficult for the Hmong to overcome differences. Moreover, the Hmong have had to face many problems to overcome the hundred-year cultural and technological barriers between the two cultures. Consequently, their initial phase of adapting to life in the United States was extremely difficult and challenging. The United States was not only unprepared to assist the Hmong, but pre-judged the Hmong from the very beginning. Many policymakers within the U.S. government considered the Hmong and other highland refugees from Laos as "not suitable for resettlement in the United States."[12] While some American officials, organizations, and citizens did what they could to help the Hmong, others expressed outright anti-Hmong refugee sentiment. Newspapers and other media often portrayed the Hmong refugees as "stone age" or "primitive" people. Not only did American media view the Hmong negatively, some Central Intelligence Agency (CIA) agents who had worked with the Hmong in Laos also expressed anti-Hmong sentiment. In discussing the acculturation difficulty of Hmong refugees, Jim Parker, who was a CIA adviser in Laos during the war years, said, "I don't feel like we abandoned them." He continued to say, "the United States is not the best home for them [Hmong]," and "they're a Stone Age people."[13] Others would have picked up any small, negative, or strange aspect of the Hmong and their culture to highlight, and then exacerbate on it. One book, for example, claims that "early marriage made Hmong mothers the most prolific in the world, with an average fertility rate of 9.5 children per woman."[14] Worst of all is the comment made in 1987 by U.S. Senator Alan Simpson, who was the ranking minority member of the Senate Subcommittee on Immigration and Refugee Affairs. He called the Hmong "the most indigestible group in society."[15] As a result, the Hmong American community faced not only acculturation problems, but also negative stereotypes and prejudice from some people in the public and few policymakers. Such debasing words gave rise to a host of other pressing issues and problems for the Hmong.

As a Hmong proverb says, "If a small calf survives, it will be a bull, and if an orphan survives, she or he will be a woman or man." Those Hmong who were resettled in the United States have survived; they have thrived and become productive citizens in their adopted country. The Hmong continue to enrich their local communities socially, economically, and culturally. Among a few success stories, the Hmong in St. Paul have turned the ghetto Frogtown on University Avenue in St. Paul, Minnesota, into vibrant housings and thriving businesses, shops, and restaurants. In educational attainment, the Hmong have made strides in higher education. For instance, data of 2015 the ACS showed 17 percent of Hmong Americans hold bachelor's degree or higher, compared to 17 percent for Cambodians, 14 percent for Laotians, and 27 percent for Vietnamese Americans.[16] After four decades, the Hmong have made modest gains in social, economic, and political accomplishments. This is a testament to those critics who believed otherwise of the Hmong refugees' adjustment and adaption to their new country. The following is devoted to the discussion of diversity among Hmong American communities and their adaption to different local communities.

DIVERSITY OF HMONG AMERICANS AND THEIR ADAPTION TO DIFFERENT LOCALITIES

Over the past forty years, the Hmong have come a long way; they have overcome many socio-economic challenges and cultural barriers. The Hmong have strived and adapted well to their new social, cultural, political, and economic environment. As the Hmong have been slowly integrating into the mainstream, they have become very diverse in their adaptation to local American communities. The Hmong in Michigan, for example, own and operate nearly two hundred restaurants, whereas there are few restaurants owned by the Hmong in Fresno. However, the Hmong in Fresno and the Central Valley are well known for their small and specialty crop farming. The Hmong in Washington State grow and sell flowers to local farmers' markets as well as to restaurants and other businesses. Some Hmong in Tennessee, North Carolina, and other Midwestern states are involved in poultry and other animal farming. Members of the Hmong American community are also diverse in terms of education, economic development, religion, and political affiliation. Although most elected officials of Hmong descent, such as Mee Moua, Cy Thao, Tou Xiong, and others, are affiliated with the Democratic Party, many Hmong are also known to be members of the Republican Party, especially the elders from the Hmong veteran community.

To illustrate the diversity or differences between each Hmong American community, the Hmong American communities of Missoula, Montana; Denver, Colorado; and Fresno, California are listed and briefly discussed below.

The Hmong Community of Missoula, Montana

The existing but small Hmong American community of Missoula has a lot to do with one single person: Jerry "Hog" Daniels (June 11, 1941–April 29, 1982), a native of Palo Alto, California, and a Montana smokejumper who became the CIA case officer assigned to be the liaison between the CIA and Maj. Gen. Vang Pao during the war years. Hog is Daniels' self-chosen call-sign and was the name known to many people who were around him. Jerry Daniels and his family made it possible for many Hmong students and Hmong refugees to come to this city. It is also Missoula where some of the first wave of Hmong refugees came to resettle. Although some of the Hmong in Missoula left in the 1980s as second migrants to California and other states, this small Missoula Hmong community continues to exist and thrive. The secondary migration in the 1980s has reduced the Hmong population in Missoula from eight hundred people in 1982 to about two hundred in 2015. These two hundred people are likely to stay for the long term as they have adapted well to this town and its people and culture. After four decades in Missoula, the Hmong in this city have evolved into a unique Hmong American community, where almost every Hmong man owns guns and hunt, and some of them own horses, and have in many ways adapted to the cowboy culture and their ways of life. On the other hand, they have preserved many aspects of Hmong religion and culture.[17] In retrospect, the first few Hmong who arrived here around 1971 were Sisouk, Cha, and Chai, children of Maj. Gen. Vang Pao. They came here to study and stayed with Wallie Mace and his wife. The Maces' daughter was married to Jerry Daniels' younger brother, so the Daniels linked them to his Hmong friends. Soon, Saykham Moua, the son of Col. Cher Pao Moua, and Khamseng Lee, the son of Col. Lee Teng, also came to study. They stayed with Mr. Stowald and his family in Missoula. Another Hmong student by the name of Chong Toua also came and stayed with Mr. Ron Jones and his family.[18] In 1973, Cha Moua was sent here by Jerry Daniels to stay temporarily with Daniels' mother and attended Hell Gate High School. In 1974, Chong Vang, a dropout cadet from the U.S. Military Academy at West Point and a son of Maj. Gen. Vang Pao, came to stay with Cha Moua temporarily. Before 1975, the Hmong in Missoula were mostly high school students, except Cha Moua, who, by that time, was a student at the University of Montana, Missoula.

In June 1975, Maj. Gen. Vang Pao, his youngest wife, and their son, Chu Long, were sent to Missoula, Montana, by agents of the CIA. In his book, *Harvesting Pachay's Wheat*, Quincy stated that the U.S. Embassy in Thailand had persuaded Washington to bend immigration rules to allow Vang Pao and his family to enter the United States.[19] A CIA agent by the code name of Zack (Joe Glasco) was sent to Missoula to tend to Vang Pao and his family's needs, and to prevent the media from accessing Vang Pao. Cha Moua, who had been in daily contact with Vang Pao and Zack, related that Zack would accompany Vang Pao and/or his wife while shopping and would pay for all the bills at the checkout stand. Cha Moua also stated that Zack did not allow anything to be in Vang Pao's name, so when the CIA wanted to buy a car for Vang Pao, they approached Cha Moua about using Cha Moua's name on the title, but the car would be for Vang Pao's use. Jerry Daniels' friend, John Really, who was a realtor, allowed Vang Pao and his family to temporarily stay in his vacant house at Miller Creek. After one month at this house, the CIA bought a house for Vang Pao at 336 Central Avenue in Missoula. A year later, the CIA bought a farmhouse in Hamilton, Montana, for Vang Pao and his family. By 1976, the rest of Vang Pao's family was resettled in Missoula as refugees. They all came to stay at the Central Avenue house and the farmhouse. The farmhouse was about twenty minutes away from the Central Avenue house, so members of Vang Pao's family traveled back and forth between these two homes. In the early 1980s, Vang Pao and his family moved to California, and both the Central Avenue house and farmhouse were sold. According to Cha Moua, who had been very close to Vang Pao from 1975 to 1981, the CIA paid for the down payment, but Vang Pao paid for the monthly mortgage payment. By the time they bought these two houses for Vang Pao, the CIA had already allocated him twenty-five hundred dollars per month. Additionally, his young wife brought ten thousand dollars with her to Missoula.[20]

As more and more refugees came to Missoula, Cha Moua became the unofficial liaison for these refugees and the larger American community; he spent much of his time helping them. Initially, he volunteered to help them as much as his time allowed. In 1977, the Hmong community and some local leaders formed the Lao Family Community of Missoula. Cha Moua became the executive director for this new organization, which was a non-profit organization, formed to help the refugee community in Missoula.[21] In 1979, Moua Sue, a former member of the National Assembly of Laos, and his family were resettled in Missoula. The community continued to grow and by 1983, the Hmong Missoula community grew to about eight hundred people, but news of farming and kinder weather in California, and other factors, drove the Hmong en masse to California. As of the year 2015, there were about fifteen families remaining in Missoula; about six of these families belong to the Moua Clan, the clan of Moua Sue and Cha Moua. Although the majority of the Hmong in Missoula in the 1980s, including the family of Maj. Gen. Vang Pao, had left this city to other parts of the United States, the Hmong have, overall, left their footprints on this city. There are, for example, within the metropolitan of Missoula, Hmong Street, and Moua Lane. Cha Moua left Missoula to go to California, not as a second migration, but to follow his job. He is now retired and lives in Merced, California. Moua Sue continued to live in Montana until 2002, when his family moved to Spokane, Washington; he died in Spokane that same year. The life of Moua Sue is another unique story that reflects the struggles of the Hmong as well as the rooting of the Moua

Clan in Missoula. It is also a story of courage and resilience to realize his own goals, and it is worthy for discussion, as follows.

Moua Sue was the first Hmong of Houa Phanh Province to be elected to the National Assembly of Laos. He went from being an orphan with only a third-grade education to becoming a two-term People's Deputy in Houa Phanh Province from 1967 to 1974. He was one of the three Hmong who served in the National Assembly, when it was dissolved in 1974. He was first elected at the end of 1966 and re-elected in 1972, and served until 1974, when the National Assembly was replaced by the National Political Consultative Council.[22]

Moua Sue was born in 1930 in Ban Pak Kha, Sam Neua District, Houa Phanh Province, Laos. Ban Pak Kha was about twenty-five kilometers from the town of Sam Neua. His father died when he was young, and he grew up with only the guidance of his mother and his four older brothers. In the early 1940s, his uncle, Chia Long Moua (the younger brother of his father), hired a Lao tutor to teach basic education to his sons and nephews, including Moua Sue. After only two years, the tutor had to return home. As one of the older pupils of his tutor, he was often asked by the tutor to help clean the classroom and do other tasks. Before the tutor left, he took the young Moua Sue to a jar, where he kept his silver coins. He told Moua Sue, "You watch the silver coins in this jar. If I do not return to this village in three months, then you keep all these silver coins and use them to buy whatever you need." Due to the war, the tutor left and never returned. Moua Sue took the silver coins as told. He used them as capital seeds for trading goods in the area. The young Moua Sue did very well in his trading. It needs to be added here that after his tutor left, Moua Sue went to a public school in Sam Neua Town for one year. He received a total of three years education. He stopped going to school because of World War II; the Japanese began to arrive in Laos and things became chaotic, and people were fearful of a looming war.

As mentioned above, the young Moua Sue used the money left to him by his tutor as capital seed for a trading business. During one of his trading trips to a Hmong village known as Ban Houei Moune, he met a girl he liked very much. He returned home and asked one of his uncles to go with him to ask for her hand in marriage. His uncle did and that is how he got married to his first wife.[23] Soon after he married his first wife, he joined the army of the French Indochina to fight against the Japanese. Because he had three years of education, he was promoted to the rank of sergeant, overseeing more than ten village soldiers or Auto-Defense de Choc (ADC). In 1946, after the Japanese returned home, Moua Sue and his soldiers became part of the French army fighting with the then New Lao Issara Movement or the Lao for the Independence of Laos. Unfortunately, one of the bombs carried by his soldiers accidentally exploded, killing one soldier and injuring Moua Sue and another soldier. Moua Sue was wounded at his knee. The pellets went inside his knee, and as a result, he spent one year in Vientiane undergoing many surgeries to remove the pellets and repair his injury. During the one year he stayed in Vientiane, he was exposed to city life and modernization. When he returned home to Houa Phanh, his injury had healed and he had seen farther than any person in his own village. He recalled being young, energetic, and highly motivated; he continued to do trading business and network with other leaders of Hmong and non-Hmong ethnic groups. By the mid-1950s, Moua Sue had become a successful trader. He often went out to buy goods in Xieng Khouang or other towns and brought them back to sell in his region. His trading caravan included thirteen horses and a three person-team, such as himself and two assistants. One assistant was his older brother Chia Xeng Moua and the other was his adopted son, Kua Neng. The three of them rode on three horses, and the other ten horses were used for transporting goods and merchandise. He gained respect from the villagers and others, and as a result, he was made a village chief. By 1960, he became a sub-district chief or Tasseng, trying to stay neutral between the Pathet Lao and the Royal Lao government. The Pathet Lao, however, suspected that he was not loyal to them because most of his relatives joined the ADC of the Royal Lao government. They tried to arrest him, so he and his relatives in Pak Kha escaped to Houei Ngou, where he helped to organize Battalion Volunteer 12B and placed it under Military Region II; he became a company commander under Battalion Volunteer 12B. While serving as company commander, he continued to trade, often buying goods from Vientiane and other towns, and then selling them to people in his region. He became the "rich company commander" and as such some of his brothers in arms—"company and battalion commanders"—were envious of him, but he was much liked by the people in the region. In 1965, he wanted to run for a seat in the National Assembly of Laos, and was seeking a way to submit paperwork for his candidacy. He was, however, blocked by Maj. Gen. Vang Pao and was discouraged by Touby Lyfoung. Maj. Gen. Vang Pao had someone else in mind as a candidate and Touby Lyfoung did not think Moua Sue had the needed education and credentials to run for a national political office. Unfortunately, those deputies elected in 1965 served only one year; they were terminated due to political complications. In 1966, he was ready to run for political office and asked for no one's opinion. He said he had a feeling that he would win and that he could do the job. When he inquired about getting all the paperwork to file for his candidacy, he was told by the staff of Ministry of Interior that the minimum educational requirement for candidacy is a certificate of sixth-grade completion. He quietly went to Long Cheng to see Major Moua Sue, who allowed him to use Major Moua Sue's certificate of sixth-grade completion as both of them have the same name. The major had an eighth-grade education; therefore, he did not have a need at the time for a certificate of sixth-grade completion. Moua Sue filed for candidacy and was elected to office by the end of 1966. In January 1967, he officially became the first Hmong of Houa Phanh Province to serve in national office in the National Assembly of Laos, as a People's Deputy from Houa Phanh Province. He said he did not worry about not knowing what to do, he just wanted to give his very best. Once elected to office, he said, he had a secretary to help him and he could do just as well as any other educated deputies. He said he might be a better deputy because he spent most of his out of session time visiting the people. Most of the other deputies, he said, spent their time in Vientiane in the comfort of air-conditioned rooms and city life. In his second term in office, he suggested to the prime minister to make it a requirement for all Cabinet and National Assembly members to marry war widows. He said this requirement would minimize poverty and other sufferings of war widows and their children. It was a laughing matter to most members of the National Assembly, but he was serious; he suggested it from the point of view of someone who saw so much suffering of war widows and their children. They were not only deprived of their husbands and fathers, but were also under abject poverty. He did what he could to help any Hmong in Vientiane who sought his help. Consequently, he became popular among his Hmong, and followers of other ethnic groups, because he approached them according to their customs and traditions. Furthermore, he knew their needs and issues. He offered his home in Vientiane to any Hmong and his constituents who traveled to Vientiane.

He said he helped people because it was the right thing to do, and sometimes, he might break the rules to get things done. He was certain he would be re-elected for a third term, if the National Assembly was not dissolved in 1974. It should be noted here that the National Assembly was dissolved in 1974 in accordance with the Peace and National Reconciliation Agreement, which was signed on February 21, 1973, between the Royal Lao government and the Communist Pathet Lao. The implementation of this peace agreement led to the formation of the Provisional Government of National Union and the National Political Consultative Council (NPCC) in April 1974; the NPCC served as the legislative body of the new coalition government. His last wish was to become a member of the Council for the King; that wish that never happened. He and his family left Laos to go to Thailand in 1975 and stayed in a refugee camp in Thailand for four years. The family left the refugee camp in Thailand on October 18, 1979, to go to Missoula, Montana. Shortly after they arrived in Missoula, Moua Sue and nine other refugees went to work for Big Sky Cookie Company. Moua Sue worked there as janitor, and after two weeks, he related to Cha Moua that he felt so bad that he had to clean restrooms and do other dirty tasks. Cha Moua, who is his nephew, told him to stop working if he felt that the job did not fit him well. Cha Moua then spoke to the Forest Department in Missoula, and they designated an area in Blue Mountain for Moua Sue to cut wood and sell so that he could get some money from selling the wood he cut. He loved this new job as he worked under no one and worked very independently. He worked in this job until June of 1983, when he, his second wife, and their children moved from Missoula to Billings, Montana. His first wife and her children continued to live in Missoula and later moved to Spokane, Washington. In Billings, his second wife worked as a janitor for a local hospital. Moua Sue bought an acre of land and worked mostly on this land. Moua Sue and his second wife and their children lived in Billings until 2002, when he and his second wife moved to Spokane to be closer to the first wife and her children. By the time they moved to Spokane, Moua Sue's health was not only failing, but critical as his kidneys had failed. He was on dialysis every day. He died in Spokane in 2002 at the age of seventy-two.

While he was in Billings, he was physically isolated from relatives and friends, but he was still influential among his clan members. The Moua clan under Moua Sue's leadership was well organized. Most of the Moua clan members were actively involved in their annual meetings in which Moua Sue acted as their honorary chair. Moua Sue had worked hard to push and promote education and economic self-sufficiency for members of his clan. When asked about his words of wisdom, he said, "Set goal, work hard for it, and earn your own merits." Also, "Believe in yourself, earn your money, and take only whatever power the people give to you or you earn from the people."

Moua Sue had two wives. He had eight children with the first wife and five with the second wife. The eight children with the first wife are Muas, Huas, Toog, Txos, Paj, Kub, Ntxawg, and Mos. The first son, Muas, died young, and the third son, Toog, died in Spokane. The second son, Huas, served in the U.S. Army and retired as a captain. He lives with his family in California. The other children live all over many cities, some in Spokane, others in California. The five children with the second wife are Txoov, Khej, Kaus, Tsab Mim, and Koob.

Moua Sue was a pathfinder in his homeland as well as in his adopted country, the United States of America. With the belief in himself, a pioneering spirit, and a practical approach to life, he became the first Hmong in northeastern Laos to serve in the pre-1975 National Assembly of the Kingdom of Laos. With these qualities and his determination to be independent and self-supportive, members of his extended family have made Montana their home. They have become self-sufficient and are well adapted to Montana, land of the big sky and cowboys. After forty years in Missoula, the small Hmong community there has evolved and adapted to their physical, social, economic, and political environment. About half of the fifteen Hmong families in Missoula, for example, engage in mobile restaurants, serving Asian foods at many major events, such as county fairs, Native American pow wows, and local festivities. Some drive miles and miles to sell food. Reportedly, a few of them have come to Idaho Falls and to Reno to sell their foods during major events there. When there are no major events in the region, they drive their food trucks to local shopping centers or to large work places to sell their foods. These Hmong capitalize on their appearance as Asian, and market their foods as Chinese, Thai, and other Asian foods. These types of work allow them the freedom to do what they like to do and to work independently. Moreover, in a good year, their income during the summer alone can support them for the entire year, so they have the winter to tend to other activities or to come to California to visit family and attend the Hmong New Year celebrations in Fresno and Sacramento. Only one Hmong, who is a college graduate from California, works for the State of Montana as a computer specialist.

Another sign of their adaptation to Montana is their strong bond with hunting traditions and horseback riding. Almost every Hmong man owns a gun and a hunting bow, and they would not do anything except go hunting during the open season.

When the hunting season is over, they like to go fishing and enjoy the snow. During the summer, many Hmong go out to harvest huckleberry, which provides them with extra income. In a good year, a couple can bring home up to ten thousand dollars per season. Unlike the Hmong in Fresno and the Twin Cities of St. Paul and Minneapolis, when the Hmong in Missoula get together, they tend to talk about hunting and fishing. They talk about who might get the top hunting trophy award of the year. And, when they go out deer hunting, it is not the meat that they go after; it is the horns they want as their trophy for the year. Moreover, many Hmong in Missoula own horses, and when they go out to hunt elk and deer, they ride on their horses and use some of them to transport their supplies; they might stay for a few days away from town.

In general, the Hmong in Missoula continue to retain many aspects of Hmong traditions, customs, religion, culture, and identity. More so, they tend to preserve the tradition of rituals of Hmong life stages, such as birth, marriage, and death. Most of them continue to practice the Hmong religion.

The Hmong Community in Denver, Colorado

Hmong began to resettle in Denver since early 1976, and among those earlier settlers were Yang Chee, Major Ly Fu, and many others, who have helped and guided the community to be what it is today. Although Hmong community leaders estimate the Hmong population in Denver to be about six thousand, the 2010 U.S. Census counted it to be only 3,859. The population make-up of the Denver Hmong American community is an example of the diversity of the Hmong American background as this community includes Hmong refugees and immigrants from many parts of the world. The Denver metro area is home to most of the Hmong in Colorado; it is a small, but growing Hmong community, estimated to be between 3,959 to 6,500 people. Of this population, there are at least seven Hmong Chinese immigrants, one Hmong Argentinian family of eleven people, and about five French Hmong families. There was one Hmong Australian family who lived in Denver for a few years, but they moved to California in 2006. The rest of them were initially Hmong refugees; some have been in Denver since 1976, when they were initially resettled there, whereas others moved in and out of Denver throughout the last twenty-five years.[24]

Hou Wanlin, who is one of the mentioned seven Chinese Hmong in Denver, has a unique and interesting immigration story. He came to Denver, Colorado, in December 1999 to visit his fiancé. A month later, they were married and he has since lived with his wife. He and his wife have two children as of 2007.[25] Hou Wanlin was born and raised in Yunnan Province, the People's Republic of China. His father was a Chinese civil servant, so he grew up in the city and enjoyed the privilege of being a city dweller, including having an education. He is one of the most educated young Hmong persons in Yunnan Province. He graduated from law school in Yunnan and went to work for the Yunnan First Construction Company as a staff attorney, which was a very prestigious position for him, because he was from a Hmong minority background. He was pleased with his job and the working environment, and had the potential to quickly climb up the ladder in his career. Being a staff attorney of such a large and prestigious company, he was on his way to become a top prosecutor, criminal defender, or a judge. But his heart was with a woman who lived thousands of miles away from China; she was a Hmong American.

Hou's love affair began when he was in law school. In his early years in law school, he began to show an interest in Christianity and had spent his free time studying this religion and attended their church activities. Those activities led him to become acquainted with and eventually meet a young Hmong American Christian woman in 1995. Their acquaintance grew into a love relationship. She visited him in Yunnan several times, and eventually, he proposed to her and asked her to come to stay with him in China. She refused, but proposed that he come to visit her in the United States so that they could get to know each other better. He accepted her proposal and came to visit her in

December of 1999; they were married a month later. He and his wife started a new life together in Denver, where he had to start his life from the bottom up. He not only abandoned his life in China, but his profession as well. He started college all over again; this time, he decided to study accounting. He reasoned that accounting would be more appropriate for him because his English and cultural skills were not strong enough to practice law in the United States. He became a naturalized citizen of the United States in 2005 and then earned his bachelor of science degree in accounting in 2006. He invited his parents to the United States to attend his commencement in the summer of 2006. They came and decided to stay to help him and his wife take care of their two young children. They applied for and were granted permanent residence status in 2006. Hou is not only a productive new immigrant to the United States, but also plays a very active role in the leadership of the Denver Hmong community. In 2007, he was the treasurer for the local Hmong Association and has been very active in his church and other community activities. He is now a general accountant for CoBiz Financial and Investment Accountant at Great West Financial. He lives with his family in Greenwood, Colorado.

The Hmong Community in Fresno, California

With a population of more than thirty thousand, the Fresno metropolitan area is now home to the second largest Hmong population, after only the Twin Cities of St. Paul and Minneapolis in Minnesota, which have a Hmong population of more than seventy thousand.[26]

In many of my articles, I describe the Hmong community in Fresno as a secondary migrant community. I wrote that Fresno was not one of the selected sites for the initial Indochinese refugee resettlement, so there were no Hmong in Fresno before 1977, until one Hmong family moved from Merced to Fresno, and this family began to persuade their relatives and friends to come to Fresno.[27] By 1979, there were only five Hmong families in Fresno, however the number grew very fast; by the end of 1980, more than two thousand called Fresno their new home, and two years later, there were more than ten thousand Hmong living in Fresno. By 1995 the population grew to about thirty-five thousand. The community began to change in 1996, when the Fresno Hmong community began to move out of California in what is called the "Third Hmong Migration."[28] By the year 2000, the Hmong in Fresno numbered around twenty-five thousand and lost its place to the Twin Cities of St. Paul/Minneapolis as the largest Hmong concentration in the United States. By this time, the Twin Cities of St. Paul/Minneapolis reportedly had a Hmong population of more than fifty thousand and became the capital of Hmong Americans. The Fresno Hmong population grew to more than thirty

Figure 5.1.   Hmong New Year gathering in Fresno, circa 2008.
Kou Yang.

thousand in 2010, and it is known as the second largest Hmong American community in the nation.

By the year 2015, the Fresno Hmong community appeared to be adapting well, yet many pressing problems continued to exist. Many Hmong continue to farm, but the number appears to be declining as the younger Hmong seem to prefer working in types of jobs other than farming. As such, Hmong are found to be working in many professions throughout the city; it is easy to find Hmong working from fast food restaurants to upscale sushi bars, from assembly line workers to computer skilled jobs, from kindergarten to twelfth-grade teaching to university-level teaching, from instructional superintendent in Fresno Unified School District to associate vice president for enrollment services at California State University, Fresno. In the Bliatout Plaza within the Asian Village there are many shops, including V-Nai Mini Mall with at least forty small Hmong shops, selling goods ranging from herbal medicine to clothing, from beauty products to general goods from China and other countries. Additionally, it is home to many offices and other businesses, such as a supermarket, three restaurants, one dental clinic, one medical clinic, one pharmacy, and several other shops. The Bliatout Plaza was owned by Sam Bliatout from 1999 to the spring of 2015. Bliatout bought the building in 1999 for a price of almost three million dollars and sold it in the spring of 2015 for six million dollars. The building generates between sixty thousand to seventy thousand dollars per month, which is more than enough to cover staff salary, building maintenance, and mortgage payments, plus tax, insurance, and utilities. The loan for the building was paid off at the end of 2013.[29]

There are also many Hmong offices and businesses that are located outside of the Bliatout Plaza on the west side of Asian Village. These offices and businesses include the Fresno Center for New Americans, Excel Travel, Bobby Yang Medical Clinic, and other businesses. The Fresno Center for New Americans is the largest Hmong mutual assistance organization in Fresno, serving not only Hmong, but also Khmer, Lao, Iraqi, and other new refugees from the Middle East and elsewhere. Asian Village has slowly been a concentration of Hmong businesses, and the hut that can generate tax to the city, a contribution by the Hmong to Fresno. Other major Hmong businesses in Fresno include Asia Supermarket, Golden Bowl Supermarket, Bingo Supermarket, and so on. Another contribution to Fresno is their annual New Year celebration, which is held from Christmas to the end of December. The Hmong New Year celebration in Fresno is a highly celebrated and well-attended event. It attracts approximately fifteen thousand people per day to its venue at the Fresno County Fairground; about half of these New Year participants come to Fresno from out of state and other countries. They stay in hotels, get their meals from local restaurants, and rent cars from local car rental companies. Therefore, these New Year participants contribute generously to the local economy. They also add to the cultural diversity and richness of the city.

The Hmong in Fresno and the Twin Cities of St. Paul and Minneapolis have become urbanites and are very active in social and political events. When the Hmong in these cities get together, they tend to talk about education, politics, and hot topics for the day. The hot topics for September and October in 2015 were on the Lao Family Community of Minnesota and other radical groups like the ones who call themselves HmongLand or Hmoob Teb Chaws. Regarding the Lao Family Community of Minnesota, the issues surrounded the mishandling of money and potential corruption,[30] and for the HmongLand group or HmoobTebchaws, the issues were on potential fraud as this group was reportedly investigated by the local police as well as the Federal Bureau of Investigation. The Federal Bureau of Investigation warned the Hmong community leaders about potential financial scams from this group.[31] Xeng Xiong, leader of HmongLand, was arrested in March 2016 for defrauding Hmong elders, and he was convicted in January 2017 for one count of wire fraud and one count of mail fraud.[32]

As for young Hmong professionals who felt compelled to preserve their diaspora experiences in the United States, they managed to develop educational exhibits about the Hmong. In 2015, many young and educated Hmong spent their free time and energy working on Hmongstory40, an exhibition of their forty years in America. The end products, which included timelines, historical documents, artifacts, and photos, were exhibited in the museum of the Hmong New Year in December of 2015 in Fresno, California.

Social and Economic Contributions of Hmong Americans

Although Hmong refugees have initially struggled to overcome many challenges and difficulties, for many, the journey to adapt to this country continues to be ongoing. Forty years have now passed, and so the question is, "Where are the Hmong now, in their journey to become Americans?" Through resilience and perseverance, many individual Hmong refugees have shown remarkable success in both entrepreneurial spirits and mainstream political arenas. Additionally, they have made some progress in education as well as business entrepreneurial success. I will highlight a few of them in the following.

1. Art and Literature: More and more young Hmong are engaging in various forms of art. Mai Der Vang was the winner of the prestigious 2016 Walt Whitney Award. She was born and raised in Fresno, California, and is now a teacher at Clovis Community College. According to the *Fresno Bee*, Mai Der Vang holds "a Bachelor's degree in English at the University of California, Berkeley, and a Master of Fine Arts degree at Columbia University. While at Columbia she won the Corrente Poetry Fellowship. Her poems have been published in *Ninth Letter*, *The Journal*, *The Cincinnati Review*, *The Missouri Review Online*, *Radar* and *Asian American Literary Review*, among other publications."[33] The books *Bamboo Among the Oaks* (2002), *How do I Begin?* (2011), and *To Live Here* (2014) are examples of the growing community of creative Hmong American writers and poets. The Center for Hmong Arts and Talent in the Twin Cities of Minnesota testifies to a small but growing community of Hmong artists. The Twin Cities are also home to a few well-known Hmong artists, such as Xeexeng Lee and Cy Thao. Xeeseng Lee is a studio artist and art teacher. He teaches art at Blake School and lives in St. Paul, Minnesota. On his website, he lists his recent commissions as murals for the city of Wadena, the St. Paul Dragon Festival, Concordia University, Northpoint Wellness Center, and others.[34] Cy Thao, a State Representative who served in the Minnesota Legislature from 2002–2010, is a painter and creator of "The Hmong Genocide and Immigration," which tells stories of Hmongs' long journey of diaspora. Standing out among all Hmong artists is Yer Za Vue, who is an animation artist working on many major projects for Disney. On her website, she writes, "My passion for drawing and painting led me to attend The Kansas City Art Institute, where I received my BFA in Illustration in 1993. After interning at Hallmark Cards and Disney Feature Anima-

tion, I relocated to Orlando, Florida, where I spent over [ten] years working for Disney on traditional animated films and my list of credits include *The Little Match Girl, Brother Bear, Lilo & Stitch, John Henry, Tarzan, Mulan, Pocahontas,* and *Circle of Life.*" She has also "directed numerous animated shorts including *Fido, Cinderella, Bubbles, Masterpiece Makeover, Ethos,* and *Paper Indians.*"

Yer Za Vue is the quietest and least known person in the Hmong American community, but is a giant artist among American artists and impressionists. Reportedly, her awards include second place 2014 Los Gatos Plein Air, Fifteenth Annual American Impressionist Society, 2014 National Juried Exhibition, Grand Prize Quick Draw Pacific Northwest Plein Air, 2014 Paris in the Park Blocks Portland Art Museum, 2014 Plein Air Easton, Pacific Northwest Plein Air, Portland Art Museum Invitational, Lake Oswego Invitational, Hillsboro Plein Air, and Eugene Plein Air. Yer Za Vue has been featured in *Willamette Weekly Portland,* Oregon Public Broadcasting (PBS), and *The Oregonian.* She teaches animation at the Art Institute of Portland.[35]

2. Business Entrepreneurship: The idea of doing business is new to the Hmong, so it takes a long time for some of the young Hmong to learn the trade and accumulate needed capital seed. As of 2015, cities with larger Hmong population, such as the Twin Cities of Minnesota, Fresno, and Milwaukee, have a shopping building of thirty to two hundred shops. Other Hmong businesses include home healthcare services, grocery supermarkets, real estate, insurance service, and professional services, such as chiropractic, dental, and medical clinics. Hmong in different parts of the country tend to focus on different types of business that are suitable for their area. In Milwaukee, for example, the Asian Market Phongsavan, which is owned by Tou and Pai, has sixty-nine vendor stalls and a food court of nine restaurants, including three sandwich shops on its first floor. The second level has office space available for medical clinics, chiropractic care, insurance needs, hair salons, and Hmong book stores, among others. In the back of the facility is a twelve thousand-square-foot open multi-purpose space made available for celebrations such as the Hmong New Year, birthday parties, graduation parties, and others.[36] The Hmong in Michigan own and operate nearly two hundred restaurants; most of them are outside the metropolitan area of Detroit to avoid competition from other Asian restaurants. The Hmong restaurant business in Michigan began with one person, Nou Ying Kue, who brought his dream of owning a restaurant from Philadelphia to Detroit in the late 1970s. The idea of owning a restaurant started when Nou Ying Kue was working as a dishwasher in a Chinese restaurant in Philadelphia in 1976. He noticed that the restaurant was extremely busy, so he kept thinking about owning his own restaurant. Later, he went to work for another Chinese restaurant, where one of the

chefs, who was a Thai Chinese, decided to teach Nou Ying to cook Chinese food. After mastering all the needed Chinese cooking techniques, the chef demanded that the owner hire Nou Ying Kue to help him as a cook. He became a cook and started to call and consult his uncle, Wang Tru Hang, about opening their own restaurant. At first, no one paid much attention to him, but insistency persuaded his relatives and friends to support his idea. In 1978, Nou Ying and his family moved to Michigan to take on the new challenge. Nou Ying and his five partners each raised about fifteen thousand dollars as capital seed for the new restaurant. They took the risk of opening the restaurant of Nou Ying's dream in 1981, known as Chee Peng. It was in Petoskey, a small town in northwest Michigan. The restaurant became quite successful, and so the six did not stop there, but continued to open more restaurants—at the rate of one per year. Chee Peng, meaning "Capital Seed," was franchised out to Wisconsin, Minnesota, and California. Starting this very first restaurant, the Hmong in Michigan now own nearly two hundred restaurants. Unlike the Hmong Americans in Michigan, the Hmong in the Central Valley of California, for example, are heavily involved in farming where they produce fresh vegetables, crops, and fruits that are further distributed to retail stores across the country, especially in areas where there is a concentration of Hmong and other Asian populations. In Washington State, the Hmong Americans invest heavily in floral businesses by growing and selling flowers, a new trade they learned in this country.

As for the Hmong in the Midwest, there seems to be a mix of small businesses and retail shops. For instance, the Hmong Village Shopping Center in the Twin Cities of Minnesota, which was open in 2010, houses more than two hundred vendors that include office space, grocery stores, food courts, batik textiles, farmers' market, barber shops, pharmacies, specialty shops, and kiosks. This Hmong Village mall creates hundreds of jobs and generates about three thousand dollars a day for the City of St. Paul. As of 2015, the Hmong Village Shopping Center is co-owned by eight individual Hmong entrepreneurs: Shongleng Yang (three shares), Paul Vang (two shares), and one share for each of the following co-owners: Yong Yia Vang, Brandon Vang, Archie Vang, Kevin Vang, Tony Vang, and Chue Fue Thao. The Hmong Town Market Place in St. Paul is another prime example of the growing Hmong entrepreneurship. Although this market place is much smaller than the Hmong Village Shopping Center, it has about one hundred similar shops and venders, and creates hundreds of jobs for Hmong and non-Hmong.

Shongleng Yang, who is one of the eight co-owners of the Hmong Village Shopping Center in St. Paul, Minnesota, and one of a dozen of Hmong American millionaires, has not only an interesting story, but a Hmong version of the American "rags to riches" odyssey. He is one of five children of his parents. His mother died when he was only five years old, and he was raised by his father with the help of his older brothers and sisters. He had a few years of schooling in Laos before he escaped to the refugee camp in Thailand in 1979. He came to Thailand with his cousins, and five of them stayed in a small hut in the refugee camp, where he only remembers hunger and misery. He stayed in the refugee camp for one year and three months before resettling in the United States in 1983. He arrived in Los Angeles on April 1, 1980, when he was fifteen years old; he came with the mother-in-law of his oldest brother and her two daughters. They stayed in Los Angeles for three months before moving to Chicago, Illinois, to join his four cousins, who had lived together with him in the refugee camp. The mother-in-law of his older brother and her two daughters went to Appleton, Wisconsin, to be closer to their relatives. Shongleng and his four cousins stayed together in a small apartment in Chicago. They were single and not eligible for public assistance, so they worked as they could to support themselves. In 1984, he moved to Columbus, Ohio, to work as a Hmong community job developer and continued his education there. Unfortunately, the refugee program ended in less than a year, but fortunately, he met Nou Ying Kue, who opened the first Hmong restaurant in Michigan, and learned of the success of his restaurant business. So, he began to think about doing business or owning his own restaurant. In 1985, Shongleng went to Travers City in Michigan to learn cooking and restaurant business from Nou Ying Kue. After completing his training, he moved to Minnesota to open a restaurant with Dr. Yang Dao, Dr. Neng Zong Yang, and others. After two years of working at this restaurant, Shongleng realized that it was not easy for him to be in this business because he is physically small and short; he could not handle two woks at the same time. He thought to himself that he could not do this work for the rest of his life, and therefore must change his business career. He began to visualize about others, who are educated and have easier jobs, and earn a good living. He decided to go back to school; he attended a GED class in the early morning before the restaurant opened. It took him a year to get his GED. At the same time, his uncle, Wa Thao Yang, had been preaching the idea of doing business and working for oneself as the way to get rich and move up the social ladder in the United States. Property investment was the main topic of discussion at the time, so he bought his first duplex house for fifty thousand dollars when he was still single. Fortunately, the unit he rented out covered his monthly mortgage payment, so he only paid for the tax, the insurance, and the utility bills for the duplex. Soon after he bought the duplex, he married Zoua Vang from St. Paul, Minnesota. Unfortunately, their restaurant as mentioned above had to be closed because the landlord wanted to sell the building. Shongleng and his wife had to start all over; fortunately, they found labor jobs at a producer company, which paid them $5.50 per hour or $11.00 an hour for two persons. He compared their combined wage to his cousin, who had a bachelor of arts degree and earned $12.50 an hour. Shongleng and his wife discussed their future and agreed that she would continue to work at the producer company and Shongleng would work part-time at a restaurant, so that he could attend college. He did what he and his wife had planned, but it was very hard for him to work part-time and attend school almost full-time. Moreover, his grades were not good and he was not happy about it. At the time, he met a recruiter for a home care agency; it sounded less stressful, so Shongleng went to work as a personal care assistant to one of his elder relatives, who needed such service. He worked as a personal care assistant for six hours a day, seven days a week, and had more time to study. More time to study meant taking more units. He took sixteen credits every quarter, and it took him three and a quarter years to earn his bachelor's degree in business administration in 1993 from National University in Minnesota.[37]

Soon after he graduated from college, the owner of the home health care agency that he worked for made a very attractive and generous offer to him: if Shongleng Yang could recruit more Hmong clients to his home health care agency, the owner would create a new home health care agency for him to run. He took the offer and went from being a manager to president of the new agency. He did an excellent job and was amazed by the income generated from his own efforts to the new agency. After a while, he realized that the job of managing the home health care agency was not difficult and it was something that he had the skills and ability to do. After only one year on this job, Shongleng offered to buy the health care agency from the owner, but the owner did not want to sell. He, however, encouraged Shongleng to open a new one with his help. In March 1995, Shongleng started the paperwork for his new health care agency and the business was opened in May 1995. As a token of support, the owner of his previous employer transferred five clients from the previous health care agency to Shongleng's new one. These first five clients helped Shongleng to not only start, but keep the door of his business open for the first month or two. Home health care provides personal care for people with disabilities and the elderly at their homes by assisting them with bathing, grooming, cooking, housekeeping, shopping, and by accompanying them to doctor's visits. Home health care agencies' income is derived from federal or state medical assistance. For a client to get their services, they must have a need for long-term care and medical necessities requiring personal care. Moreover, in the State of Minnesota, a client must be referred by a family physician for the needed services. Shongleng Yang's home health care agency grew from five clients in May of 1995 to more than 197 clients in 2008. As of 2008, his agency has 201 employees (both part-time and full-time) with 745 hours of service per day. His home health care agency continued to do well until 2013, when it, like other businesses, began to experience varieties and complex problems. Many of these problems arose from Shongleng's trust and confidence in his staff. Because of him trusting his staff, he paid more attention to other business projects and often traveled out of town. By the time he realized it, the home health care agency was going downhill; much of it had to do with the staff failing to do their jobs, and there were many violations of state rules and regulations. In the end, he closed his home health care agency at the end of 2013. Since then, he has been focusing on other business projects, such as the Hmong Village Shopping Center, in addition to other businesses in Laos. He has, for many years now, been experimenting with poultry, rubber trees, and other farming businesses in Laos.

3. Corporate America: A small number of young Hmong have also reached the boardroom of corporate America. One of them is Lee Yang, who is now the vice president for finance in the Kaiser Permanente Corporation. He previously served as western region finance director of United Airlines and as senior vice president for finance of Logitech. Between 1995 and 2005, Yang was actively involved with major milestones including the launch of Ted as United entered the low-cost carrier market. With over two thousand flights daily, Yang, at the time, held a prominent position at United Airlines, the world's second largest airline.

Lee Yang was born in Muong Cha, Xieng Khouang Province, Laos, to Yongva Yang and Blia Vang. His family escaped from Laos to Thailand in January of 1976, when Lee was just a child. On August 30, 1979, Lee and his family left Thailand to travel to Tennessee via San Francisco. The family started their new lives in America in Memphis, Tennessee, and they were there for four years with almost no Hmong community and many acculturation difficulties. In August 1983, they moved from Memphis to Merced, California, to reunite with other family members and to be with the larger Hmong concentration in the Central Valley of California.

Lee Yang began his school in America in Memphis in 1979 as a fifth grader, and, like other refugee children, his major barriers were the English language and American culture. After a few years in school, he managed to overcome some of the mentioned barriers and did well educationally. He continued his schooling in Merced in 1983, and he went on to Merced High School. Upon his completion of high school, he entered the University of California, San Luis Obispo, and graduated with a bachelor of arts in economics. He recalled being the only Hmong student at that campus without a car and any friends. He had to walk to work and to school on foot. He said he cried almost every week, but he survived. In 1996, he was accepted to the master's in business administration program at Stanford University and did well. He graduated with a master's in business administration in 1998 and became the first Hmong person to graduate from Stanford with a master's in business administration. He also holds a doctorate degree from California State University, San Francisco.[38]

Few young Hmong have entered the financial market and related firms. One of them is Chong K. Moua, who is a general partner with Boathouse Capital, which is a private equity firm based outside of Philadelphia. Chong K. Moua has been with Boathouse Capital, which has managed more than $350 million in funds, since 2008. He previously served as vice president for American Capital in Philadelphia, and has also worked with AIG Global Investment Group in New York and Wachovia Securities.

4. Education: In 1975, the Hmong of Laos had only one person who held a doctoral degree, and it wasn't until 1982, when a Hmong American earned his doctorate in the United States. Now, more than one thousand Hmong Americans have earned their doctoral degrees. Data from the 2015 ACS indicated that 17 percent of Hmong Americans age twenty-five or older hold bachelor's degrees or higher, compared to 17 percent for Cambodians, 14 percent for Laotians, and 27 percent for Vietnamese Americans;[39] it is improving but not yet at the preferred level. According to data of the 2013 ACS, 17 percent of Hmong American women twenty-five and older have earned a bachelor's degree compared to 15.4 percent of Hmong American men; this is a major shift from previous decades.[40] It is worthy to note that the Hmong population is very young, and many Hmong who have graduated with a bachelor of arts degree are under the age of twenty-five; the 2013 ACS did not include these young Hmong. Another important fact is that by the year 2015, Hmong students had enrolled in many universities, including Stanford and Harvard; Stanford has fifteen Hmong students and Harvard has about seven. In California, nine out of the ten campuses of the University of California system have Hmong students. Only the University of California, San Francisco, has no Hmong students, but it does have two Hmong on its faculty in the School of Medicine, Fresno Medical Education Program. Dr. Tou Mouanoutoua, a cardiologist, and Dr. John Moua, a pediatric pulmonologist, are both assistant clinical professors in the mentioned program. As of 2015, the University of California at Berkeley has twenty-four Hmong students; at Davis, 175; at Irvine, 70; at Los Angeles, 25; at Merced, 121; at Riverside, 38; at San Diego, 22; at Santa Barbara, 30; and at Santa Cruz, 71.[41] Overall, the number of Hmong students enrolled at the University of California system has slowly increased over the years. Data from the University of California Disaggregated Enrollment and Degrees show that there were 383 Hmong students attending the University of California in 2012, 449 in 2013, 586 in 2014, 582 in 2015, and 569 in 2016.[42]

At the kindergarten to twelfth-grade level, many Hmong have become teachers and some have moved up the ladder to serve in various leadership capacities. At least one known Hmong has now been serving as instructional superintendent of a large school district. This person is Mao Misty Her, who was appointed in 2011 as instructional superintendent in the Fresno Unified School District. She is a bilingual daughter of a school janitor, and she is a mother and wife who has an energetic and strong personality. She has the reputation of being an effective teacher, capable school principal, and having excellent people and communication skills. In retrospect, there were no Hmong teachers in Fresno Unified School District until 1991, when Cher Vang was hired to teach at Wolters Elementary School.[43]

Strong pressure from the community and great demand within the Fresno Unified School District led to a gradual and slow hiring of many young Hmong; now more than one hundred teachers of Hmong descent are teaching in the Fresno Unified School District. It should be noted here that prior to the hiring of Cher Vang in 1991, schools in the Fresno Unified School District often used various resources they could find, such as Hmong interpreters to help with translation or to perform other tasks. A case example is the use of Chue Her, who was a night custodian for Mayfair Elementary School and the father of Mao Misty Her. He performed additional duties, such as translating and cultural brokering, and was a liaison between parents and the school.[44] Chue Her's hard work and perseverance paved the way for the success of the next generation; his daughter became instructional superintendent in the same school district he had worked in for many decades. His son became a physician assistant, and he has another daughter and son in education as well.

In addition, as of 2015 there are many Hmong who are school principals in California, Minnesota, and Wisconsin. Many Hmong have previously served, or are currently serving, as trustees of many school districts in California and Minnesota. The St. Paul Public Schools, for example, has, since 1992, had Hmong serving on its Board of Education; as of 2015, Chue Vue is the sitting member of this Board of Education. At the university level, many Hmong have slowly risen to take on leadership roles. In the summer of 2015, Malisa Lee was named associate vice president for enrollment services at California State University, Fresno. She is the first Hmong to hold such a leadership position.

Previously, she was the assistant vice chancellor for enrollment management at the University of Nebraska-Omaha. She holds a doctorate in higher education with a concentration in public policy from the University of Michigan. She also holds a bachelor's degree from the University of California, Santa Barbara, in sociology and Asian American studies, and a master's degree from the University of Southern California. She was born in Moline,

**Figure 5.2. Malisa Lee, associate
vice president for enrollment
services, California State University,
Fresno.**
Malisa Lee.

Illinois, and her family moved to Fresno in the mid-1980s. On July 2, 2016,
Thy Yang was named assistant vice president for international education at
Norwich University in Northfield, Vermont. She is an expert on international
education and has worked in this field for St. Cloud State University, Minnesota, and other universities in Michigan, North Dakota, and Kansas. Several
Hmong have previously served or are currently serving as department chair
and in other leadership capacities. I have previously served as department
chair of ethnic and gender studies at California State University, Stanislaus.
Professor Neal Thao, as of 2015, is the chair of the department of social
work at Metropolitan State University in St. Paul, Minnesota. Since 2004,
Lee Pao Xiong has held the directorship of the Center for Hmong Studies at
Concordia University Saint Paul and has been instrumental in keeping this
center running as well as keeping the International Conference on Hmong
Studies alive and well. Lee Pao Xiong also teaches political science/Ameri-
can government and eight courses that are part of the minor in Hmong Studies at Concordia University, St. Paul. Anthony K. Vang is the coordinator of
the master of arts in education and multilingual/multicultural education at

California State University, Fresno. Chia Y. Vang is the director of graduate studies in the Department of History at the University of Wisconsin, Milwaukee. About thirty-five Hmong Americans hold tenured and tenure-track university teaching appointments, and nearly one-half of them are women. Among these professors of Hmong descent is Dr. Mouatou Mouanoutoua of the University of California, San Francisco, Fresno Medical Education Program. He is one of the first few Hmong to study pharmacy in the 1980s. After completing his pharmacy program at the University of the Pacific in 1988, he opened a pharmacy in Fresno and ran this pharmacy until 1993, when he sold the pharmacy and entered medical school. He earned his MD from Ross Medical School in 1998 and completed his internal medicine residency with Aurora Sinai/St. Luke's Medical Centers, University of Wisconsin Medical School-Milwaukee Campus in 2001. From there, he spent another three years as cardiology fellow at the Aurora Sinai/St. Luke's Medical Centers, University of Wisconsin Medical School-Milwaukee Campus. Additionally, he spent another year as chief of cardiology fellow with this institution before returning to California. In the summer of 2005, he accepted the teaching appointment as assistant professorship with the University of California, San Francisco, Fresno Medical Education Program. Additionally, he is a practitioner of cardiology and might be the lone Hmong American in his field. Table 5.2 lists known Hmong Americans who hold tenured and tenure-track university professorships.

Of the above faculty, four are tenured full-time professors, sixteen are associate professors, and the rest are assistant professors. Fourteen of these are females, which is about 40 percent of the thirty-five tenured and tenure-track American professors of Hmong descent. Altogether, California has fourteen of them; Minnesota, eight; Wisconsin, nine; Oregon, two; and one for each of the states of New York and Pennsylvania. Additionally, there is one professor emeritus,[45] one retired professor, and several adjunct faculty and lecturers. There are also many Hmong who teach at the community college level, such as Dr. Leena Her, who teaches full-time for Santa Rosa Community College in California. It should be noted here that a few Hmong teach or serve in various capacities in religious teaching institutions. On July 9, 2015, the Concordia Seminary, St. Louis, announced that Rev. Laokouxang (Kou) Seying would be joining its faculty as associate dean for urban and cross-cultural ministries and associate professor of practical theology beginning with the 2015–2016 academic year.[46] In retrospect, there was no Hmong teaching at the university level until 1991, when Thao Yang was appointed as assistant professor of chemistry at the University of Wisconsin, Eau Claire. It was unthinkable in the late 1970s that there would someday be Hmong teaching at higher learning institutions or serving as administrators. It is an uphill battle,

Table 5.2.   American Tenured and Tenure-Track Professors of Hmong Descent

No	Name	Gender	Rank	Department and/or Institution	State
1	Yer Jeff Thao	M	Associate professor	Curriculum & Instruction-Education, Portland State University	OR
2	Yer Za Vue	F	Associate professor*	Foundation Art, Art Institution of Portland	OR
3	Thao Yang	M	Associate professor	Chemistry, University of Wisconsin, Eau Claire	WI
4	Vincent Her	M	Associate professor	Ethnic and Racial Studies, University of Wisconsin, La Crosse	WI
5	Chia Y. Vang	F	Associate professor	History, University of Wisconsin, Milwaukee	WI
6	Pao Lor	M	Associate professor	Education, University of Wisconsin, Green Bay	WI
7	May Vang	F	Associate professor	Education, Concordia University of Wisconsin,	WI
8	Maysee Yang Herr	F	Associate professor	Education, University of Wisconsin,Steven Point	WI
9	Yang S. Xiong	M	Assistant professor	Ethnic Studies, University of Wisconsin,Madison	WI
10	Nengher Vang	M	Assistant professor	History Department, University of Wisconsin, Whitewater	WI
11	May Vang	F	Assistant professor	Curriculum and Instruction, University of Wisconsin,, White Water	WI
12	Vang Xiong	M	Assistant professor	Ethnic Studies, Minnesota State University, Mankato	MN
13	Pao Lee	M	Assistant professor	Sociology, St. John Fisher College-Rochester	MN
14	Mai Na Lee	F	Associate professor	History, University of Minnesota	MN
15	Neal Thao	M	Associate professor	Social Work, Metro State University	MN
16	Zha B.Xiong	M	Associate professor	Social Science, University of Minnesota	MN
17	Pa Der Vang	F	Associate professor	Social Work, St. Catherine University	MN
18	Shoua Yang	M	Associate professor	Political Science, St. Cloud State University	MN
19	Pao Vue	M	Assistant professor	Sociology, St. John Fisher College	MN
20	Pa Her	F	Assistant professor	Social Science, New York City College of Technology	NY

#	Name		Rank	Field, Institution	State
21	Aline Lo	F	Assistant professor	English, Allegheny College	PA
22	Surge Lee	M	Professor	Social Work, California State University Sacramento	CA
23	Kajua B. Lor	F	Associate professor	Pharmacy, Touro University California	CA
24	Ka Va	M	Associate professor	Bilingual/Multicultural Ed., California State University Sacramento	CA
25	Mayyoua Vang	F	Assistant professor	Educational Leadership and Policy Studies, California State University Sacramento	CA
26	Mouatou Mouanoutoua	M	Associate professor	Cardiology, University of California at San Francisco (Fresno Campus)	CA
27	John Moua	M	Assistant professor	Pediatric Pulmonology, University of California at San Francisco (Fresno Campus)	CA
28	Ma Vang	F	Assistant professor	Humanities and Arts, University of California at Merced	CA
29	Anthony K. Vang	M	Associate professor	Literacy & Early Education, CSUF	CA
30	Song Lee	F	Associate professor	Counseling, California State University Fresno	CA
31	May Lo Thao	F	Professor	Biology, California State University Stanislaus	CA
32	Christopher Vang	M	Professor	Teacher Education, California State University Stanislaus	CA
33	Bao Lo	F	Assistant professor	Ethnic Studies, California State University Stanislaus	CA
34	Der Thor	M	Assistant professor	Physiology, Dugoni School of Dentistry, University of the Pacific	CA
35	Paoze Thao	M	Professor	Linguistics & Education for the Liberal Studies, California State University Monterey Bay	CA

* The academic rank of Yer Za Vue at the Art Institute of Portland has not yet been verified. It is known that Yer Za Vue has been teaching at the Art Institute of Portland since 2006; therefore, she could be either an associate or full professor by 2015. Many media and other sources identify her as professor, but the 2008–2009 Catalogue of the Art Institute of Portland list her and their entire full-time faculty as "Instructor." As such, her academic rank could either be instructor, associate professor, or professor. Yer Za Vue is a renowned American artist and an impressionist. Permission Released Letter on file.

but the number above shows that barriers have slowly been broken, although the glass ceiling remains much stronger to break into.

5. High-tech and Science: Many young Hmong are now scientists and high-tech researchers in various fields, including biology and bio-chemistry research, physics, and high-tech researchers at Intel. Two Xiong brothers, Cheng and Laj, work for Intel Corporation. Cheng Xiong, for example, is a senior process engineer, lithography, of the Portland Technology Transfer and Manufacturing Group at Intel Corporation. In short, his work is to create the process to put pattern on computer chips. He holds a bachelor of science degree in environmental engineering from the University of California, Riverside, and both his master of science and doctoral degrees in chemical engineering from the University of California, Los Angeles.

Laj Xiong, the younger brother, graduated from Clovis East High School in 2003 and attended the University of California at Berkeley. While there, he majored in chemical engineering and conducted undergraduate research under the tutelage of Professor Clay Radke until he graduated in 2007. In 2008, he began working at the University of California at Riverside, under the tutelage of zeolite and hydroxide exchange fuel cell expert Yushan Yan, again majoring in chemical engineering, with a focus in materials and energy. In 2011, however, Laj moved to Newark, Delaware, along with his research group, when his adviser took an offer from the University of Delaware, prompting a move to the east coast, where he eventually graduated in 2015. Laj's graduate work includes the design, development, and characterization of novel polymer membranes for energy applications, such as the energy-efficient capture of carbon dioxide from flue gas, and as a membrane inside water-remediation electrolyzers. As of February 2016, Laj Xiong resides in Hillsboro, Oregon, where he works for Intel Corporation, developing the technology for the newest, cutting-edge microchips.[47]

There are a small but growing number of young Hmong working in Silicon Valley; most of them work for high-tech and related companies, but a few of them work for high-tech companies, but not in the high-tech field. Laolee Xiong, for example, is working for Facebook as its learning management systems administrator. Other young Hmong in Silicon Valley work for many other high-tech firms including SanDisk, Linked, Tesla, and Genentech. Among the computer scientists who work elsewhere in the United States is Jee Vang, who is a senior data scientist at Korverse Inc. He was born in a Thailand refugee camp and came to the United States when he was just two weeks old. Jee Vang graduated from Clovis High School in central California when he was sixteen years old, and went to Georgetown University, where he earned his doctoral degree in computational sciences and informatics. There are also Hmong scientists and engineers working in many fields and labs, including the biochemical lab of the University of Wisconsin at Eau Claire; the biological lab of California State University, Stanislaus; the Federal Lab of OSHA in Alaska; and the *National Aeronautics and Space Administration* (*NASA*). Cheng Moua and Mai Lee Chang are the two known Hmong engineers working for *NASA*. Below is Cheng Moua's account of his journey to become an engineer with NASA.

Cheng Moua is the first Hmong to work for NASA and has been with NASA since 2001. He said his family is among those first waves of Hmong refugees who came to the United States in 1976. In 1981, his family moved from Santa Ana, California, to the Fresno area to farm. Cheng graduated from Clovis High School in 1986 and continued his education at California State University, Fresno. In December 1990, he graduated from California State University, Fresno, with a bachelor of science degree in electrical engineering and was offered a position with the Air Force Flight Test Center at Edwards Air Force Base in California. He worked for the Air Force for ten years as a flight test engineer and covered F-16, B-1, and Air Borne Laser Programs. While working at the Air Force he was offered multiple scholarships as part of a training program to continue his education. He took the offer and completed his first master's degree in electrical engineering from California State University, Fresno, while working full-time. In 1998 Air Force offered him an additional full scholarship in order to cover his salary and to further develop his technical skills. This offer enabled him to attend Cal Poly Pomona where he graduated with a master's of science in electrical engineering, with an emphasis in communication engineering. In 2001, he started his NASA career at NASA Armstrong Flight Research Center in Edwards, California, as a flight control engineer. He worked on the X-45, F-15 Intelligent Flight Control System, and F-15 Quiet Spike Program as a flight control engineer performing stability analysis. As his roles and responsibilities grew he was later promoted to be the NASA chief engineer on the X-48 Flight Project overseeing all technical aspects of the project. His desire was to improve, and learning led him to another educational opportunity at the University of Washington in Seattle, where he focused his study on aeronautics engineering with an emphasis on flight control. While he was working part-time and studying part-time, an opportunity to take on a bigger role at NASA Armstrong presented itself to him in 2012, at which time he became the project manager of the Vehicle Integrated Propulsion Research (VIPR) Project. He has been leading and managing the VIPR Project since 2012. The VIPR Project is a large partnership between multiple NASA centers, other federal agencies (the Federal Aviation Administration, Air Force, U.S. Geological Survey), industries (Boeing, General Electric, Rolls Royce, Pratt & Whitney), and many universities.[48] The second Hmong working for NASA is Mai Lee

Chang, who is currently an engineer at the NASA Johnson Space Center in Houston, Texas.

6. Hollywood and the Filmmaking Industry: A few young Hmong have ventured into Hollywood and the movie industries. Brenda Song, for example, is a Disney Channel actress/teen star and is of Hmong descent, known for *The Suite Life of Zack & Cody*, *The Suite Life on Deck*, and *Wendy Wu Homecoming Warrior*. Another rising star in mainstream film and television industries is Doua Moua, who was born in the refugee camps in Thailand. He grew up in Minnesota and is a graduate of Marymount Manhattan College. He is best known for his mean and evil role as Fong/Spider in Clint Eastwood's 2008 film *Gran Torino*. Other films on Moua's resume include *Don't Whistle*, which won best picture at the Fargo Film Festival, and *LALO*, and was the winner of best film at the New York Latin Film Festival. He also performed in Hilary Swanks' production company's *Resolve* and *Uncertainty*, which was distributed by IFC, and *Prisoners*, which was selected in various film festivals. Moua also appeared in M. Night Shyamalan's *The Last Airbender*. In his biography, he wrote that, "As a young actor he has had the privilege of creating various roles such as the role of Hong in *King's Man* opposite Joe Estevez, where he played a woman/transvestite." His other films include National Lampoon's *Dirty Movie* starring Christopher Meloni (star of "Law in Order: Special Victims Unit") and Mario Cantone (from "Sex in the City"). His resume shows that he has also appeared in an array of television programs, such as Comedy Central's "Michael & Michael Have Issues," Nickelodeon's "The Naked Brothers Band," ABC's "One Life to Live," The Sundance Channel's "The Captive," and CBS's "Blue Bloods" with Donnie Wahlberg and Tom Selleck. In addition to films and television programs, Moua has performed in many off-Broadway and off-off-Broadway productions, including Richard Greenberg's play "Take Me Out," where he played the role of Takeshi Kawabata, for which he received good reviews and was singled out by the *New York Post* for giving a "terrific" performance. He is also an inspired writer.[49]

A few other Hmong also appeared in *Gran Torino* (2008) and in hundreds of low-budget and low-tech Hmong movies. More and more young Hmong are now engaging in filmmaking. One of the many emerging Hmong filmmakers is Chao Thao, who is known for her work on A Daughter's Debt (2014), Kev Ntsiag To (2011), and The Hunting Ground (2015). She is a graduate of the University of Southern California School of Cinematic Arts, and her thesis film was *A Daughter's Debt*. She was a Princess Grace Foundation Award Winner in 2012. The Princess Grace Foundation Award is "dedicated to identifying and assisting emerging talent in theater, dance and film by awarding grants in the form of scholarships, apprenticeships and fellowships."[50] Another Hmong documentary filmmaker is Kao Choua Vue. On her website, she describes herself as an independent documentary filmmaker, story teller, and educator. She has worked in youth media for ten years. She enjoys youth media because she believes it is an important tool that empowers youth and gives them a voice. In 2010, she founded the first Hmong film festival in Minnesota called Qhia Dab Neeg (storytelling) Film Festival, which takes place annually. That same year, Kao Choua received the Jerome Travel and Study Grant, which allowed her to travel to Laos in 2014. Her video, titled *Tso Plig: Let the Spirit Fly*, was accepted in the 2011 MNTV Showcase. Currently, she is working on a short narrative about a Hmong refugee family in the 1980s in Minnesota and their introduction to fishing. The list of her short films includes *Cry in 1982* (2015), *Our Sisters Taken* (2015), *Tso Plig: Let the Spirit Fly* (2011), *Daughters* (2009), and *Whispers From the Vietnam War* (2006).[51] A selected list of other Hmong filmmakers includes, but is not limited to, Sao Chang and Pac Vaj, who directed the film *3 Lub Tooj Npab* (2008), and Abel Vang, who directed the film *Nyab Siab Zoo* (2009). The list also includes Bryan Vue, who is the writer, producer, and director of *The Stranger (2009) and Journey to the Fallen Skies* (2010). Others, such as Phoua Porsha Chang, who is a Hmong teacher from Sacramento, California, and has an academic background in American Sign Language/ deaf studies, creates short films as a hobby. Her credits include *Tsev Xaw Naag (Leaky Roof)* (2015), *Mi Tes Mi Taw (Hands and Feet)* (2014), and *Ib Sij Huam (In a Glimpse)* (2013).[52] Phoua won an award for Mi Tes Mi Taw at the Qhia Dab Neeg Film Festival for "Most Compelling" story in 2014.

7. Law: Although the Hmong American community did not have their first lawyer until 1987, when T. Christopher Thao became a member of the Minnesota Bar, the number of American lawyers of Hmong descent has steadily increased during the last twenty years. For instance, the growing number of Hmong lawyers has led to the creation of the Hmong Minnesota Bar Association. Many Hmong lawyers have specialized in a multitude of different fields ranging from immigration to criminal defense, and civil law to business law. Most still practice law in private clinics and a few are working in local and state governments. However, in 2014 Paul C. Lo made history when he was appointed to the Superior Court in Merced County in the state of California by Governor Jerry Brown. Paul C. Lo is the first Hmong to graduate from the Law School of the University of California, Los Angeles. He is very active in community and public services, and became the first native of Laos to hold an elected office in California when he was elected in 2001 to the Board of Trustees in the Merced City School District. He is the founder of the Southeast Asian American Professional Association. His community and public services include being a past president of Hmong National Development and

Figure 5.3. Paul C. Lo, circa 2015.
Paul C. Lo.

a foundation board member of the University of California in Merced. As of 2016, he is a board member for Mercy Medical Center and Southeast Asian American Professional Association. He is a pastor for the Lao Evangelical Church in Merced and the secretary for the Lao Evangelical Church Headquarters.

Paul C. Lo's other community services include past memberships with the Board of Directors of Merced Red Cross (Merced-Mariposa Chapter), Central California Legal Services, Boys and Girls Club of Merced, and Merced College Legal Clinic. Additionally, he was the chairperson of Lo Society Education Council and the vice president of Lo Collegian Association of Stockton. He is a graduate of the class of 1995 of the Merced Leadership Program (Merced Chamber of Commerce) and was president and co-founder of the Hmong Student Union at the University of California, Davis. Paul C. Lo is often sought out to speak to community groups and gatherings, especially in the California Hmong community and beyond. Judge Lo is a great role model not only for the younger Hmong generations, but for the youth of other ethnic groups as well. His legal specialties include personal injury, business and corporate transactions, employment law, general civil litigation, and criminal defense. His practice in law has greatly benefited the Hmong and other ethnic communities in central California.

Paul C. Lo began his education in the United States in fifth grade in Colorado in 1979. In 1981, his family moved to Stockton, California, as part of the Hmong secondary migration. There, he went to middle school and high school. He graduated from Tokay High School in 1987 and went on to study at the University of California, Davis, where he founded the Hmong Student Union and became its first president. In 1991, he graduated from University of California, Davis, with a bachelor's degree in economics, and during that same year, he was admitted to the School of Law at the University of California, Los Angeles. Paul C. Lo went on to graduate from University of California, Los Angeles, in 1994 with a Juris Doctor. He is the first attorney of Hmong descent to join the California Bar Association.

Paul C. Lo, like most Hmong, came from a large extended family. He is the oldest child of eight children born to his parents, Chong Xe and Sai Lee Lo. He was seven years old when the government of Laos collapsed to the Communists in 1975. Paul C. Lo is a native of Sayaboury, Laos, and attended school there for only one year (first-grade education) before his family escaped from Laos to Thailand. They stayed in the crowded and impoverished refugee camps in Thailand for four years before resettling in the United States in 1979. They came to Denver, Colorado, and stayed there until 1981, when the family moved to Stockton, California. His parents continue to reside in Stockton, California. Paul lives in Merced, California, with his wife and their five children.[53]

In April 2017, Kashoua "Kristy" Yang, aged thirty-six, was elected to the Milwaukee County, Wisconsin, Circuit Court. She is the second American judge of Hmong descent. She came to the United States thirty years ago, when she was only six years old. She grew up in Sheboygan, Wisconsin, with her ten siblings and her parents. She is the third oldest child, married young, divorced, and returned to school. She eventually graduated from the University of Wisconsin-Madison Law School in 2009 and became a lawyer in Milwaukee, practicing family law. She remarried her ex-husband, Long Thao, who is the father of her three children.[54]

8. Political Participation: In 1991, twenty-two-year-old Choua Lee became the first Hmong woman to hold an elected office when she became a member of the St. Paul School Board of Education. Since then, many young Hmong have run for office and gotten elected. In 1992, Ya Yang was elected to the Board of Education in the Wausau School District in Wausau, Wisconsin. In 1993, Thai Vue, won a seat in the Board of Trustees of the Lacrosse School District in Lacrosse, Wisconsin. In 1995, Neal Thao was elected to the St. Paul School Board of Education and served two terms on the school board. In 1996, Joe Bee Xiong was elected to the City Council of Eau Claire, Wisconsin, and became the first Hmong to serve as an elected member of a city council in the United States. The Hmong American community in Minnesota made history (again) on January 29, 2002, when Mee Moua, a Hmong female lawyer, was elected to the Minnesota State Senate. In that same year, Cy Thao was also elected to the Minnesota State Assembly. Mee Moua went on to

serve in the Minnesota Senate until 2010, when she resigned from office to be the president and chief executive officer of the Asian Americans Advancing Justice Center in Washington, District of Columbia. In April of 2015, there were eight Hmong Americans holding public offices including State Senator Foung Hawj in the Minnesota State Senate; Noah Lor in the Merced City Council (termed out in November of 2016) in Merced, California; Steve Ly in the Elk Grove City Council of Elk Grove, California; Dai Thao in the St. Paul City Council of St. Paul, Minnesota; Blong Yang in the Minneapolis City Council of Minneapolis, Minnesota; Tou Xiong in the Maplewood City Council of Maplewood, Minnesota; Michael Xiong in the Eau Claire City Council of Eau Claire, Wisconsin; Somxai Vue in the Thornton City Council of Thornton, Wisconsin; Chue Vue in the St. Paul School Board of Education in St. Paul, Minnesota; and Kaying Thao in the Roseville School Board of Education in Roseville, Minnesota. While a few of these office holders were termed out by the end of 2015, many young Hmong were also elected to office by the end of 2015 and 2016. In November of 2015, for example, Tou Xiong was elected to Maplewood City Council in Minnesota. He is the first American-born Hmong to hold a political office. Xiong is a graduate of William Mitchell College of Law and also holds a bachelor of science in economics from St. Cloud State University. In April of 2016, Yee Leng Xiong, at twenty-two years old, was elected supervisor of Marathon County in Wisconsin. He is the youngest among his peers; he was born and raised in Wausau, Wisconsin. Mary Thao was also elected in April of 2016 to the Board of Education in Wausau, Wisconsin. The election in November 2016 brought more young Hmong Americans to the political scene. Steve Ly was elected mayor of the City of Elk Grove in California and became the first American mayor of Hmong descent. Lee Lor was elected to the Merced County Board of Supervisors; she became the first Hmong to hold such an office in California. Also, Mai Yang Vang won a seat on the Board of Education for Sacramento City Unified School District, and G. Brandon Vang was elected to the Board of Trustees for Sanger Unified School District in Sanger, California. Outside of California, Foung Hawj was re-elected to the Minnesota Senate, Fue Lee was elected to the Minnesota State Assembly, and Susan Kaying Pha won a seat on the City Council of Brooklyn Park, Minnesota. As of January 2017, fifteen Hmong Americans hold political offices: 1) Foung Hawj, Minnesota State senator; 2) Fue Lee, Minnesota State assemblyman; 3) Susan Kaying Pha, Brooklyn Park City Council member, Minnesota; 4) Blong Yang, Minneapolis City Council member, Minnesota; 5) Dai Thao, St. Paul City Council member, Minnesota; 6) Tou Xiong, Maplewood City Council member, Minnesota; 7) Chue Vue, St. Paul School Board member, Minnesota; 8) Charles Vue, Eau Claire School Board member, Wisconsin; 9)

Michael Xiong, Eau Claire City Council member, Wisconsin; 10) Yee Leng Xiong, Marathon County supervisor, Wisconsin; 11) Mary Thao, Wausau School Board member, Wisconsin; 12) Steve Ly, Elk Grove City mayor, California; 13) Lee Lor, Merced County supervisor, California; 14) Mai Yang Vang, Sacramento City School trustee, California; and 15) G. Brandon Vang, Sanger School trustee, California. Minnesota continues to lead other states in having more Hmong holding political offices as seven out of the above fifteen political office holders are in that state. Hmong women continue to make progress in this field as five out of the fifteen political office holders are female; as mentioned above, Hmong American women were the pioneers in running for and being elected to office. Choua Lee, who was elected in November of 1991 to the Board of Education of St. Paul Public Schools, became the first Hmong and Indochinese refugee to run and be elected to office. In 2002, Mee Moua, a female lawyer, was elected to the Minnesota Senate, and she became the first Hmong and former Indochinese refugee to hold a state office.

The Hmong American community is known to be very active in the American political system, and as such many young Hmong have learned the needed skills to not only run for office, but to run a political campaign. An example is Louansee Moua, who was the chief of staff for the former City of San Jose Vice Mayor Madison Nguyen (2005–2014) and campaign manager for the 2016 California State Assembly, District 27 election. Louansee has also become another political story of the Hmong. Her political experience, communication skills, and fundraising ability made her a well-known political strategist to not only candidates of Hmong descent, but to others as well. Prior to becoming campaign manager and then chief of staff to Madison Nguyen in 2005, Louansee Moua had worked on the campaigns for Jesse Ventura, former governor of Minnesota; Roger Moe, former Minnesota Senate majority leader; and the late U.S. Senator Paul Wellstone. Louansee was press secretary for Roger Moe for his governor campaign and was the communications director for Mee Moua's successful 2002 state senate campaign.

The 2005 election of Madison Nguyen to the San Jose City Council brought both Nguyen and Moua to the spotlight. Nguyen, a former Vietnamese refugee woman, hired Moua, who is a former Hmong refugee woman from Minnesota, to manage her campaign. It turned out to be not only a very successful campaign for Nguyen, but for *all* former Indochinese refugees as well. Madison Nguyen is the first former refugee from Indochina to hold a seat in a large American city.[55]

9. U.S. Armed Forces: Many thousands of young Hmong have volunteered to serve in the U.S. Armed Forces, and many of them have made the ultimate

sacrifice. Thai Vue, aged twenty-two, from Willow, California, was killed in action in Iraq on June 18, 2004, and Qixing Lee, aged twenty-two, from Minneapolis, Minnesota, was killed by improvised explosive device in Taji, Iraq, on August 27, 2006. Another soldier, Kham Xiong, aged twenty-three, from St. Paul, Minnesota, was among those thirteen American soldiers killed at Fort Hood, Texas, in 2009 by a military psychiatrist. He was shot senselessly while preparing for deployment at a hospital in Fort Hood. All of the three served in the U.S. Army.

Many American officers of Hmong descent continue to serve honorably in the U.S. Armed Forces. Yee Chang Hang, for example, is a colonel in the U.S. Army and is the first officer of Hmong descent to have served as battalion commander. As of 2016, he is serving as the director of Land Supplier Operations for the Defense Logistics Agency, Land and Maritime. Col. Hang is the first Hmong to have graduated from the U.S. Military Academy at West Point. Upon graduating from the U.S. Military Academy in June of 1991, Yee Chang Hang was commissioned as a second lieutenant in the U.S. Army and has since served in numerous leadership and staff positions. He has been deployed to many countries, including the Republic of Korea, Germany, Bosnia-Herzegovina, Afghanistan, Kuwait, and Iraq.

Col. Hang is the recipient of the 2004 Pioneer Award of the Hmong National Development, cited as the first to graduate from West Point. The second colonel of Hmong descent in the U.S. Army is Col. Vamin Saichu

Figure 5.4.   Col. Yee Chang Hang, U.S. Army, circa 2015.
Col. Yee Chang Hang.

Cha, who is a lawyer and a graduate of the Law School of the University of Nebraska, Lincoln. As of 2016 he is the commander of the 658th Regional Support Group, stationed in Yongsan, South Korea.

Those who have reached the rank of lieutenant colonel include, though not limited to, Lt. Cols. Tou Thiang Yang, Ge Yang, and Tong Vang (retired). Lt. Col. Tou Thiang Yang, who is a pharmacist and in the Medical Corps, is the first Hmong to reach the rank of lieutenant colonel. He has been stationed in many countries, including Germany, South Korea, and other foreign countries. Additionally, he was a part of the first medical staff to be deployed in Iraq in 2003. He is the recipient of many military awards, including Meritorious Service Medal, Humanitarian Service Medal, Army Commendation Medal, Junior Pharmacy Officer of the Year, Army Achievement Medal, and National Defense Medal. Since 2015, he has been stationed in Fort Hood, Texas, serving as the chief of pharmacy in charge of eleven pharmacies spreading throughout the base and the surrounding civilian towns. Lt. Col. Tong Vang is the second Hmong to graduate from West Point Military Academy; he is from the class of 1993. Additionally, he holds a master of arts degree in literature from Northwestern University. Prior to his retirement from the army a few years ago, he was the U.S. Military Attaché at the U.S. Embassy in Ghana. Chief Chuepheng Lo is one of those retired commissioned officers of Hmong descent. Chief Lo retired in 2012 as a major from the U.S. Army after twenty years of service as a military police officer in a variety of command and staff positions in the United States and overseas; he served one operational tour in Kuwait and served one combat tour in Iraq. His military awards and decorations include the Legion of Merit, Purple Heart, Bronze Star, Combat Action Badge, Parachutist Badge, and German Efficiency Badge (Silver Award). Chief Lo continued his law enforcement career as police operations major at Fort McCoy, Wisconsin; as deputy chief of police at the Naval Weapons Station Seal Beach Detachment in Fallbrook, California; and is currently the chief of police at Defense Logistics Agency San Joaquin in Tracy, California.

Chief Lo joined the U.S. Army after receiving a Reserve Officers' Training Corps commission and a bachelor of arts in philosophy from the University of California, Santa Barbara. He also holds a master in business administration degree from Saint Martin's University.

Born in Samthong, Xieng Khouang, Laos, his family came to the United States as Hmong refugees of the Secret War in Laos. He was only seven years old when the family arrived in the United States. Chief Lo and his family first arrived in Goodland, Kansas, in 1976 and then moved to Denver, Colorado, in 1979 before calling Stockton, California, home in 1981. As of 2016, Chief Lo, his wife Helen, and their four children reside in Ripon, California.

On April 12, 2017, the University of California at Merced named Chou Her as police chief of the campus. Chou, who was born in Laos and came to the United States at the age of three, has served the University of California, Merced, community since the campus opened in 2005. He became the third police chief of the University of California campus and the second police chief of Hmong decent. Before joining University of California, Merced, in 2005, Her was a deputy sheriff for the Merced County Sheriff's Department for five years and a probation officer for Stanislaus County for nearly a year. Chou Her, who has lived most of his life in Merced, holds an associate's degree in administration of justice from Merced College, a bachelor's degree in criminal justice, and a master's degree in public administration from California State University, Stanislaus.[56]

Many young Hmong have also reached higher ranks of non-commissioned officers. Shua P. Yang (retired), for example, reached the rank of master sergeant before his retirement in November of 2011. He has twenty-three years of service in the U.S. Army and has been previous deployed to Desert Shield/Storm; Saudi Arabia; Operation Restore Hope; Somalia; Joint Task Force Falcon; Sarajevo; Bosnia; Operation Iraqi Freedom 2005–2006; Iraq; and Operation Iraqi Freedom 2009–2010 in Iraq. He was born in Laos and his family was resettled in Sheboygan, Wisconsin, in the United States when he was nine years old. He graduated from Sheboygan South High School in 1986 and attended the University of Wisconsin, Milwaukee, for two years before joining the army in November 1988. During his twenty-three years of service, Master Sergeant Shua P. Yang has received numerous awards and medals including two Bronze Stars, three Meritorious of Service Medals, five Army Commendation Medals, nine Army Achievement Medals, Joint-Commendation Medal, NATO Medal, Kosovo Campaign Medal, Global War on Terrorism Service Medal, two Iraqi Campaign Medals, Kuwait Liberation Medal (Government of Kuwait), Kuwait Liberation Medal (Kingdom of Saudi Arabia), two Joint Meritorious Unit Awards, and the Meritorious Unit Commendation Award. He also earned the Combat Action Badge, the Basic Parachute Patch, and the Hungarian Parachute Patch.[57] He represents many young Hmong who have or are currently serving in the U.S. Armed Forces; they, like other Americans, give their very best to protect and defend their country, the United States of America. There are also many Hmong who have already graduated from the Air Force Academy and other academies. Major Ted Yang, for example, is a graduate of the Air Force Academy, class of 2004. Yang is a native of Fresno, California.

10. Other Contributions: Many young Hmong have entered other various professions, such as civil servant, journalism, commercial piloting, and so on. Data from the three-year estimates of ACS from 2008–2010 indicated

that Hmong Americans have a higher rate of working as government workers. The rate for Hmong Americans who worked as government workers or civil servants is 12 percent compared to 8.3 percent for Laotians, 8.6 percent for Cambodians, and 9.7 percent for Vietnamese Americans.[58] Kimiko Moua Vang is an example of a young Hmong who has made a career as a civil servant. Kimiko earned a bachelor of arts in sociology, with a minor in ethnic studies, and a master of social work from California State University, Stanislaus. Kimiko started her social work career in child welfare at Stanislaus County Community Service Agency. There, she worked in many different child welfare programs, including the drug-endangered children multidisciplinary team with law enforcement agencies and the district attorney office. After a few years, she joined the Merced County Human Services Agency as a supervisor in child welfare. Kimiko was later promoted to program administrator, overseeing the adoptions and home assessment programs, child welfare training, and the Westside Services Center. While overseeing the training program, Kimiko developed the Southeast Asian Family training, which is now a required training for all new social services staff. In this position, she also created the Hmong Women's Initiative (HWI), a first-of-its-kind county program that offers culturally and linguistically sensitive services to Hmong women and families in the county. The HWI offers workshops covering a variety of topics and issues, and a safe environment for engaging discussions. In addition, with Hmong women stakeholders and community partners, the HWI organized the Hmong Women's Conference. Although it was held in Merced, California, the conference attracted over four hundred participants representing all age groups from throughout the Central Valley. In November of 2015, Kimiko was promoted to deputy director of the Merced County Human Services Agency, overseeing the Employment Services Branch and becoming the first Hmong in California to have reached that level of management position in a county agency. In her current position, Kimiko is responsible for the oversight of employment and training programs, staff development for more than six hundred employees, and motherhood and fatherhood programs. Kimiko is continuing to expand the HWI program, which now offers a Hmong Women's Support Group, and will soon offer a Hmong Men's Support Group. In addition to her social services and management experience, Kimiko is the first, and currently the only, Hmong bilingual licensed clinical social worker in Merced County. Her clinical experience includes working with adults and children with trauma and sexual abuse history. Kimiko believes in strengthening the community by building capacity. To this end, she is providing clinical supervision to the next generation of Hmong bilingual licensed clinical social workers. Kimiko is actively involved in the community and has been a past member of the Merced Building Healthy Communities hub. She is a founding member of the grassroots group Kashia, a founding member and president of the Hmong Social Worker Association, and the current president of the Southeast Asian American Professional Association.

Similarly, Doualy Xaykaothao is among those who work as journalists. She is a correspondent for Minnesota Public Radio News, covering race and culture. In addition to her previous journalist work in New York City; Washington, District of Columbia; Los Angeles; Portland; and Dallas, she spent a decade reporting overseas for NPR from southeast and northeast Asia.[59] Doualy Xaykaothao was born in Laos and raised in Texas. Another newspaper reporter and columnist is Nonhia Lee of the *Fresno Bee* in central California. Like Doualy Xaykaothao and BoNhia Lee, another anchor women is Gia Vang, who is reporting for Fox 26 News in Fresno, California, and Boua Xiong, who is a reporter for KARE TV 11 in the Greater Minneapolis-St. Paul area. A few Hmong have entered other unusual professions, such as commercial piloting and university staffer. Yeng Vang is known to be a captain for Delta Connections, which is part of Delta Air Lines. Mai Hu Vang is assistant director of Diversity and Inclusion Programs at Harvard University. Tsu Ya is the director of Admissions and Academic Services for the Graduate Division at the University of California, Merced. He has fifteen years of experience working in higher education and has worked for both the California State University system and the University of California system. Tsu Ya oversees recruitment, admissions, academic policies, and academic services for the graduate division. Additionally, he serves as a staff consultant to the Graduate Council. Tsu Ya holds a master of business administration and a bachelor of science degree from California State University, Stanislaus. He is currently in the doctoral program at Northeastern University. In May 2015, Mai Hu Vang was appointed Harvard University's *assistant director of Diversity and Inclusion Programs,* Office of the Assistant to the President for Institutional Diversity and Equity. Prior to that, she was the special assistant to the Chancellor of Equity and Affirmative Action at the University of Wisconsin Stevens Point. Vang holds a master of science degree in educational leadership and policy analysis from the University of Wisconsin Madison, and a master of education and a bachelor of science in elementary education, both from the University of Wisconsin, Stevens Point.[60]

Brazing a different field is May Kao Hang, who is the president and CEO of the Amherst H. Wilder Foundation, a nonprofit organization dedicated to improving lives in the greater Saint Paul community and beyond through direct services, research, and community building. Similarly, Kaying Hang is the Senior Program Officer at Sierra Health Foundation in the Sacramento Region Health Care Partnership. Previously, she was associate director for Grantmakers Concerned with Immigrants and Refugees, where she worked with foundations, affinity groups, public policy groups, and immigrant rights organizations. There are a few young Americans who work as staffers for members of the U.S. Congress and those who serve as community activists. Chao R. Lee, for example, is a senior staffer for U.S. Congresswoman Betty McCullum, who represents Minnesota's fourth congressional district. Among those who devote their time to serve as activists for the Hmong American community and beyond are Tou Ger Xiong in the Twin Cities of Minneapolis-Saint Paul area. This list serves as a sample of young Hmong Americans who have entered diverse professions in both public and private sectors. Consequently, they give their very best to their community and the United States of America, their adopted country.

11. Strengthening of Relationships between the United States and Their Former Homeland: The close diplomatic relations between the United States and Laos were never totally broken after the war, and in 1992 the two countries restored full diplomatic relations at the ambassadorial level. In December 2004, the United States granted its Normal Trade Relations to Laos, expanding the relations between the two countries. Granting Normal Trade Relations to Laos was made partly possible because of strong lobbying made by many former refugees from Laos, who are now citizens of the United States. During the initial phase of Laos's request to gain full membership of the World Trade Organization, many European nations were not very supportive of the process because Laos did not make efforts to initiate reconciliation with its former citizens, especially the Hmong, who are now living on the European and the American continents. To deal with this issue, a European humanitarian dialogue center based in Geneva, Switzerland, had sponsored many private meetings in Geneva between a special envoy from Laos and some key persons from the Hmong expatriate community. As a result, Laos gained full World Trade Organization membership in early 2013. Vang Rattanavong, the former Lao People's Democratic Republic ambassador to the United States, has publicly acknowledged the economic contributions to Laos from Hmong Americans who have returned to visit relatives in that country. In 2013, the Lao Multi-Ethnic Solidarity Committee, which was led and made up of large numbers of Hmong Americans, raised more than eight thousand U.S. dollars to help flood victims in Laos.[61] Another example of giving back to Laos are the efforts to build libraries and schools for the people of Laos. Xia Vue Yang and his group in Sheboygan, Wisconsin, for example, have been able to raise more than forty thousand U.S. dollars to build a library in Xieng Khouang Province, Laos. They claimed their efforts as a way to teach people how to fish, not just giving them fish.[62] In addition to the above library, Hmong Americans have built schools and others for the people of Laos. Susan and Arick Xiong of Fresno, California, have built two

schools for the people in Laos. The first school was built in Phawai Village in Xieng Khouang Province. This school building, which was completed in 2015, has six rooms with four bathroom stalls with septic systems, a year-round water well, and electricity. The total cost was a little over sixty-two thousand U.S. dollars. This cost includes the construction and all furnishings and educational materials for the classroom. Their second school is projected to be built in 2017 for the people of Phone Cheng Village in Xieng Khouang Province. This school building is for preschool students, and it has two classrooms, two bathroom stalls with septic systems, electricity, and water well establishments for year-round water access. The cost of construction of this school building is budgeted at thirty-five thousand U.S. dollars. Their selection of these villages is based on the levels of need and the growth potential for these villages based on family households and children. Additionally, they were selected based on the commitment of the villagers to collaborate and assist in the construction of the school. The villagers of these two villages have agreed to contribute at least 10 percent of the total cost, whether in monetary form or labor. Susan and Arick Xiong are co-founders of the A Hopeful Encounter, Inc., a non-profit organization established with a vision to create learning environments and build schools in an effort to promote growth and development in southeast Asia, specifically in underserved communities.[63] Many Hmong have also returned to Laos to live or do business. One of them is Jim Vang, who went to Laos in the 1990s; he built the Mekong Breeze, a mid-size hotel in Vientiane, Laos. He has since stayed in Vientiane to run other business projects. Sam Bliatout is another Hmong American who has been doing business in Laos since the 1990s.

One of the many contributions Hmong Americans have made to the economy of Laos is through their remittance of money to relatives and friends in Laos. Sam Bliatout, who is very familiar with the transfer of money by Hmong Americans to their relatives and friends in Laos, estimated that up to five hundred thousand dollars is sent daily to Laos, and more so during the New Year. He estimated that there are at least fifty MoneyGram shops owned and operated by Hmong Americans throughout the United States, and on average, each one of them sends ten thousand dollars per day to Laos. Two of these MoneyGram shops are in the Bliatout Plaza in Fresno, California, and Sam Bliatout said that each one of them is allowed to send only up to twenty-five thousand dollars per day, but they usually maximize their accounts by noon of each day.[64] Further, MoneyGram is not the only option for Hmong Americans to send money to their relatives in Laos. Many of them use Western Union, wiring from their banks to relatives' accounts inside Laos, or they use other alternatives, such as passing money to relatives who will visit Laos. Furthermore, most individual Hmongs who visit Laos would spend at least three thousand to five thousand dollars, not including the airfare ticket. Many Hmong Americans have also bought cars, houses, and land for their relatives inside Laos. Some of them lend capital seed money to open businesses in Laos.

The United States is now the most talked about country in Laos. People in almost every village and town in Laos know someone or has a relative in the United States. Despite there being conservatives in Laos who still distrust the United States from the Second Indochina War, the people's connections and family ties from their separation during the war is an inevitable bond between the diaspora and the people of Laos. Many Americans who go to Laos to do business or become involved in government affairs are none other than former Indochinese refugees and their American-born offspring. Paul Herr, for example, is now the country coordinator in Laos for a project of the Asian Development Bank. Many Hmong in rural Laos and Vietnam know the telephone area codes of Fresno, California, and St. Paul, Minnesota. Many young Hmong in Vietnam use the Romanized Phonetic Alphabet, the most widely used writing language of Hmong Americans, to browse Hmong American websites. More interestingly, many young Hmong in Vietnam use the term *soun (ສູນ)* to refer to zero. It is a term the Hmong borrow from the Laos word *soun*, which is derived from the Sanskrit word "शून्य" (SUNYA), which is zero. Transnational influence on all sides has already began. More and more Hmong Americans have for the past ten years visited Laos. Many have bought gifts and artifacts from Laos to their children who were born in the United States. Many college students of Hmong descent also participate in educational tours of Laos and other Asian countries, attempting to learn more about the birthplace of their parents and grandparents.

Worthy of mention are the unexploded ordnances (UXO) in Laos. It has been a pain in the neck and a barrier for both Laos and the United States to fully close their chapter on the Secret War. The U.S. Air Force carried out 580,000 bombing missions against Laos during the Secret War from 1962–1975. That breaks down to about one planeload of bombs dropped every eight minutes, twenty-four hours a day, for nine years. The United States dropped over two million tons of bombs in Laos, more than all the bombs dropped during World War II. Up to 30 percent of those bombs did not explode. UXO do not discriminate between soldiers, civilians, children, or animals. Bomblets are hidden underground, waiting for someone to step on them or be dug into. When they do, an explosion ensues. Many people have died, and many more are severely injured. "More than [twenty thousand] people have died at the hands of the remains of cluster munitions in Laos and an estimated [twelve thousand] more victims are in need of assistance, Legacies of War has found."[65] Many of these victims are children who were

born long after the war. "The U.S. spent $2 million ($17 million in today's
dollars) per day for nine years to bomb Laos, but only an average of $4.2
million a year for clearance of unexploded ordnances and victims' assistance
over the past [twenty] years, according to Legacies of War."[66]Although the
U.S. Congress has allotted for 2016 the amount of more than nineteen million
dollars for UXO clearance in Laos, it is far from enough to clear the UXO in
that country. One of the main reasons for such a low allotment of funds from
the United States to clear the UXO in Laos is, just like the Secret War itself,
not well known to the U.S. Congress and the American public. To raise the
awareness of the American public and the U.S. Congress, a few members
of the U.S. Congress, such as Betty McCullum, who represents Minnesota's
fourth congressional district, and Mike Honda, of California's seventeenth
congressional district, have written letters to members of the U.S. Congress
about UXO and the need to clear these UXO. Many former refugees from
Laos have also continued to voice the need to clear UXO in Laos. For example, I wrote in 2015 an opinion piece, entitled "Prof. Kou Yang: The Deadly,
Horrible Mess We Made Still Plagues Indochina."[67] This piece, which was
published by the *Modesto Bee* and many other newspapers, became a voice
to strongly advocate for the United States and other Vietnam War parties
to provide needed funds to clear and clean the UXO and Agent Orange in
southern Laos and Vietnam. My piece and other voices, in addition to the
advocacy of the U.S. Legacy of War, have kept this issue alive. Before U.S.
President Barack Obama visited Laos in September 2016, his administration
had pushed to provide more funds to clear the UXO in Laos. Deputy National
Security Adviser Ben Rhodes, who visited Laos in the fall of 2015, has said
about Obama's September visit to Laos that, "It's about settling history's account and meeting our responsibility." And, "this president, both because of
his willingness to resolve painful issues in U.S. foreign policy and his focus
on Southeast Asia, is uniquely suited to do that. There is the potential for this
to be a truly historic visit."[68] The exact amount of aid packet is not known,
but President Obama is very likely to offer more U.S. funds for the clearance
of UXO in Laos; he visited Laos in September of 2016.

It was a truly historic visit when U.S. President Barrack Obama visited
Laos in early September 2016. First, he became the first sitting U.S. president to visit Laos, and he was well-liked by people from all walks of life in
Laos. Second, President Obama acknowledged the Secret War and pledged
$90 million to help with survey and clearance of unexploded ordnance and
remnants of U.S. bombing in Laos.[69] Last, the United States and Laos have
opened a comprehensive partnership, and to inaugurate this new partnership
a Presidential Joint Declaration was made by President Obama and Laos
President Bounnhang Vorachit. The Presidential Joint Declaration consists

of twenty items that are under ten major categories: Political and Diplomatic Cooperation, War Legacy Issues, Humanitarian Cooperation, Trade and Economic Ties, Education Cooperation, Health and Nutrition, Environment, Security, Promotion and Protection of Human Rights, and People-to-People Ties.[70] The implementation of the Presidential Joint Declaration will likely further strengthen the relationship and partnership between the two countries. It is hoped that the U.S. presidential visit, the U.S.-Laos partnership, and the mentioned efforts made by Hmong Americans will speed up the closing of the war chapter so a new chapter can be opened, which will benefit the people of both Laos and the United States.

THE PASSING OF THE WAR-ERA GENERATION

Looking back, forty years is a very long time; a generation is gone and another emerges. Most Hmong Americans today were born after the Secret War in Laos. This also means that many of the war-era generation have already passed on; many leaders and elders of the war years are gone. A selected list of the passing Hmong elders and leaders is discussed in the following.

On the Pathet Lao side, Faydang Lobliayao, the politician and figurehead of the Hmong under the Pathet Lao died on July 12, 1986, and was buried in Nong Het, Xieng Khouang, Laos. He was one of the many sons of Lo Bliayao, the leader of the Hmong in Xieng Khouang during the first part of the twentieth century. Although Faydang was not a member of the Lao People's Revolutionary Party (the Communist Party of Laos), the Pathet Lao made use of his name to rally the Hmong to support their cause. He became one of the vice presidents of the Lao People's Supreme Assembly after the Pathet Lao officially took over Laos on December 2, 1975. The post of vice president of the People's Supreme Assembly is a ceremonial one with no power. His half-brother, Nhiavue Lobliayao, who was an alternate Politburo member of the Lao People's Revolutionary Party in the 1980s, also died in his native land of Nong Het on June 16, 1999.[71] He was buried next to his father, Lo Bliayao, and on the ground of his ancestral home in the Nong Het District. Nhiavue was born in 1915 to Kaitong Lo Bliayao and his second wife, May Yang (Maiv Yaj). He was the only son of May who also had four daughters with Lo Bliayao. He was a half-brother of Faydang and Chong Tou, the elder sons of Lo Bliayao. Nhiavue was the last son of Lo Bliayao to have lived until 1999. As a member of the Lao People's Revolutionary Party, he was a key player behind the scene during the war years. In my article, "The Passing of a Hmong Pioneer," I wrote that Nhiavue was a prominent member of the Lao [People's] Revolutionary Party and a key player during the war years (from the late 1940s to the 1970s). In the 1980s, Nhiavue Lobliayao was an alternate Politburo member of the Lao People's Revolutionary Party (a.k.a. Phak Pasason Lao, or Lao Communist Party). He ranked twenty-first in the Central Committee of the party; he probably held that rank since the 1970s when the party was

> still secretly operating behind the Neo Lao Hak Sat (Pathet Lao or Lao Patriotic Front). In the 1980s, he was also named head of the Office of Nationalities. During the war years, he was reputed to be much closer to the core of the decision-making body of the Lao Revolutionary Party than his half-brother, Faydang Lobliayao. Faydang, who was not even a member of the party, was a figurehead for the Hmong on the side of the Pathet Lao.[72]

Col. Paseuth Fong Ya, the former commander of the Pachay Battalion and the commander of the subdivision of Xieng Khouang Province in 1975, was assassinated in October 1975. He was a key military player after the death of Col. Ya Thotou in January 1961, the founder of the Pachay Battalion. Among all Hmong military officers under the flag of the Pathet Lao, Ya Thotou stood out as the most well-known and well-recognized officer. He was highly decorated and recognized nationally during the war years as well as in the post-war Lao People's Democratic Republic.

In my *Laos and Its Expatriates in the United States*, I wrote about Ya Thotou as follows:

> Because Ya Thotou was a nephew of Lo Bliayao and a first cousin of Faydang Lobliayao, he was not considered a sympathizer of the French and their Partisans. The Partisans raided the village of Ya Thotou and his clan in Nong Het. Ya Thotou and his people escaped to Vietnam and joined the Viet Minh. Under the Pathet Lao, Ya Thotou founded his military unit, the *Ba Tou Unit*, named after Ya Thotou, and was made up mostly of his own relatives and friends. The unit fought very well and quickly caught the attention of Kaysone Phomvihan, who changed the unit's name to *Pachay Battalion* after Pachay, the legendary Hmong leader, who led the above mentioned rebellion against the French from 1919 to 1921.[73]

Col. Ya Thotou, who died from a single car accident in 1961, was posthumously honored as a hero of the Land of a Million Elephants by the post-1975 government of Lao People's Democratic Republic. Also, a statue of him was erected in Phonhsavanh, the capital of Xieng Khouang Province, in February 2015 to commemorate his contributions not only to the Pathet Lao movement during the war years, but also to the Lao People's Liberation Army. The statue is erected in Phonhsavanh because it is located near the Plain of Jars, the home base of Ya Thotou's Battalion 2, which made him stand out as the commander who saved not only his troops, but the future of the Lao People's Liberation Army. His birthplace is also in Nong Het, which is not far away from this city.

Ya Thotou is cited for saving Battalion 2 of the Pathet Lao Forces in May 1959. At the time, the Pathet Lao only had two battalions; Battalion 1 was stationed in Xieng Ngeune in Luang Phrabang and Battalion 2 was based in the Plain of Jars and was commanded by Col. Ya Thotou. A coalition government was formed in 1958 in an attempt to bring peace and national reconciliation to the country, but the process did not go well as planned. In May of 1959, Battalion 2 of the Pathet Lao was besieged by troops of the Royal Lao Army to disarm them. To safely and peacefully escape out of the besieged camp, Ya Thotou, the commander of Battalion 2, came up with a plan to get all of them safely out of the beleaguered base. Knowing that his base was surrounded by forces of the Royal Lao Army, Ya Thotou ordered his troops to hold a party with loud music and dance during the night. While the sound of music went on loudly, he ordered his troops to break up into many small groups, and that each group was to quietly disappear into the dark of the night with specific instructions to be regrouped in a specific point far away from their besieged base. The plan worked perfectly; all members of his troops were safely out, and before daybreak, the musicians and singers were also safely out. Before sunrise, soldiers of the Royal Lao Army stormed the base to find an empty camp; no one was there. Soldiers of Battalion 2 safely sneaked away and regrouped in a safe location. The Pathet Lao claimed this military tactic as the one that led them to victory in 1975; the survival of this battalion led to the continuity of the military movement of the Pathet Lao. Unlike Battalion 2, members of Battalion 1 were disarmed by troops of the Royal Lao Army, and its members were mixed with soldiers of the Royal Lao Army. Thus, Battalion 1 no longer existed. To commemorate Ya Thotou's genius military tactics and the survival of Battalion 2, the post-1975 government of the Lao People's Democratic Republic continues to hold a celebration on the anniversary of this special military event, and many speeches have been made about this event as well as Ya Thotou, the commander of the Battalion 2, and his men. It is worthy to note here that the celebration to mark the fifty-fifth anniversary of the above event, which took place on May 18, 2014, was not an auspicious one. A plane carrying high-ranking officials to the event crashed, killing Lt. Gen. Douangchay Phichit, deputy prime minister and minister of defense; Thongbanh SengAphone, minister of public security; and two other high-ranking officials.[74] Since 1975, many books have been written about Ya Thotou or have mentioned his contributions to the Communist movement in Laos during the war years.[75]

Ya Thotou was born in 1916 in Nong Het District to a prominent Yang clan. His father was Ya Xaychou and his mother was a sister of Lo Bliayao.

As a nephew of Lo Bliayao, Ya Thotou grew up in a political family. During World War II, Ya Thotou and his relatives remained neutral between the French and the Japanese. After World War II, the French returned and Faydang Lobliayao escaped from Nong Het to join the Viet Minh in Vietnam. Because of being neutral to both the French and Japanese, Ya Thotou and his relatives were oppressed and often harassed by the Partisans of the French. Consequently, Ya Thotou also joined the Viet Minh and later the Pathet Lao. Upon joining the Viet Minh and the Pathet Lao, Ya Thotou was assigned to recruit soldiers and founded, as mentioned above, the Ba Tou Unit, which became the Pachay Battalion. As of 2016, Pany Yathotou, the daughter of Yathotou, is the third member of the Politburo and president of the National Assembly of Laos. She is a key figure in the government of the Lao People's Democratic Republic, and the only female member of the Politburo of the ruling party, known as the Lao People's Revolutionary Party.

Pany Yathotou was born on February 18, 1951, in Nong Het District, Xieng Khouang Province, Laos. She received both her high school and college education in north Vietnam. She started her career in the banking system and rose very rapidly to be the governor of the National Bank of Laos in the

Figure 5.5.   Pany Yathotou, the president of the National Assembly of Laos, circa 2012.
Kou Yang.

mid-1990s. She was elected to the National Assembly of Laos in December 2010 and rose up very quickly to be vice president of that institution. In 2011 and 2016, Pany Yathotou was elected member of the Politburo and then appointed president of the National Assembly of Laos.

Pany Yathotou stood out as the first and only woman to have ever held the post of governor of the Bank of Laos, the president of the National Assembly, and the Third Member of the Politburo of the Lao People's Revolutionary Party (The Communist Party of Laos).

On the side of the Royal Lao government, Touby Lyfoung, the post–World War II paramount political leader of the Hmong of Laos, was sent to re-education camp in November 1975 and reportedly died in 1979. With almost a high school education, Touby, the son of Ly Foung and grandson of Lo Bliayao, represented the first educated generation of Hmong leaders in Laos. The French sought his help during World War II, and after the war in 1945, the French and King Sisavang Vong rewarded him generously. Before reaching the age of thirty and before the end of the decade of the 1940s, Touby had already held the office of district mayor of the Hmong, deputy governor of Xieng Khouang Province, and more importantly, he was conferred by King Sisavang Vong the title of "*Phaya Damrong Rittikay*–ພະຍາ ດຳຣົງ ຣິດທິໄກ" (loosely translated as the *Lord of Far Reaching Authority*). He was recognized as the first minority of Laos to have risen up to national political affairs; he held many national posts, including vice president of the National Assembly of Laos, member of the King's Council, deputy minister of information, minister of justice, minister of human services or social welfare,[76] minister of health in the tri-party government formed after the 1962 Geneva Accords, and deputy minister of posts and telegrams from 1974 to November 1975 under the Provisional Government of National Union.

In his *The Politics of Heroine in Southeast Asia*, Alfred McCoy wrote that Touby once said of Maj. Gen. Vang Pao, "He is a pure military officer who doesn't understand that after the war there is peace. And one must be strong to win the peace."[77] Touby was a gifted politician and proud of his Hmong heritage and identity; he had been seen wearing Hmong outfits to attend many socio-cultural events. Reportedly, he had very good people skills, and as a result, he worked well with people from all walks of life and all ethnic groups. He was very comfortable dining with a rural and poor Hmong family as well as with foreign ambassadors and the king. Those who knew Touby Lyfoung well said that Touby was intelligent, mature, courageous, daring, competent, self-confident, decisive, charismatic, and approachable.[78] In summary, Touby brought the Hmong from the highlands to the provincial and national affairs of Laos. And, in many ways, he was the political voice and the face of the Hmong of Laos.

With only an eleventh-grade education, Touby's work experience served him well; he was fluent in Lao and French, and spoke limited Vietnamese. Sayasith Yangsao, one of his nephews who had lived with Touby's family for many years, said that his uncle's French was at the college level.[79] Although Touby Lyfoung did not have a college education, he was the champion of education for his family and his Hmong people. When he was the deputy governor of Xieng Khouang Province, he made extra efforts to get Hmong children to school and persuade Hmong parents to send their children to school. George L. Barney, who studied the Hmong in Xieng Khouang during the mid-1950s, noted that Touby was very influential in getting Hmong children to register for public school.[80] His efforts to get an education for himself and his people started much earlier. While studying in elementary school in Xieng Khouang Town in the early 1930s, Touby and Tougeu had talked about and promised each other that they would commit themselves to education and return to help the impoverished Hmong in their remote villages as well as helping the Hmong gain access to education.[81]

In early May of 1975, Touby Lyfoung called key members of his extended family, including Dr. Yang Dao, for a meeting in his home in Vientiane. During the meeting Tougeu had urged Touby to leave Laos by saying, "Touby and I must leave as we have fought against the Viet Minh and Pathet Lao for more than [thirty] years. It is no longer safe for us to stay." At the end of the meeting, Touby concluded that he would leave Laos and told members of the family to also leave at their own will.[82] Tougeu Lyfoung and his family left Laos on July 2, 1975, to Thailand and then to France. So, why did Touby not follow through with his decision to leave Laos in 1975? The answer has not yet been found.

Touby Lyfoung died in the re-education camps in northeastern Laos. According to an anonymous source,[83] in late November of 1975, all ministers, including Touby, were told that the next ministerial meeting would be held in Sam Neua Town, Houaphanh Province, the stronghold of the Pathet Lao, and the presence of every minister was requested. Every minister was allowed to be driven there by his or her personal driver. After a day or two in Samneau Town, the ministers were told that the agenda and meeting activities would last much longer than anticipated, so they should send their personal drivers home to Vientiane first. Touby's personal driver was Vangleng Lyfoung, one of his grandsons, who came home to Vientiane to tell the family that his grandfather was staying behind longer than expected. That was the last news the family ever heard about Touby Lyfoung. He did not come home as expected. There was no news about Touby until 1979, when the family received a letter from Touby detailing the news that he had heard about his family going to other countries and the marriage of his daughter Gao Hnou in

Figure 5.6. From left to right: Tougeu Lyfoung, Touby Lyfoung, and Dr. Yang Dao, circa May 16, 1974.
Dr. Yang Dao.

France. Reportedly, Touby was sent to a re-education camp, known as camp Sop Hoa or camp No. 5, which was reserved for former high-ranking officials of the previous government, including the former king and members of the royal family and ministers.[84] Camp Sop Hoa is reportedly located in Vieng Say in Houaphanh Province, which was the stronghold and headquarters of the Pathet Lao during the war years. In 1985, a letter from the Government of the Lao People's Democratic Republic was sent to Tia that her father, Touby Lyfoung, had died of natural causes in 1979. Tia is the oldest daughter of Touby Lyfoung, who continued to stay in Vientiane with her husband and family after the war. There are various accounts of the causes of Touby's death. One account indicates that he died in the re-education camps in 1979 due to malnutrition.[85] Another account says Touby along with many ministers from the non-Pathet Lao side were chained and deprived of food and other basic needs, and as a result, all of them died of malnutrition, but Touby Lyfoung died of a single bullet shot from a guard. This account also indicates

Touby was deprived of food and basic needs; therefore, he had lost so much weight that he may have been in the state of delusion; he might have used strong words with the guard, who shot him.[86] What is certain is that Touby Lyfoung, the rhino among the elephants,[87] died in 1979 in the re-education camps in northeastern Laos.

Tougeu Lyfoung, the younger half-brother of Touby, passed away on February 10, 2004, in southern California. When the young Tougeu earned his baccalaureate from Lycée de Khaidinh, Vietnam, in 1942, he became the first minority in French Indochina to have such a prestigious educational diploma; he was among a handful of the people in Laos to have had such an education. He also completed his law studies from the Ecole National de la France d'Outre Mer in France. Thus, Tougeu is the first Hmong of Laos to have been trained in a law school in France. Tougeu had served Laos in many capacities, including member of the King's Council, member of the National Assembly, president of the Lao Supreme Court, and the general director of the Royal Lao government's Ministry of Justice. He was the third Hmong in the Kingdom of Laos to be conferred the title of Phaya, the most prestigious title of the Kingdom of Laos. The other two were Touby Lyfoung and Major General Vang Pao. His full title is Phaya Toula Pasith Tougeu Lyfoung. The title Phaya Toula Pasith (ພະຍາ ຕຸລາ ປະສິດ) can be loosely translated as "Lord of the Scale of Justice."

Tougeu Lyfoung was known as a man with dignity, integrity, and honor. Additionally, he lived up to his title as the "Lord of the Scale of Justice" because he held justice and fairness above all. He was also a task-oriented, neat, very efficient, and focused person; these qualities made him an excellent student, fair judge, good legal scholar, and outstanding bureaucrat.

In 1949, Tougeu Lyfoung married Sisamone Thammavong, his love at first sight. They celebrated their fiftieth anniversary in March 1999, five years before his passing in southern California on February 10, 2004. She was a nurse when he met her in Vientiane, Laos. It is said that he followed her with his Peugeot (the most prestigious bicycle at the time), and had followed her time after time until she could not refuse his love for her.

After their marriage, he rested his bicycle in their Vientiane home to re- mind him of his love and passion for his wife. In one of his many speeches during the 1994 Hmong New Year banquet in Fresno, Tougeu showed to the audience a picture of his wife taken before their marriage in 1949. He said that he fell in love with her the very first time he saw her and has loved her ever since. Prior to their departure from Laos to France in 1975, Sisamone Thammavong Lyfoung, who is fluent in Hmong, was very active with the Red Cross and the International Women's Club, assisting the needy, such as refugees, orphans, widows, and so on. In recognizing her humanitarian work,

King Sisavang Vatthana awarded her a medal, and Queen Khamphouy also awarded her another medal. Tougeu has credited her for reminding him of the need for them to visit their Hmong people during their early years in France. Tougeu and Sisamone have seven children: five daughters and two sons.

It is worthy to note here that I interviewed and met with Tougeu Lyfoung several times in 1999. Tougeu appeared to have a clear and good memory as he correctly recalled past events, dates, and time prior to 1975. He talked passionately about his childhood in Hmong villages when he had no shoes and wore very simple Hmong clothes. His other memories include his experience in Luang Prabang with the then Crowned Prince Sisavang Vatthana, who was the future and last king of Laos. He said the Crowned Prince took him to do net-fishing, gardening, and other activities. He recalled that the Crowned Prince was very a good diver and could dive without assisted equipment for a long period of time.

Tougeu Lyfoung said that he was pleased and surprised with the progress the Hmong have made over the last sixty years. He said the Hmong have taken a giant step in developing themselves, and their progresses are beyond his expectations. Reflecting on his past—to his school years, his career, and leadership—he said, "It was not easy at all." He made it because of his self-discipline, goal-oriented, and hardworking commitment. What does he miss the most? He said he misses his Hmong village life filled with freedom and farming activities, meaning the life before he entered the war and involved himself with local and national affairs in Laos. What does he regret the most? From 1961 to 1974, while he was burdened with the Justice Department's responsibilities, he saw a need to create a Hmong Student Center in Vientiane, where Hmong students could stay while studying in Vientiane—far away from their families. He regrets not having met this necessary need.

In the late 1990s, Tougeu and Sisamone Lyfoung spent most of their time in Santa Ana to practice his first profession, agriculture and gardening. After high school, he went to study agriculture in Hanoi, but his education was interrupted by World War II. He has since then loved to plant flowers and do gardening. Tougeu and his wife also loved to travel and visit family and friends. They visited China and other countries, in addition to France and places in the United Sates.

Tougeu Lyfoung died in southern California on February 10, 2004, of pneumonia, blood complications, and kidney failure. He was eighty-three years old. His traditional Hmong funeral was held in Fresno, California, which has the second largest concentration of Hmong Americans. During this last rite of passage, people from all walks of life came to pay their last respects. These people included Prince Soulivong, the son of the Crowned Prince, and grandson of the last king of Laos; and Chao Panya Souvanna

Phouma, one of the sons of the late Prime Minister Prince Souvanna Phouma. Others included members of the House of Phouan Principality or House of Xieng Khouang, many former Lao and Hmong politicians and military officers, and many American politicians and community leaders.

Tougeu Lyfoung, the Lord of the Scales of Justice, was the first minority in French Indochina to have a high school education, the first Hmong to receive a law education in France, and the first Hmong and minority in Laos to serve in the King's Council and be the general director of the Ministry of Justice. He was the last of the three Lyfoung brothers who rose up during World War II, and went on to the national stage of post–World War II national affairs of Laos.[88]

It should also be mentioned here that Toulia Lyfoung, who was appointed to the First National Assembly of Laos in 1947, became a refugee to France and died there. Reportedly, he was a member of the committee to draft the first national Constitution of Laos and he had fought hard to include all people of Laos as citizens of the country. Toulia is a half younger brother of Touby and a younger brother of Tougeu; he was one of three Lyfoung brothers who played a major role in helping the French during the occupation of the Japanese in Laos during the early 1940s. Also, Mao Soua Lo Bannavong, the step-sister of Touby, Tougeu, and Tou Lia, was the first Hmong woman in Laos to have run for a national office in Laos. She returned from France to Laos and launched in 1958 an unsuccessful campaign for a seat in the National Assembly of Laos. She left Laos for France in 1981 and died there in 1985. She was one of the first educated Hmong women in Laos. After completing sixth grade in Laos, she went to study in Hanoi for two years. She later married Sattasinh Bannavong and then accompanied her husband to France, where she also studied politics and leadership. She was fluent in Hmong, Lao, French, Vietnamese, and also spoke Chinese.[89]

The list of other civilian leaders who have passed on includes, but is not limited to, Youatong Yang, Touxia Thaoxaochay, Moua Sue, Ly Tou Yia, Lycheu Lynhiavu, Lyteck Lynhiavu, and so on. Also, Pakao Her, co-founder of the Chao Fa resistant movement in Laos, was assassinated in 2003 in Thailand and was buried in Fresno, California.

Prior to 1975, only eight Hmong had served as members of the National Assembly of Laos. These Hmong are Toulia Lyfoung, Tougeu Lyfoung, Touby Lyfoung, Ly Tou Yia, Ly Cheu Lynhiavu, Moua Sue, and Lao Chue Cha. Six of these seven Hmong have already passed away prior to 2015. Lao Chue Cha, known in the United States as Lawrence Cha (Npliaj Tswb Tsab), is the only person still living as of 2015. Below is a brief biography of Lao Chue Cha.

Lao Chue Cha was born in 1929 in Kio So, a village near the border of Thailand, in Sayaboury Province, Laos. He came from a prominent Hmong family in Sayaboury District. His father, Lao Chu, was a leader of many villages and was a very well-known person in the region. The fifteen-year-old Lao Chue Cha was sent to school in Sayaboury Town in 1946; there he attended first-grade through third-grade education. In 1949, his father heard about Father Yves Bertrais, a French Catholic missionary, and his private school in Kio Kacham in Luang Phrabang Province, which emphasized the French language. His father decided to send Lao Chue there for his education, hoping that he would get a good education and become proficient in the French language. He ended up studying with Bertrais for two years. It needs to be noted here that Father Yves Bertrais (1921–2007) was not only a good teacher, but the co-inventor of the Hmong language, generally known today as the Romanized Phonetic Alphabet, and was instrumental in providing school and shelter for many Hmong children to receive an education. Lao Chue Cha, Yang See, and Dr. Yang Dao are among those who benefited from the tireless efforts of Father Bertrais.

After Laos gained its limited autonomy under the French Union in 1949, Prince Khamphanh Panya, the provincial governor of Sayaboury, urged Lao Chu Cha's father to bring the young Lao Chue Cha back from Kio Kacham

Figure 5.7.   Lao Chue Cha, circa 2008.
Kou Yang.

to Sayaboury Town. In late 1950, the young Lao Chue Cha returned to Sayaboury Town. Shortly after his return, the Governor of Sayaboury sent him
and another Hmong by the name of Lao Ou Lee to Vientiane to study nursing
aid. In order to cover their basic needs, the government provided each one
of them with a scholarship of about eight hundred kip per month. They spent
nearly three years in Vientiane, and Lao Chue Cha successfully passed the
exit examination in 1953, but Lao Ou Lee did not. Lao Chue Cha returned to
Sayaboury Town and left Lao Ou Lee back in Vientiane to refresh his studies.
Upon his return to Sayaboury, he was assigned to work in the town's infir-
mary. At the time, he was one of a few Hmong individuals in the region to
hold a civil servant job. Being in this position, he learned to work effectively
with the Lao and had many Lao friends. His family was well connected with
many powerful Lao families, including the family of Prince Rattana Panya,
the provincial governor of Sayaboury and a half-brother of the late King
Sisavang Vatthana.

Lao Chue Cha worked as a nurse aid until 1969, when there was an opening
of one slot for any nurse aid to learn radiology in Vientiane. He volunteered
for the slot and went to study radiology in Vientiane, graduating in 1971.
While in Vientiane, the capital of Laos, he learned that there was widespread
corruption by high-ranking government officials and military officers. He was
not happy with what he had learned. Upon his returned to Sayaboury Town
in 1971, he began to think about ways to minimize corruption and other problems facing the nation. He decided to be a part of the solution and declared
his candidacy for a seat in the National Assembly. There were only three seats
allotted for Sayaboury Province, but there were twelve candidates, including
him; therefore, his chances were very slim.

Fortunately, he won and became one of three people's deputies from Sayaboury Province. In early 1972, Lao Chue Cha (a.k.a. Laurence Cha) took the
oath of office to serve in the National Assembly of Laos. He became the
first Hmong in the northwestern region of Laos, including Sayaboury, Houa
Khong (Luang Namtha), and Luang Phrabang, to be elected to the National
Assembly. To implement the 1973 Peace Agreement, the National Assembly
was dissolved in 1974, and was replaced by a new NPCC. Lao Chue Cha was
not selected to serve on the new NPCC.

Lao Chue Cha and his family left Laos on May 25, 1975, for Thailand and
stayed in a refugee camp for one year before resettling in San Diego, California, in November of 1976. He and his family lived in San Diego, California,
from 1976 to 1982. They then moved to Porterville, California, and have been
there ever since. Currently, Lao Chue Cha lives with his family in Porterville,
California, and is actively helping his community and has been attending
many social and cultural activities in Fresno, California.[90]

The list of Hmong military leaders who have passed away include Major General Vang Pao; Colonels Yong Chue Yang, Neng Chu Thao, Ly Nou, Lysyblong Lyfoung, Cher Pao Moua, Lee Lo, Shoua Yang, Naokao Ly-foung, and Shong Leng Xiong; Lt. Cols. Hang Sao, Ly Xang, and Chou Peter Vang; and so on. The exact number of Hmong who held the rank of colonel is not known, but a partial list of Hmong military officers in the Nam Phong Refugee Camp in 1975 shows fourteen full colonels. The full list, however, is much larger. According to Col. Moua Sue,[91] who once served as the chief of staff for Military Region II, there were eight colonels of Hmong descent who served in the regular forces of the Royal Lao Army in Military Region II, and twelve who served under the Special Guerrilla Units (SGUs) in Military Region II. They are listed below:

- Colonels of Hmong descent in the regular Royal Lao Army: 1) Neng Chue Thao (Neej Tswb Thoj), 2) Shoua Yang (Suav Yaj), 3) Toupao Ly (Lis Tub Pos), 4) Naokao Lyfoung (Nom Kos Lis Foom), 5) Syblong Lyfoung (Xws Nplooj Lis Foom), 6) Ly Nou (Lis Nus), 7) Tou Lue Moua (Tub Lwj Muas), and 8) Cher Pao Moua (Txawj Pov Muas).
- Colonels of Hmong descent in the SGUs: 1) Moua Sue (Muas Xwm), 2) Tou Long Yang (Tub Looj Yaj), 3) Ly Teng (Lis Teeb), 4) Nhia Lue Vang

Figure 5.8.   Military Region II military officers of Hmong descent, circa 1968. The ranks indicated in the photo are their highest military ranks in 1975, not their ranks in 1968. All of them wore the uniform and Armed Forces cap badge of the Royal Lao Army, though about half of them served as Special Guerilla Unit officers.
Xia Vue Yang.

(Nyiaj Lwm Vaj), 5) Youa Tru Vang (Ntsuab Rwg Vaj), 6) Vang Xeng
Vang (Vam Xeeb Vaj), 7) Saidang Xiong (Xaiv Ntaj Xyooj), 8) Shongleng
Xiong (Shoob Leej Xyooj), 9) Tong Vang Lo (Tooj Vam Lauj), 10) Lee Lo
(Lis Lauj), 11) Youa Pao Xiong (Ntsuab Pov Xyooj), and 12) Yong Chue
Yang (Ntxoov Tswb Yaj).

As listed above, there were twenty colonels (both regular forces and SGU)
of Hmong descent in Military Region II in 1975, and it is assumed that more
than one-third of them have already passed away.

Yong Chue Yang (Ntxoov Tswb Yaj), one of the abovementioned colonels, passed away in 1997 in Sheboygan, Wisconsin. Below is a brief mention
of his military career.

According to his son, Xia Vue Yang, Yong Chue Yang was born on September 5, 1930, to Chong Vue Yang and Mee Vang. At the time of his birth,
the family lived in the village of Hav Kab Kawb about twenty kilometers
away from Nong Het Town (Rhino Lake), Xieng Khouang, Laos. When he
was about eight years old, he was sent to school and became a classmate of
Vang Pao, the future major general and commander of Military Region II.
World War II reached Laos in 1945, so the young Yong Chue Yang returned
home to help his parents work on their farms. A year later, he married Plia
Lor, when he was about sixteen years old, and soon he was recruited by the
mayor of Pha Vene to serve as his personal secretary, the position he held
until 1954, when the French were defeated in the historic Dien Bien Phu
Battle, which led to the signing of the 1954 Geneva Agreement, granting independence to Cambodia, Laos, and Vietnam, and partitioning Vietnam into
North and South Vietnam.

Again, Yong Chue Yang returned home to help his family work on their
farms and fields, leading a simple Hmong life. In early 1961, Yong Chue
Yang was recruited by then Lt. Col. Vang Pao to join his newly formed
SGUs. As one of those young Hmong with basic education, he rose through
the ranks very quickly. He soon became company and then battalion commander. From 1969 to 1972, Yong Chue Yang was the commander of Battalion 21 stationed in Ban Na, and then became a military advisor of Military
Region II from 1969–1972. In 1972, when he was just a lieutenant colonel,
he was the acting commander of Groupement Military II with the command
center located on top of a bare mountain between Phou Bia and Phou Pha
Xay. Lt. Col. Yong Chue Yang coordinated with the commander of Regiment
33 under Col. Boualiane, who came from Military Region III in Savannakhet,
to guide T-28 pilots to drop bombs on enemy positions near Phou Pha Xay. In
early 1973, Yong Chue Yang was officially promoted to the rank of colonel,
when the war had almost come to an end. In mid-May of 1975, Col. Yong

Chue Yang's family was one of those 120 families or twenty-five hundred people on the list that Maj. Gen. Vang Pao handed to the Americans as people to be evacuated from Long Cheng to Nam Phong, Thailand. They, indeed, were evacuated to Nam Phong on May 14, 1975. Consequently, Col. Yong Chue Yang and his family, like thousands of other Hmong, became refugees in Thailand. He and his family came to the United States in August of 1976 and were settled in Sheboygan, Wisconsin. Like other Hmong refugees, Col. Yong Chue Yang had to start his life all over; he became an employee of Eclipse Manufacturing, and then Ametek, Inc., where he worked until his retirement in the summer of 1993. Yong Chue Yang was the founder of the Hmong Mutual Assistance Association of Sheboygan and also the co-founder of Yang Wang Meng Association, and he continued to play a major role in helping Hmong refugees in their early years of their resettlement in the United States. Col. Yong Chue Yang died in 1997 and was buried in Sheboygan, Wisconsin, his adopted hometown.

Among all Royal Lao military officers of Hmong descent, Major General Vang Pao[92] stood out as the most well-known and the key military player during the Secret War in Laos. Those who have worked for him and knew him well, such as Lyblong Lynhiavu, described Vang Pao as "very active, courageous, intelligent, determined, confident, daring, and a hardworking man with splendid qualities, and capabilities. He did not have much education, but he was unquestionably a very capable military leader. . . . [He was also] a highly spiritual individual and superstitious. . . . He believed that if he asked, the spirits would tell him what was yet to come or how events would unfold."[93] On the negative side of Vang Pao, Lyblong Lynhiavu wrote that Vang Pao was "hot tempered, and impatient" and "was easily swayed and manipulated by cunning and dangerous individuals."[94] Also, Lynhiavu claimed that Vang Pao, despite having many excellent and noble qualities, certainly had his weaknesses and fell under the spell of corruption, undesirable activities, and murderous intentions. Lynhiavu listed the assassination attempt on the life of then Lt. Ly Fu in 1957 as one example of the murderous intentions of Vang Pao; gambling was another example of Vang Pao's many undesirable activities.[95]

Vang Pao began his military career in the late 1940s with the French forces in Indochina, graduated from the Done Hene Officer Academy in 1952, and then became a commissioned officer in the Royal Lao Army. From 1965 to 1975, Vang Pao became the commander of Military Region II of the Royal Lao Army, overseeing military affairs of the provinces of Xieng Khouang and Houa Phanh. He, too, was the first Hmong and ethnic minority who had reached the military rank of major general in the Royal Lao Army and of commander of a Military Region. Military Region II is located along the borderlines with China and Vietnam, which was one of the battle zones where all the heavy fighting and bombing runs took place. As such, Military Region II experienced the most intensive fighting, savagery, and destruction that today is still marked by bomb craters. Also, soldiers of Military Region II consisted of many ethnic groups; the Hmong were proportionally larger in number, and they were hit the hardest and received most of the attention from the press. As a result, soldiers of Military Region II were often portrayed as the faces of the SGUs, though Military Regions I, III, and IV also had SGU soldiers imbedded in their troops.

After resigning his commission as the commander of Military Region II,[96] he left Laos on May 14 for Thailand and stayed there from May 14 to early June of 1975. He then made a brief visit to France before coming to Missoula, Montana, in June of 1975. In the United States, Vang Pao continued to play a major role in the affairs of the Hmong refugee community; he played an instrumental role in founding many organizations, including Lao Family Community, Inc., Hmong Council, Inc., and the United Front for the National Liberation of Laos or *Neo Hom Kou Xat* in the Lao language (also known as "*Neo Hom*") as a resistant movement in exile. When the Neo Hom was founded in 1981, the organization also formed a government in exile with Phaya Outhong Souvannavong as the head of state, Maj. Gen. Vang Pao as the commander in chief of the Army of National Liberation, and Maj. Gen. Thonglith Chockbengboun as his deputy. The organization also include many other important pre-1975 politicians, such as Sisouk Na Champassack, the former deputy prime minister and minister of defense.[97]

On June 4, 2007, agents of the Federal Bureau of Investigation and the Bureau of Alcohol, Tobacco and Firearms arrested Maj. Gen. Vang Pao and nine other conspirators of the *Neo Hom*, charging them with a plot to overthrow the Communist government of Lao People's Democratic Republic,[98] which violated the federal Neutrality Act. The accused were charged with conspiracy to plot and overthrow the government of Laos and to kill, maim, or injure persons in a foreign country with which the United States was at peace. Vang Pao and his accomplices were put on trial multiple times. However, in September of 2009, federal prosecutors decided to drop all charges against Vang Pao on humanitarian grounds. Charges against the others were also dropped later in that same year, although open investigations remain on those cases.

On December 22, 2009, Maj. Gen. Vang Pao publicly announced his decision to visit Laos in the upcoming year. Shortly afterwards, the government of Lao People's Democratic Republic responded that he may return to Laos, but that his death sentence imposed by the Lao court in 1975 still stood.[99] It should be noted here that on September 5, 1975, six rightists were tried in absentia in Vientiane, convicted, and sentenced to death, five were sentenced to life imprisonment, and twenty were convicted and sentenced to jail. Those sentenced to death were Phoui Sananikone, former president of the National Assembly and right-wing politician; Prince Boun Oum Na Champassak, former head of the Royal House of Champassak and right-wing politician; Major General Vang Pao, former commander of Military Region II; Major General Kouprasith Abhay, former deputy commander in chief of the Royal Lao Army; Major General Oudone Sananikone, former director general of the Defense Ministry; and Major General Thonglith Chockbengboun, former commander of Military Region V.[100]

Vang Pao was one of the three Hmong who were conferred by the King of Laos the title Phaya, and his title is "Phaya Nora Pramok" or "ພະຍາ ນໍຣະປະມົກ." The other two, as mentioned above, are Touby Lyfoung and Tougeu Lyfoung. Maj. Gen. Vang Pao, one of the most recognized military officers of the Royal Lao Army, died in Clovis, a city near Fresno, California, on January 6, 2011, at the age of eighty-one. His funeral was held in Fresno, California, but he was buried at Forest Lawn in Glendale, southern California.

One of the first two Hmong graduates from the prestigious Done Hene Officer Academy in Savannakhet, Laos, was Major Ly Fu (Lis Fwm). The first of these two was, as mentioned above, Maj. Gen. Vang Pao, who graduated in 1952.

Two years younger than Major General Vang Pao, Ly Fu was born in 1932 in the region of Nong Het, Xieng Khouang Province in Laos. He completed his sixth-grade education in 1950 and is considered more educated than Vang Pao, who reached only a third-grade education. He joined the French army in Laos in 1950 and received many trainings, including weaponry, corporal academy, and sergeant academy, before being admitted to the most prestigious officer academy in Done Hene in Savannakhet. He graduated from this academy in 1954, just before the end of the Dien Bien Phu Battle, in which the Viet Minh defeated the French forces. He missed the opportunity to be deployed there to help the French forces. After graduating from the respected Done Hene Officer Academy, Ly Fu returned to his Company 14 in Xieng Khouang, and was given the rank of Aspirant in the French army system. Normally, it takes six months of post-graduation to move up to the rank of second lieutenant, but the army considered his case a special situation; therefore, they promoted him to commissioned officer at the rank of second lieutenant before the end of his six-month probation. Soon after his return to Company 14, the army expanded Company 14 to become Battalion 21. Consequently, he was commissioned to command Company 16 under Battalion 21, and Vang Pao, who had just been promoted to captain, became commander of the new Battalion 21. In the mid-1950s, Ly Fu was commissioned to go to Houa Phanh Province. While he was there, he organized an Auto-Defense Corps, known then as ADC (self-defense corps). It was a success for both the organization of the ADC and his ADC's resistance against the Pathet Lao troops. As a result, the military command center in Vientiane highly respected Ly Fu, and whenever he went to Vientiane to report to the military command center, they treated him as a sub-division commander.

In late 1956, he was ordered to get back to his old Company 16, which was based in Phou Pha Luam, and was one of many companies under Battalion 21, commanded by then Major Vang Pao. This post put him between a rock and a hard place. In April of 1957, Major Vang Pao ordered Ly Fu to go to Muong Peune to arrest several soldiers, who were absent without official leave. He responded that the soldiers absent without official leave did not go to Muong Peune, but to the Plain of Jars. If they want to follow their soldiers, he told Vang Pao, they need to go to the direction of Plain of Jars. Vang Pao said, "Alright, do as you say." The next morning, Vang Pao came to Ly Fu's house and asked Ly Fu to return the travel permit issued by Vang Pao. Ly Fu was suspicious of Vang Pao's behavior, so Ly Fu decided to depart late to avoid any potential problem awaiting him along the way. Two soldiers and Ly Fu departed late as planned and were on their way for only four or five kilometers from the base when assassins fired several rounds of ammunition at Ly Fu, hitting and breaking his right leg and damaging several teeth of his horse. He fell from his horse and it ran away. Ly Fu told one of his two soldiers to go back to his Company 16 and ask them for help. He ordered the second soldier to stay with him and watch for the return of the assassins. On the way to their military base, his soldier encountered two Hmong soldiers by the names of Lue Vang (Lwm Vaj) and Yao Thao (Yob Thoj). These two men belonged to Vang Pao's battalion and were stationed in his base. They inquired information about Ly Fu's condition, and when they learned that he was alright, one of them said, "We must go back and finish the job." Ly Fu's soldier told them that he will kill them first, if they want to further harm his boss. The two soldiers walked away. His soldier reached Company 16, and many soldiers came to help Ly Fu, who wanted them to take him to Muong Peune, far away from Vang Pao. They did, and many hours later, they arrived in Muong Peune and Ly Fu received basic medical attention there. The next day, the chief of military internal investigation (known in the army as Office #2) in Muong Peune came to see Ly Fu to investigate the assassination attempt on him. Ly Fu gave him all the information he had and anything that linked this assassination attempt to Major Vang Pao. He was later airlifted from Muong Peune to Vientiane for medical treatment.[101]

After this incident, Ly Fu began to connect all the dots and realized that Maj. Vang Pao wanted to kill him. Before this incident, Vang Pao told Ly Fu to join him to rebel and declare Houa Phanh and Xieng Khouang Provinces as Hmong territory. Ly Fu refused, but suspected that Vang Pao only wanted his yes answer so that Vang Pao could use it for the government of Laos to arrest and charge Ly Fu for treason. The second event involved the false use of Ly Fu's name by Major Vang Pao to send a telegram to Touby Lyfoung. Vang Pao secretly drafted a telegram in Ly Fu's name to Touby Lyfoung, telling Touby that Ly Fu wanted to rebel and separate Houa Phanh and Xieng Khouang to be a Hmong territory. Vang Pao gave the memo without Ly Fu's knowledge to two Hmong telegram operators and ordered them to send it to Touby. The two operators read the memo and were very concerned as it indicated that Ly Fu was its author and that Ly Fu wanted to rebel. They approached Ly Fu and shared the content of the memo with him. Ly Fu told them not to send the telegram as it was not his telegram, and it could be dangerous to him and people around him. A day later, Major Vang Pao called Ly Fu to his office and loudly told him, "If you want to know something, come to me, do not go to our subordinates." As a result, the memo was not sent, but Vang Pao had since then held his grudge against Ly Fu. The third event involved Vang Pao sending three assassins to kill Ly Fu without success. Mrs. Ly Tou, whose shelter was just next door, saw three soldiers secretly entered Ly Fu's shelter, looking for him without asking anyone. Two of them carried Thompson rifles that only soldiers in Vang Pao's base had. Ly Fu also said that Vang Pao was very jealous and envious of Ly Fu's successes in Houa Phanh Province and he [Vang Pao] was afraid that Ly Fu would rise very quickly to be his rival or achieve higher ranks than Vang Pao. Allegedly, this assassination attempt on Ly Fu's life was not the first or the last. Yang Shonglue,[102] the Mother of Hmong Language, for example, was allegedly assassinated by Vang Pao's order. Col. Khamhou Boussarath also told Ly Fu privately that Vang Pao had attempted to assassinate him once.[103] In his *The Liver and the Tongue*, Lynhiavu also alleged that Vang Pao ordered the assassination of Ly Fu and the successful assassination of Col. Tong Va Lor (Tooj Vam Lauj) "for criticizing the unjust treatment of ordinary soldiers and the general's corruption."[104]

After the assassination attempt, Ly Fu was sent by Toulia Lyfoung to Japan, so that he could get both medical treatment and physical therapy. It took him six months to get his broken leg healed and well enough to the point where he could almost walk normally. By the time he was ready to return to Laos, he was able to speak limited Japanese, using simple conversations; he had lost something, but then gained something else in its place. Ly Fu said that the six months spent in Japan opened his eyes to the world outside of Laos; it broadened his perspective, enhanced his problem-solving skills, and enabled him to be more compassionate and forgiving. Ly Fu said that he kept saying to himself, "Vang Pao wants to take my life, but I refuse to do the same to him." Since then, Ly Fu kept telling people that the Hmong should not use the assassination attempts on his life as an excuse to divide the Hmong people, especially between the Ly and the Vang clans and their descendants. Ly Fu wants this bitter relationship to end with him and Major General Vang Pao. He also said he wants the next generation to take these assassination attempts as a lesson and as shortcomings of their past leaders; officers turning guns at each other should never happen again in the future or in any society. He said, "If we can tolerate and cooperate with each other, we will go farther and be better than the past. If we can put our jealousy, envy, grudge, prejudice, and selfishness aside, and work together, we will be stronger and in a better position to develop our people. Imagine how much more Maj. Gen. Vang Pao and I could do for the Royal Lao Army, and more importantly, for our Hmong people, if the two of us, the first two Hmong, who graduated from the Officer Academy, and the first two Hmong who became commissioned officers of the Royal Lao Army can work together."

Figure 5.9. Major Ly Fu, circa 1971. Ly Fu, in the formal Royal Lao Army service uniform, was an Army Major at the time. On his shoulders is his military sholder insignia (with the rank of Major). Photo courtesy of Ly Fu.

Ly Fu said, after the assassination attempts, the military command center in Vientiane sent Major Khamsouk to take over Major Vang Pao's battalion and ordered Major Vang Pao to leave to the military command center in Vientiane for six months. Ly Fu said he does not know what happened to Vang Pao inside of the command center in Vientiane. After his treatment in Japan, Ly Fu returned to Xieng Khouang and became the commander of both the Auto-Defense and ADC of Xieng Khouang Province.

After the Kong Le Coup in 1960, Major General Phoumi, the new defense minister, who knew that Vang Pao had previously attempted to assassinate Ly Fu, transferred Ly Fu to Savannakhet. Ly Fu was assigned in 1961 to work in the Ministry of Veterans Affairs in Vientiane and was promoted to major in 1962. Initially, he was made the director of the veterans affairs of Vientiane Province, but later, became the bureau chief of foreign relations; he had language skills in French and Japanese, in addition to his Lao and Hmong. In 1967, he received a scholarship to study English and social welfare in Australia for almost two years; therefore, he also learned how to speak, read, and write English.

Upon his return to Vientiane in 1970 from Australia, he was appointed vice director of rehabilitation for war veterans. In early 1975, his superiors recommended that he be promoted to lieutenant colonel, but before it could be officially granted, the promotion had to be approved by top officials of the Royal Lao Army and the Ministry of Defense. The turmoil and upheaval of that year delayed the official granting of all promotions, including his. Consequently, he ended up leaving Laos in September of 1975 with only the rank of major. He rose slowly through the ranks in the Royal Lao Army because of two major factors: first, he had not been deployed to the frontlines since the early 1960s, and second, he was assigned to the Ministry of Veterans Affairs, doing only office and management work. His language skills in many languages, attention to details, excellence in paperwork, and thoughtful actions were all a blessing and a curse; it was a blessing because everywhere he went, he was assigned to office jobs doing paperwork, and people around him liked his work. It was a curse because office jobs in the military equates with slowness in promotions.

His family arrived in Colorado Springs, Colorado, on September 29, 1976, and stayed there for only three months before moving to Denver to join a small Hmong community. His family lived in Denver until 2001, when they moved to California, where the weather is friendlier to older people and where they could stay closer to many of their relatives and friends. They have since made Sanger, California, their home. Major Ly Fu lives with May Nhia Vue (Maiv Nyiaj Vwj), his wife of sixty-five years. He jokingly said that he lives long and is happy because he does not have a lot of money and problems, so he is at peace and sleeps well every night.[105]

Dr. Yang Dao, a well-known Hmong American leader and scholar, officially retired in 2005, contributing to the end of a generation or the phasing out of the older leaders and their leadership.

Yang Dao earned his Ph.D. in social sciences from Sorbonne University-Paris in 1972, making him the first Hmong of Laos to hold a Ph.D. He returned to Laos in 1972 and became the head of the Human Resource Department of the Ministry of Planning for the Royal Lao government. In 1974, Yang Dao was appointed to the NPCC, which was established under the 1973 Peace and National Reconciliation Agreement between the Royal Lao government and the Communist Pathet Lao.[106] In May of 1975, Dr. Yang Dao and his family became refugees in Thailand, and while in the refugee camp in Thailand, Dr. Yang Dao played an important role in advocating for Hmong refugees to be included in the U.S. and French refugee resettlement programs. In June of 1976, Dr. Yang Dao and his family took political asylum in France and then came to the United States in 1983. Between 1983 and the latter part of the 1990s, Dr. Yang Dao held numerous positions, including staff of the University of Minnesota's College of Education and lecturer in the College of Liberal Arts of Hamline University and Metropolitan State University. He also served as a southeast Asian cultural specialist, assistant director in the English language learner department, and director of the Multi-Language Communications Office in the Communications and Public Information Department of St. Paul Public Schools. From 2002 to 2005, he lectured on Hmong contemporary history, culture, and traditions in the Asian Cultures and Literatures Department of the College of Liberal Arts in the University of Minnesota.

Dr. Yang Dao is the author of *Vanguard of Development* in French (1975) and *Hmong at the Turning Point* in English (1993). He is the co-author of *The Fabulous Adventure of the Poppy People* in French (1978); *The Dragon, the Master of Sky and his Seven Daughters"* in French (1978); *French-Hmong Dictionary* (1980); *Handbook for Teaching Hmong-Speaking Students* in English (1988); and *Minority Cultures of Laos* in English (1992). He has also contributed to a number of books, including *Hmong in the West* (1982), *Hmong Forum* (1990), *Hmong/Miao in Asia* in English (2004), and *The Impact of Globalization and Transnationalism on the Hmong* in English (2009). His more than ten articles have appeared in many journals and magazines, including *Les Temps Modernes, La Documentation Francaise, Hmong Studies Journal*, and so on. He is also a Hmong musician and has composed the first Hmong modern songs (1965–1968) including "Hnub Twg Txoj Kev Sib Paj Caij Vaj" meaning "When Cooperation Rules the World, Our Humanity

Will Shine" in 1968. Dr. Yang Dao is very active in the Hmong American community and beyond. He is a co-incorporator of Hmong National Development and co-founder of the Laotian Multi-Ethnic Alliance for USA-Laos Friendship.

Yang Dao was born in 1943 to Yang My No and Her Ker. With a scholarship from the French Colonial Administration of Indochina (Cambodia, Laos, and Vietnam) in 1950, he started elementary school at the French Petit Lycee Yersin in Dalat, South Vietnam. From 1954 to 1959, he pursued his studies at the French catholic middle school of Paksane, Central Laos, and in June of 1960, he finished tenth grade at French High School Lycee de Vientiane, the capital of Laos. Afterwards, his education was interrupted for two years by the civil war in Laos. In September of 1962, with the help of French missionary Father Yves Bertrais, Yang Dao went to France to resume his French education in a high school in Arras on the border of Belgium. In June of 1964, he successfully passed the national examinations for the French high school baccalauréat at Lycee Henry IV in Paris and earned his high school diploma. With scholarships from the French government and, later, the United Nations for Education, Science, and Culture Organization, he was able to successfully pursue his undergraduate education and complete his Ph.D. in social sciences from Sorbonne University-Paris in 1972. Dr. Yang Dao and his wife, Ly Mo, have five children: three daughters and two sons. Dr. Yang Dao speaks and writes Hmong, Lao, French, Vietnamese, English, and has a good command of the Thai language.[107]

As the first Hmong of Laos to earn a doctorate, he became a role model for young Hmong and played many influential roles in the Hmong American community. His retirement in 2005, in addition to the passing of Maj. Gen. Vang Pao and many other older leaders, marked the end of a generation and the passing of the baton to the younger Hmong American educated leaders. The next generation of Hmong American leaders is very likely to step away from their predecessors, who tended to practice traditional leadership, which is paternalistic in nature. The leadership concept of one paramount leader is also gone with the older generation. There will now be many young leaders and Hmong in various fields with various expertise who will now serve as leaders in their own fields. Having more than one leader is probably best for the Hmong as their leadership will continue generation after generation, and this process will lead to democracy, equality, and prosperity. The very young Hmong American constituents in the twenty-first century, who grew up and have been educated in the United States, would expect their leaders to be more democratic, proactive, progressive, inclusive, and pragmatic. Additionally, they would expect their leaders to deliver on what they preach and be accountable for what they do or don't do. Many young Hmong today do have the potential to lead, speak, or advocate on behalf of the Hmong American community. Many of these do have leadership potentials and other capabilities, and can serve as advocates on behalf of the Hmong community. Mee Moua, who stepped down in February 2017 as president and executive director of Asian Americans Advancing Justice, and former Minnesota state senator, has and will continue to be the face and voice of the Hmong and other Asian Americans in Washington, District of Columbia. Although she has stepped down as president and executive director of Asian Americans Advancing Justice, Mee Moua continues to stay in Washington, District of Columbia, actively involved in important issues related to Asian Americans.

She is listed in November of 2015 by Washingtonian.com as one of the most powerful women in Washington, District of Columbia.[108] Paul C. Lo, Esq., the California Superior Court judge in Merced County, has been the face of the Hmong in the legal system and has continuously spoken on behalf of the Hmong in the last two decades. He has served the Hmong community in many capacities, including being the past immediate president of Hmong National Development, Inc. Foung Hawj, Minnesota state senator, represents a new generation of Hmong leaders, who are bilingual-bicultural. Blong Xiong, another politician and former member of the Fresno City Council in California, continues to be very active and represents the interest of the Hmong in Fresno, as well as in other regions. Bao Vang, the executive director of Hmong American Partnership and Hmong National Development, is another mover and shaker at the regional and national level. Xoua Thao, M.D., J.D., M.P.H., and president of the Hmong Nationalities Organization, Inc., has served in the past as the president of Hmong National Development, Inc., and undoubtedly will continue to be the voice and face of Hmong Americans. Mao Misty Her, the instructional superintendent of Fresno Unified School District, is not only an educational leader, but a visionary Hmong leader as well. She is a strong voice for the Hmong and is a strong force behind Hmongstory40, which was exhibited in Fresno in December of 2015 and put on display during the Fresno Hmong New Year. Malisa Lee is a leader in higher education and can bridge the gap between the Hmong and higher education. Lastly, Doualy Xaykaothao and Gia Vang represent the face of the Hmong in the media, showing the positive images of the Hmong to the public and being role models for the Hmong youth.

There are also many young Hmong who are most likely to be the faces of the Hmong in the larger American public. They include Brenda Song, the Disney actress; Doua Moua, the actor and writer; Yer Za Vue, the artist and impressionist; Lee Yang, the senior vice president for finance of Kaiser Permanente Corporation; and Col. Yee Chang Hang of the U.S. Army. Additionally, there are Cheng Xiong and Laj Xiong of Intel, Cheng Moua and

Mai Lee Chang of NASA, and Thao Yang, a biochemist at the University of Wisconsin-Eau Claire. These young Hmong might represent other young Hmong's quest to enter the world of high-tech and science.

The selected list above is incomplete as there are many other Hmong American achievers; nevertheless, this list indicates small but significant contributions of Hmong Americans to the arts, American culture, higher education, economy, and social milestones. Despite the many success stories, these new Americans continue to face many challenges and struggles in educational attainment especially with the high school dropout rate, health disparity, high unemployment, and poverty in the communities. An analysis of the ACS data from 2007 to 2013 places the Hmong poverty rate at 25.6 percent compared with 24.6 percent for Bangladeshi, 19.4 percent for Cambodians, and 15.5 percent for Vietnamese.[109] One possible explanation of the unusually high rate of poverty is that the Hmong tend to live in central California and the Midwest, where the cost of living, and level of income, tends to be lower.

NOTES

1. Major General Vang Pao did not come to the United States as a refugee, but as tourist with a Lao passport. Reportedly, the Thai government did not want him to stay in Thailand for fear that his stay would strain their diplomatic relationship with the soon to be new government of Laos, so they asked him to leave Thailand. According to the remarks of Xuwicha (Noi) Hiranprueck during the symposium on "The History Behind The Hmong Refugee Exodus," Major General Vang Pao did not want to leave Nam Phong Refugee Camp in Thailand. But was lured by Central Intelligence Agency agents and Thai secret agents to take a vacation in France and after a few days in France, he and his youngest wife were secretly sent to Missoula, Montana, in the United States. They took him to Missoula because some of his children were sent there earlier for schooling and Missoula is also the hometown of his Central Intelligence Agency case officer, Jerry "Hog" Daniels.

2. Quincy, Keith. 2000. *Harvesting Pa Chay's Wheat*. Eastern Washington University Press.

3. Dao, Yang, personal communication. November 3, 2016. According to Yang Dao, this Thai general diplomatically told Vang Pao that after a few years abroad, he may quietly return to Thailand. Also, that Vang Pao's son, who is attending the U.S. Military Academy at West Point, may come to Thailand and join the Thai Armed Forces after his graduation.

4. Lyblong Lynhiavu noted that a fortune teller had predicted in 1955, when Vang Pao was only a lieutenant, that he would become a very important man, his fortune would rise, and he would have a lot of power. But his fortunes depend completely on his wife, Niam Ntxhiav (known as Elder Mother). "When the time comes that Xia Thao is no longer with him, Lt. Vang Pao will only experience misfortunes and

calamities." Not long after Xia Thao's death in 2007, misfortunes found Vang Pao, who was arrested in 2007 and died in 2011. While Vang Pao was in jail, both of his two wives at home—Chia Moua (Txiab Muas) and Song Moua (Ntxhoo Muas)—drove from Santa Ana to visit him in Sacramento; their car was hit by another car, and they were both seriously injured. Chia Moua eventually died on August 22, 2009. Since then, Lynhiavu said Vang Pao continued to experience misfortunes and one problem after another; even Col. Ly Tou Pao, his brother in-law and closest ally, broke away from him in 2009. Consequently, his power and influence gradually declined. See Lyblong Lynhiavu. 2015. *The Liver and the Tongue: Memoir of Lyblong Lynhiavu.* Self-published, p. 94, footnote #10.

5. Yang, Pia, personal communication. September 26, 2015.

6. The account of the resettlement of Hmong in Missoula, including the Major General Vang Pao, is from Cha Moua, personal communication. September 2, 2015.

7. See, for example, Kou Yang. 2003. "Hmong Americans: A Review of Felt Needs, Problems, and Community Development." *Hmong Studies Journal*, 4:1–23. http://hmongstudies.com/YangHSJ4.pdf.

8. Yang, Kou. 2009. "The Experience of Hmong American: Three Decades in Retrospective Review." In G. Y. Lee, ed. *The Impact of Globalization and Transnationalism on the Hmong. Center for Hmong Studies Press.* Saint Paul, MN: Concordia University. http://concordia.csp.edu/eNews/CSPUpdate/Documents/hmong_studies_cover .pdf.

9. Yang, Kou. "The Experience of Hmong Americans: Three Decades in Retrospective Review." Plenary Address at the *First International Conference on Hmong Studies.* St. Paul, MN. March 10–11, 2006.

10. Bosher, Susan. 1997. "Language and Cultural Identity: A Study of Hmong Students at the Postsecondary Level." *TESOL Quarterly*, 31(3):593–603.

11. Yau, Jennifer. "The Foreign-Born Hmong in the United States." *Migration Policy Institute*, January 1, 2005. http://www.migrationpolicy.org/article/foreign-born -hmong-united-states.

12. Recalled MacAlan Thompson in his remarks at the symposium on, "The History Behind the Hmong Refugee Exodus." Fresno City College. August 22, 2015.

13. Hastings, Deborah. "Suicide Was The Last Resort For Hmong Refugee— Welfare Reform Cut Benefits To Woman's Family." *New York Times*, February 22, 1998. http://community.seattletimes.nwsource.com/archive/?date=19980222&s lug=2735914.

14. Kitano, Harry H.L., and Roger Daniels. 2001. *Asian Americans: Emerging Minorities* (third edition), 154. Upper Saddle River, NJ: Prentice Hall.

15. Fadiman, Anne. 2007. *The Spirit Catches You and You Fall Down*, 189. New York: Farrar, Straus and Giroux.

16. Asian American and Pacific Islander Data: Analysis of 2015 American Community Survey Microdata. http://aapidata.com/blog/wp-content/uploads/2017/04/ aapidata_OMB_edu_asn_origin-e1492492582195.png.

17. To learn more about the Hmong community of Missoula, this author visited the Hmong there in September 2014 and also on September 28–29, 2015. In his Sep-

tember 2014 visit, he went hunting on horseback in an attempt to gain insight into the real life of the Hmong in Missoula.

18. Cha Moua said he met Chong Toua and the Jones once, but never heard from them again. Chong Toua was an orphan and was taken in by the Jones. Cha Moua had heard that Chong Toua became a highly educated man and he either works for the U.S. State Department or the Central Intelligence Agency, and as result, Chong Toua made no contact with anyone.

19. Quincy, Keith. 2000. *Harvesting Pa Chay's Wheat.* Eastern Washington University Press.

20. Moua, Cha, personal communication. March 26, 2016. According to Cha Moua, Maj. Gen. Vang Pao privately confirmed to him in late 1977 that the Central Intelligence Agency had given him a monthly allowance of twenty-five hundred dollars.

21. Moua, Cha, personal communication. September 24, 2015.

22. Most of the account of Moua Sue and his life are based on the interview this author had with him in 1998, while he was visiting California.

23. This story was told to the author by Cha Moua, personal communication. October 6, 2015. Moua Sue came to Missoula because of Cha Moua, who had been in Missoula since 1973 to attend Hell Gate High School and later the University of Montana, Missoula.

24. Xiong, Even, personal communication. November 30, 2007.

25. Hou, Wanlin, personal communication. November 24, 2007.

26. 2015 American Community Survey—Minnesota Hmong Profile: 1 Year Estimates. http://www.hmongstudiesjournal.org/uploads/4/5/8/7/4587788/2015hmongacs.

27. To read more on Hmong's Second Migration, see Bulk, Jac. 1996. "Hmong on the Move: Understanding Secondary Migration." *Ethnic Studies Review* 19(1).

28. Yang, Kou, 2013. "The American Experience of the Hmong: A Historical Review." In Mark Pfeifer, Monica Chiu, and Kou Yang (eds.). *Diversity within Diaspora: Hmong Americans in the Twenty-First Century.* University of Hawaii Press.

29. Bliatout, Sam, personal communication. November 10, 2015.

30. See Lao Family Community of Minnesota, received a legal letter from a Law Firm representing Lao Family Foundation. From Suab Hmong TV. Created on Wednesday, September 16, 2015. "Lao Family Community of Minnesota received a legal letter from a Law Firm representing Lao Family Foundation." http://shrdo .com/lao-family-community-of-minnesota-received-a-legal-letter-from-a-law-firm -representing-lao-family-foundation/. September 16, 2015 - The latest development at *Lao Family Community of Minnesota.* ... This has evolved in community concerned due to *corruption.*

31. Melo, Fredericak. "Hmong Officials Say FBI Warning of Homeland Scam." *The Pioneer Press*, October 5, 2015. http://www.twincities.com/localnews/ci_28924882/ hmong-officials-say-fbi-warning-homeland-scam.

32. U.S. Attorneys » District of Minnesota » News. "Seng Xiong Convicted After Trial of Defrauding Hmong Elders." https://www.justice.gov/usao-mn/pr/seng-xiong -convicted-after-trial-defrauding-hmong-elders.

33. Munro, Donald. "Mai Der Vang Wins 2016 Walt Whitman Poetry Award." *The Fresno Bee*, March 23, 2016. http://www.fresnobee.com/news/local/article67888247 .html.

34. See Xeeseng Hmong Artist. http://www.seexeng.com/id98.html.

35. See Yer Za Vue Fine Art. http://www.yerzavue.com/#!artist/c161y.

36. Yang, Xee. "A Hmong: Thriving, A Business In Millions." *Hmong Globe*, February 15, 2016. http://hmongglobe.com/a-hmong-thriving-a%E2%80%A8-business -in-millions/.

37. Part of Shongleng Yang's story has been published in "The American Experience of the Hmong: A Historical Review." 2013. In Mark Pfeifer, Monica Chiu, and Kou Yang, eds. *Diversity within Diaspora: Hmong Americans in the Twenty-First Century.* University of Hawaii Press. http://www.uhpress.hawaii.edu/p-8939-978082 4835972.aspx.

38. Yang, Lee, personal communication. June 18, 2016.

39. Asian American and Pacific Islander Data: Analysis of 2015 American Community Survey Microdata. http://aapidata.com/blog/wp-content/uploads/2017/04/ aapidata_OMB_edu_asn_origin-e1492492582195.png.

40. See Mark Pfeifer. "Hmong Americans in the 2013 American Community Survey." Hmong Studies Internet Resource Center, November 2014. http://www .hmongstudiesjournal.org/uploads/4/5/8/7/4587788/2013_acs_hmong_analysis_ article_for_website.pdf.

41. Seng Alex Vang, University of California Disaggregated Data (Hmong Students). https://www.facebook.com/photo.php?fbid=10104902810325634&set=a.101 00262779334934.2682289.3312916&type=3&theater.

42. University of California, Disaggregated Enrollment and Degrees. https://www .universityofcalifornia.edu/disaggregated-data.

43. See "He's First Hmong to be Fresno Teacher." *Fresno Bee*, June 26, 1991.

44. See Amy Alexander. "Affirmative Action Plan Charter Schools' Cultural Gap." *Fresno Bee*, September 26, 1991.

45. At California State University, Stanislaus, candidates must meet three criteria to be granted the rank of professor emeritus. These three criteria are as follows: 1) the candidate must be standing full professor at the time of retirement, 2) the candidate must have taught at the institution for fifteen or more years, and 3) the rank of emeritus must be granted by the faculty senate.

46. Rev. Kou Seying (Kxf. Nyaj Kub Thoj) to join faculty. http://www.csl.edu/ 2015/07/rev-kou-seying-kxf-nyaj-kub-thoj-to-join-faculty/.

47. Laj Xiong provided this author with his brief biography. Personal communication. February 2, 2016.

48. Cheng Moua provided this author with his brief biography. It is mostly in his own words. (Personal communication. July 28, 2015).

49. Moua, Doua, personal Communication. March 7, 2016. To read more about Doua Moua and his work, go to: http://www.imdb.com/name/nm1732080/?ref_=nv_ sr_1.

50. See Junehli. http://www.junehli.com/a-daughters-debt-a-usc-thesis-documen tary/.

51. See Kao Choua Vue. http://www.kaochouavue.com/.

52. Chang, Phoua Porsha, personal communication. May 11, 2017.

53. Information for the biography of Paul C. Lo was gathered over the years, spanning nearly twenty years. Most of the time, it was informal gatherings and for the purposes of teaching.

54. Vielmetti, Bruce. "Nation's second Hmong-American judge is elected in Milwaukee County." *Milwaukee Journal Sentinel*, April 4, 2017. http://www.jsonline.com/story/news/politics/elections/2017/04/04/nations-second-hmong-american-judge-elected-milwaukee-county/100037470/.

55. Yang, Kou. 2008. "Hmong American Contemporary Experience." In Ling Huping, *Emerging Voices: The Experiences of Underrepresented Asian Americans*, 410. Rutgers University Press. http://rutgerspress.rutgers.edu/acatalog/Emerging_Voices.html.

56. "Campus Mainstay Chou Her Named Chief of Police." http://www.ucmerced.edu/news/2017/campus-mainstay-chou-her-named-chief-police.

57. Information of Hmong in the military is mostly from Master Sergeant Shua P. Yang. Personal communication. September 16, 2015.

58. 2008–2010 American Community Survey 3-Year Estimates. https://www.census.gov/newsroom/releases/archives/american_community_survey_acs/cb11-tps40.html.

59. Minnesota Public Radio. Doualy Xaykaothao. http://www.mpr.org/about/people/doualy@mpr.org.

60. HOAP NEWS. "Vang Appointed Assistant Director of Diversity and Inclusion Programs." Spring 2014. http://diversity.harvard.edu/files/diversity/files/newsletter_spring_2014.pdf?m=1422562985.

61. See "Lao Multi-Ethnic Solidarity Committee's Donation Relief for Flood and Disaster Relief in Laos." http://www.laoembassy.com/.

62. Lintereur, Josh. "Hmong Giving Back to Home Country." *The Sheboygan Press*, November 24, 2011. http://pqasb.pqarchiver.com/sheboyganpress/access/2522059071.html?FMT=ABS&date=Nov+24%2C+2011.

63. Xiong, Arick, and Susan Xiong, personal communication. April 28, 2017.

64. Bliatout, Sam, personal communication. November 10, 2015.

65. Labott, Elise. "First on CNN: Obama to Push to Clear Leftover Vietnam-era Bombs." *CNN Politics*, January 25, 2015. http://www.cnn.com/2016/01/24/politics/john-kerry-laos-secret-war/.

66. Ibid.

67. Yang, Kou. "Prof. Kou Yang: The deadly, horrible mess we made still plagues Indochina." *Modesto Bee*, April 4, 2015. http://www.modbee.com/opinion/opn-columns-blogs/community-columns/article17237951.html.

68. Labott, Elise. "First on CNN: Obama to Push to Clear Leftover Vietnam-era Bombs." *CNN Politics*, January 25, 2015. http://www.cnn.com/2016/01/24/politics/john-kerry-laos-secret-war/.

69. Wan, William. "Obama pledges $90 million to help clear remnants of U.S. bombing in Laos." *Washington Post*, September 6, 2016. https://www.washingtonpost.com/world/obama-pledges-90-million-to-help-clear-remnants-of-us-bombing

-in-laos/2016/09/06/f7d9db6a-6ee1-11e6-993f-73c693a89820_story.html?utm_
term=.696ac0747827.

70. The White House, Office of the Press Secretary. "Joint Declaration between
the United States of America and the Lao People Democratic Republic." https://
obamawhitehouse.archives.gov/the-press-office/2016/09/06/joint-declaration
-between-united-states-america-and-lao-peoples.

71. To read more on Nhiavue Lobliayao, see Kou Yang. 2000. "The Passing of
a Hmong Pioneer: Nhiavu Lobliayao (Nyiaj Vws Lauj Npliaj Yob), 1915–1999."
Hmong Studies Journal 3. http://hmongstudies.com/HSJv3_Yang.pdf.

72. Yang, Kou. 2000. "The Passing of a Hmong Pioneer: Nhiavu Lobliayao (Nyiaj
Vws Lauj Npliaj Yob), 1915–1999." *Hmong Studies Journal* 3. http://hmongstudies.
com/HSJv3_Yang.pdf.

73. Yang, Kou. 2013. *Laos and Its Expatriates in the United States*, 159. PublishAmerica.

74. Ponnudurai, Parameswaran. "Air Crash Kills Senior Lao Officials, Leaves
Power Vacuum." *Radio Free Asia*, May 18, 2014. http://www.rfa.org/english/news/
laos/crash-05182014150850.html.

75. See, for example, Khammy Naotouayang. 2014. ວິລະຊົນ ທ້າ. ຍາໄຊຈູ ແລະ *52* ປີ
ຂອງສຽງປືນຈາກທົ່ງໄຫຫີນ *(Hero Thotou Yaxaychou and 52 years of the Sound of Gun
in the Plain of Jars)*. Printing House of Lao Writers.

76. Touxa Lyfounbg. 1996. *Touby Lyfoung: An Authentic Account of the Life
of a Hmong Man in the Troubled Land of Laos*, 157–82. Edina, MN: Burgess
Publishing.

77. See "Secret War, Secret Strategy in Laos." In McCoy, *The Politics of Heroin
in Southeast Asia*. http://druglibrary.eu/library/books/McCoy/book/54.htm.

78. Anonymous, personal communication. December 18, 2014.

79. Yangsao, Sayasith Lyfoung, personal communication. November 2 and 7,
2009.

80. Barney, George L. 1990. *The Meo of Xieng Khouang Province*, 5. In Joel M.
Halpern, ed. Christiansburg, VA: Dalley Book Service. http://www.renincorp.org/
bookshelf/the-meo-of-xieng-khoung_bar.pdf.

81. Lyfoung, Tougeu, personal communication. June 22, 1999.

82. Dao, Yang, personal communication. June 30, 2011.

83. Anonymous, personal communication. January 19, 2009.

84. Hamilton-Merritt, Jane. 1999. *The Tragic Mountains*, 387. Indiana University
Press.

85. Mottin, Jean. 1982. *History of the Hmong*, 54. Bangkok: Odeon Book Store.

86. Anonymous, personal communication. January 23, 2010.

87. I use the title "Rhino among the Elephants" to refer to Touby Lyfoung because
he was born in the highlands of Nong Het (Rhino Lake) District, but spent much of his
life working and living among the Lao, who are descents of the people of the Kingdom of A Million Elephants. Reportedly, Faydang Lobliayao, his maternal uncle and
nemesis, had used the name Rhino to refer to Touby Lyfoung as well.

88. Information for the biography of Tougeu Lyfoung was gathered during several meetings with him in 1999. The last meeting was on June 22, 1999. Tougeu Lyfoung, personal communication. June 22, 1999.

89. Vue, May, personal communication. September 15, 2015. May Ly Vue is a half-sister of Mao Soua Lo.

90. Cha, Lao Chue, personal communication. April 14, 2009.

91. Sue, Col. Moua, personal communication. September 25, 2015.

92. During the war years, he was known as Tswv Xyas by Hmong civilian leaders, Hnub Qub Dawb (White Star) by his Hmong soldiers, and Keo Pha Khao by his Lao soldiers and colleagues.

93. Lynhiavu, Lyblong. 2015. *The Liver and the Tongue: Memoir of Lyblong Lynhiavu*, 93. Self-published.

94. Ibid, 93.

95. Ibid, 94.

96. See National Intelligence Bulletin. May 12, 1975. http://www.foia.cia.gov/sites/default/files/document conversions/5829/CIA-RDP79T00975A027700010020-2.pdf. It says in part that "Vang Pao has acceded to Souvanna's request that he resign his command in Northern Laos. Over the weekend, he dispatched about [one hundred] of his followers and their families by air from Long Tieng to Udorn, Thailand."

97. It needs to note here that in 1989, the *Washington Post* published an article alleging Neo Home and Maj. Gen. Vang Pao ripping off Hmong refugees. See Hammond, Ruth. "Sad Suspicions of a Refugee Rip Off." *Washington Post*, April 16, 1980. https://www.washingtonpost.com/archive/opinions/1989/04/16/sad-suspicions-of-a-refugee-ripoff/9d240948-ddee-496c-86ce-e1bd9fde736e/.

98. Moua, Wameng. "Leader in Trouble: 77-year-old General Vang Pao Arrested." *Hmong Today: Twin-Cities Daily Planet*, June 20, 2007. http://www.tcdailyplanet.net/leader-trouble-77-year-old-general-vang-pao-arrested/.

99. Ganjanakhundee, Supalak. "Laos Says No to Gen Vang Pao's Plea." *The Nation*, December 15, 2009. http://www.nationmultimedia.com/2009/12/25/regional/regional_30119180.php.

100. See Douangxay Luangphasy, 2012. *Pavaxath Phongsavadan Lao (ປະວັດສາດ ພົງສະຫວະດານລາວ)*, 171. Nakhone Si Printing House.

101. According to Col. Chou Peter Vang, Touby Lyfoung negotiated with both Maj. Gen. Vang Pao and Captain Ly Fu to settle this case out secretly and of the military court. Vang, Peter Chou, personal communication. October 22, 2009.

102. See Shong Lue Yang. http://en.wikipedia.org/wiki/Shong_Lue_Yang.

103. According to Alfred McCoy, Vang Pao also attempted an assassination on Col. Khamhou Boussarath, the Xieng Khouang sub-division commander. See Alfred McCoy. 1972. *The Politics of Heroin in Southeast Asia* (first edition). Harper & Row. http://druglibrary.eu/library/books/McCoy/book/54.htm.

104. Lynhiavu, Lyblong. 2015. *The Liver and the Tongue: Memoir of Lyblong Lynhiavu*, 18. Self-published.

105. The content of this biography is gathered through many interviews with Major Ly Fu, including the interview on December 18, 2014. Disclaimer: This is a

short version of Ly Fu's long biography. Major Ly Fu, who is fluent in English, has carefully read this biography and acknowledged that the content in this biography is true to the best of his knowledge.

106. The 1973 Peace and National Reconciliation Agreement between the Royal Lao government and the Communist Pathet Lao stipulated that the two sides nominated equal nominees to the National Political Consultative Council, and the king formally appointed them to the National Political Consultative Council. Yang Dao was nominated by the Royal Lao government side, and Lo Fong, another Hmong, was nominated by the side of the Pathet Lao.

107. Biographical information of Dr. Yang Dao was gathered during my many meetings with him over the last twenty-five years. The last interview was took place at the end of 2016. Dao, Yang, personal communication. November 3, 2016.

108. Milk, Leslie. "The Most Powerful Women in Washington, DC." *Washingtonian.com*, November 12, 2015. http://www.washingtonian.com/blogs/capital comment/power-players/the-most-powerful-women-in-washington-dc.php.

109. Wilson, Valerie. "2013 ACS Shows Depth of Native American Poverty and Different Degrees of Economic Well-Being for Asian Ethnic Groups." Economy Policy Institute, September 18, 2014. http://www.epi.org/blog/2013-acs-shows -depth-native-american-poverty/.

REFERENCES

Alexander, Amy. "Affirmative Action Plan Charter Schools' Cultural Gap." Fresno Bee, September 26, 1991.

Barney, George L. 1990. The Meo of Xieng Khouang Province. Joel M. Halpern, ed. Christiansburg, VA: Dalley Book Service. http://www.renincorp.org/bookshelf/ the-meo-of-xieng-khoung_bar.pdf.

Bosher, Susan, 1997. "Language and Cultural Identity: A study of Hmong Students at the Postsecondary Level." TESOL Quarterly 31(3):593–603.

Fadiman, Anne. 2007. The Spirit Catches You and You Fall Down. New York: Farrar, Straus and Giroux.

Ganjanakhundee, Supalak. "Laos says No to Gen Vang Pao's Plea." The Nation, December 15, 2009. http://www.nationmultimedia.com/2009/12/25/regional/regional _30119180.php.

Hamilton-Merritt, Jane. 1999. The Tragic Mountains. Indiana University Press.

Hammond, Ruth. "Sad Suspicions of a Refugee Rip Off." *Washington Post*, April 16, 1980. https://www.washingtonpost.com/archive/opinions/1989/04/16/sad -suspicions-of-a-refugee-ripoff/9d240948-ddee-496c-86ce-e1bd9fde736e/.

Hasting, Deborah. "Suicide Was The Last Resort For Hmong Refugee — Welfare Reform Cut Benefits To Woman's Family." New York Times, February 22, 1998. http://community.seattletimes.nwsource.com/archive/?date=19980222&slug= 2735914.

Kitano, Harry H.L., and Roger Daniels. 2001. Asian Americans: Emerging Minorities (third edition). Upper Saddle River, NJ: Prentice Hall.

Labott, Elise. "First on CNN: Obama to Push to Clear Leftover Vietnam-era Bombs." CNN Politics, January 25, 2015. http://www.cnn.com/2016/01/24/politics/john -kerry-laos-secret-war/.

Lintereur, Josh. "Hmong Giving Back to Home Country." The Sheboygan Press, November 24, 2011. http://pqasb.pqarchiver.com/sheboyganpress/access/2522059071 .html?FMT=ABS&date=Nov+24%2C+2011.

Luangphasy, Douangxay, Pavaxath Phongsavadan Lao (ປະວັດສາດ ພົງສະວະດານລາວ). 2012. Nakhone Si Printing House, 171.

Lyfoung, Touxa. 1996. Touby Lyfoung: An Authentic Account of the Life of a Hmong Man in the Troubled Land of Laos. Edina, MN: Burgess Publishing.

Lynhiavu, Lyblong. 2015. The Liver and the Tongue: Memoir of Lyblong Lynhiavu. Self-published.

McCoy, Alfred. 1972. The Politics of Heroin in Southeast Asia (first edition). Harper & Row. http://druglibrary.eu/library/books/McCoy/book/54.htm.

Melo, Frederick. "Hmong Officials say FBI Warning of Homeland Scam." The Pioneer Press, October 5, 2015. http://www.twincities.com/localnews/ci_28924882/ hmong-officials-say-fbi-warning-homeland-scam.

Milk, Leslie. "The Most Powerful Women in Washington, DC." Washingtonian. com, November 12, 2015. http://www.washingtonian.com/blogs/capitalcomment/ power-players/the-most-powerful-women-in-washington-dc.php.

Mottin, Jean. 1982. History of the Hmong, 54. Bangkok: Odeon Book Store.

Moua, Wameng. "Leader in Trouble: 77-year-old General Vang Pao Arrested." Twin-Cities Daily Planet, June 20, 2007. http://www.tcdailyplanet.net/leader-trouble -77-year-old-general-vang-pao-arrested/.

Munro, Donald. "Mai Der Vang Wins 2016 Walt Whitman Poetry Award." The Fresno Bee, March 23, 2016. http://www.fresnobee.com/news/local/article67888247.html.

Naotouayang, Khammy. 2014. ວິລະຊົນ ທ້າ. ຍາໄຊ ແລະ 52 ປີ ຂອງສຽງປືນຈາກທົ່ງໄຫຫິນ (Hero Thotou Yaxaychou and 52 years of the Sound of Gun in the Plain of Jars). Printing House of Lao Writers.

Pfeifer, Mark. November 2014. "Hmong Americans in the 2013 American Community Survey." Hmong Studies Internet Resource Center. http://www.hmongstudiesjournal .org/uploads/4/5/8/7/4587788/2013_acs_hmong_analysis_article_for_website.pdf.

Ponnudurai, Parameswaran. May 18, 2014. "Air Crash Kills Senior Lao Officials, Leaves Power Vacuum." Radio Free Asia. http://www.rfa.org/english/news/laos/ crash-05182014150850.html.

Quincy, Keith. 2000. Harvesting Pa Chay's Wheat. Eastern Washington University Press.

Wilson, Valerie. "2013 ACS Shows Depth of Native American Poverty and Different Degrees of Economic Well-Being for Asian Ethnic Groups." Economy Policy Institute, September 18, 2014. http://www.epi.org/blog/2013-acs-shows-depth -native-american-poverty/.

Yang, Kou. 2013. Laos and Its Expatriates in the United States. PublishAmerica.

———. 2013. "The American Experience of the Hmong: A Historical Review." In Mark Pfeifer, Monica Chiu, and Kou Yang, eds. Diversity within Diaspora: Hmong Americans in the Twenty-First Century. University of Hawaii Press.

———. 2009. "The Experience of Hmong Americans: Three Decades in Retrospective Review." In G. Y. Lee, ed. The Impact of Globalization and Transnationalism on the Hmong. Center for Hmong Studies Press. Saint Paul, MN: Concordia University.

———. 2008. "Hmong American Contemporary Experience." In Ling Huping. Emerging Voices: The Experiences of Underrepresented Asian Americans. Rutgers University Press.

———. 2003. "Hmong Americans: A Review of Felt Needs, Problems, and Community Development." Hmong Studies Journal, 4:1–23. http://hmongstudies.com/YangHSJ4.pdf.

———. 2000 (Winter). "The Passing of a Hmong Pioneer: Nhiavu Lobliayao (Nyiaj Vws Lauj Npliaj Yob), 1915 1999." Hmong Studies Journal, 3. http://hmongstudies.com/HSJv3_Yang.pdf.

Yang, Xee. "A Hmong Thriving, A Business In Millions." Hmong Globe, February 15, 2016. http://hmongglobe.com/a-hmong-thriving-a%E2%80%A8-business-in-millions/.

Yau, Jennifer. "The Foreign-Born Hmong in the United States." Migration Policy Institute, January 1, 2005. http://www.migrationpolicy.org/article/foreign-born-hmong-united-states.

Chapter Six

Conclusion

Although the United Nations High Commissioner on Refugees has initially refused to consider Hmong as refugees, and the United States has labeled Hmong and other highland refugees from Laos as "unsuitable for resettlement in the United States," the strong and forceful advocacy of many individuals both inside and outside of the United States has made it possible for the resettlement of Hmong refugees into the United States. The so-called unsuitable Hmong refugees were initially faced with many acculturation problems, but gradually, they have overcome many barriers through their hard work ethics and resiliency; they have made remarkable footprints from the arts to education, from business to economic development successes, and from high-tech to political participation. The Hmong American communities have made a visible and vibrant presence of entrepreneurial success in St. Paul, Minnesota, and Fresno, California. The large percentage of a young population means that Hmong Americans have the potential to fill up many robust labor markets and industrial sectors where the current workforce will soon be retiring.

Although no study has been done on factors that contribute to Hmong Americans' many success stories, speculation can be made on a few factors:

1. American laws, such as the civil rights laws and others that provide equal opportunity in education, employment, economic development, and voting rights, do greatly protect and benefit Hmong Americans.
2. Kindergarten through twelfth-grade education is free to all children in the country.
3. Free meals are provided to all students from low-income families.
4. The American socialist system provides financial assistance and medical benefits to unemployed parents and low-income families.

5. Generous scholarships and public student financial aid are provided to promising students regardless of their ethnicity and race, who can go beyond a high school level. Many Hmong students, for example, would not have entered Harvard, Yale, and Stanford Universities without generous scholarships and financial aid.

6. Affirmative action programs that allow promising disadvantaged students to get into higher learning institutions, even though their grade point average may have been lower than students from the majority ethnic group. Moreover, affirmative action also made it possible for many young Hmong to enter various professions in the city, county, state, and federal government.

7. Educational incentives in terms of getting jobs, economic gain, and other privileges that come with an education. Jobs are usually given to the best qualified and most talented applicants, and as a result, anyone with a college education will likely get a job and possible promotions. Consequently, their economy will improve and their social standing in the community will improve as well.

8. Incentive of speaking more than one language; in California, for example, those who speak more than one language are preferred over those who speak only one language by government agencies. Additionally, they will receive extra pay for their bilingual skills.

9. Societal inclusiveness in the manner that ethnic identity is encouraged and diversity is honored and valued in school as well as in the community. The Hmong New Year in Fresno, for example, is now considered a part of the festivities of the City of Fresno. Moreover, Hmong culture and history are included in the curriculum of many universities in California, Minnesota, and Wisconsin that have a sizeable Hmong student population.

10. Unlike pre-1950 Asian immigrants to the United States, Hmong refugees did come, mostly, as families, and in Hmong culture, the family has always been the backbone of survival from the past to the present. Moreover, the strong family support system enables Hmong individuals or groups to pursue education, business enterprise, and other endeavors.

11. Lastly, the strong traditional values of Hmong culture and beliefs have been a part of their guidance where their parents and great-grandparents had always taught them the important ethics of working hard, to be independent but never be separate from the bond of extended families, and to be responsible to both one's family and one's community obligations. Some of these limited successes can also be attributed to American values where the Hmong always believe that to be successful, one must keep pursuing the American dream. This ideal is a new phenomenon that

makes the new Americans embrace American capitalism and free market opportunities.

One could argue that the remarkable success of Hmong Americans is a testament to proving all those critics wrong about their misperceptions about Hmong refugees from the early days of the resettlement where they insisted that the Hmong would not be well integrated into mainstream American society. By giving the Hmong refugees a chance with access to education and business opportunities, they (the Hmong) would do well, become economically self-sufficient, be able to own a home, and continue to be productive citizens of their new adopted country, the United States of America. In retrospect, the Hmong have been a people of diaspora for about five thousand years; their long history, as mentioned before, has been a constant struggle through series of devastating wars, long migrations, oppressions, and suppressions by outsiders. The Hmong have been pushed and pulled to be displaced from ancient China into southeast Asia, and lastly by crossing the Pacific Ocean to the Americas. After 1975, the Hmong have been further dispersed onto five continents, but no other Hmong community has adapted and been supported as well as the Hmong American community in terms of education, economic development, cultural preservation, Hmong studies, political participation, and institutions, such as the Center for Hmong Studies, Center for Hmong Arts and Talents, Hmong Cultural Centre, and Hmong newspapers, radios, and television programs. Only in the United States can the Hmong thrive and build a vibrant community. Only in the United States can the Hmong dress in their costumes and speak Hmong in public, and only in the United States can the Hmong hold their heads high and dare to enter many professions, such as law, politics, high-tech, space exploration, and university teaching.

The future of Hmong Americans depends on their very young population, who need a good education, role models, jobs, and equal opportunities. The priority of the Hmong American community should be to build a better future, rather than to keep fighting for the past. They need to learn from mistakes in the past and recognize that the past cannot be changed. They need to forge forward to the future where they can join the larger mainstream communities to build a better world with peace and prosperity. The fortieth anniversary of Hmong resettlement in the United States is an opportunity to reflect on the past, honor their legacy and experiences, and set a new direction of where to go from here. As the conventional wisdom says, "A failure to plan is a plan to fail." The leadership of this community must plan and envision what they want to have in the twenty-first century, and what the community needs from technology, globalization, third-world consumerism, and the Internet.

There is no other choice; the Hmong must change and adapt to their socio-economic, educational, and political environments, and they must do this in a responsible and sustainable way. A Hmong television reporter asked me recently during an interview about the state of Hmong America, "Will there be Hmong in the next forty years?" My answer is simply this: "If Hmong have survived the last five thousand years, and forty years in America, there is no reason for me to believe that Hmong will not survive the next forty years as a people with unique culture, history, and identity." I also added that the Hmong American forty years from now would not be the same as the Hmong American today. Culture is not static; it changes and evolves with time, political, socio-economic, technological, and educational environments. As Confucius said, "Only the wisest and stupidest of men never change." Also, Charles Darwin said, "It is not the strongest of the species that survives or the most intelligent, but rather the one most adaptable to change." Throughout our long history and diaspora experience, the Hmong have adapted and borrowed the best from others. Hmong language today, for example, includes borrowed/adopted words from Mandarin, Vietnamese, Lao, Thai, French, and English. Their food, too, is a fusion of many cultures, including, but not limited to, Han Chinese, Vietnamese, Lao, Thai, and French. In most Hmong American feastings, one is likely to find Vietnamese Pho and Chả giò, Lao Laab and Khao Poun, French salad, Thai Tom Yum, in addition to a few traditional Hmong dishes. Laotzu also said, "Nothing is softer or more flexible than water, yet nothing can resist it." Hmong need to be soft and flexible, adaptable, and as gentle as water, but flowing in a non-stop streamline. In my book, *The Hmong and Their Odyssey*, I wrote that the "Hmong, like bristlecone pines on the rock, have been exposed to all types of weather, climate and conditions, but they won't die."[1] They won't die because of *hope*. They do not disappear because of their perseverance, adaptability, strength, and pride of their identity. There will be more changes in the years to come and more obstacles are ahead of them; the Hmong need to be prepared for any challenges blocking their way and any obstacles preventing them from getting to their destination. If one cannot remove or minimize the obstacle, find a new path and get a new idea to get to where one wants to go. The conventional saying has it that "when there is a will, there is a way."

In discussing changes and cultural loss, Chao Lee said, "While the global transformation of the Hmong people have yielded some of the greatest and unprecedented positive benefits of our time like the spread of our Diaspora throughout the globe, advancements in higher education, and joining the industrialized and modernized communities; however, the drastic changes also yielded tremendous loss, i.e. our linguistics system, our culture, our customs, our religion, our traditions, and above all our heritage. These are the inevitable changes that Hmong have no choice but to accept the unacceptable. We have to face the reality as time and space travel together."[2]

The Hmong, who were pre-judged "not suitable for resettlement in America" in 1975, have now slowly risen from the rubbles of the Secret War and have contributed their very best to America. No one knows the hardships of being refugees and people of diaspora more than the Hmong. Young Hmong Americans should always remember that their ancestors were poor and desperate refugees; therefore, they must do what they can to help refugees anywhere who are now desperately in need of help and a voice. We must work hard and share our earnings with those that have needs. We must study hard and use the power of our education to serve our society, humanity, and lend our voice for those who do not have a voice.

I want to conclude this book with a thought that "good things will not come out from the sky, emerge from the sea or from any mighty being, it can only come from hard work, perseverance, dedication, commitment, and doing the right thing at the right time." Hmong must embrace science, technology, innovation, and the know-how; if they don't adapt and change, technology and globalization will change them. Taking control is better than letting something else control you and your destiny. As Laozi said, "A journey of a thousand miles begins with a single step." I urge all Hmong to take that very single step and be a part of the catalyst for the twenty-first century, and not be a victim of it.

NOTES

1. Kou Yang. 2016. *The Hmong & Their Odyssey: A Roots-Searching Journey of an American Professor*. Self-published, p. 120.
2. Chao Lee, personal communication. February 22, 2016.

REFERENCE

Yang, Kou. 2016. *The Hmong & Their Odyssey: A Roots-Searching Journey of an American Professor*. Self-published, p. 120.

Bibliography

Ahern, Thomas L. Jr. 2006. *Undercover Armies: CIA and Surrogate Warfare in Laos 1961-1973*. Center for the Studies of Intelligence. Declassified on February 19, 2009. http://nsarchive.gwu.edu/NSAEBB/NSAEBB284/6-UNDERCOVER_ARMIES.pdf.

Alexander, Amy. "Affirmative Action Plan Charts Schools' Cultural Gap." *Fresno Bee*, September 26, 1991.

Barney, George L. 1990. *The Meo of Xieng Khouang Province*. Joel M. Halpern, ed. Christiansburg, VA: Dalley Book Service. http://www.renincorp.org/bookshelf/the-meo-of-xieng-khoung_bar.pdf.

Blaufarb, Douglas S. 1997. *The Counterinsurgency Era: U.S. Doctrine and Performance, 1950 to the Present*. New York: The Free Press.

Bliatout, Bruce, B.T. Downing, J. Lewis, and D. Yang. 1988. *Handbook for Teaching Hmong-Speaking Students*. Folsom, CA: Folsom Cordova Unified School District, Southeast Asia Community Resource Center.

Bosher, Susan. 1997. "Language and Cultural Identity: A Study of Hmong Students at the Postsecondary Level." *TESOL Quarterly* 31(3):593–603.

Brown, MacAllister and Joseph J. Zasloff. 1986. *Apprentice Revolutionaries: The Communist Movement in Laos, 1930-1985*. Hoover Institution Press.

Bulk, Jac, February 1996. "Hmong on the Move: Understanding Secondary Migration." *Ethnic Studies Review* 19(1).

Cha, Dia. 2003. *Hmong American Concepts of Health, Healing, and Conventional Medicine*. New York: Routledge.

Castle, Timothy N. 1995. *At War in the Shadow of Vietnam: U.S. Military Aid to the Royal Lao Government - 1955-1975*. New York: Columbia University Press. https://books.google.com/books?isbn=023107977X.

Chan, Sucheng. 1994. *Hmong Means Free*. Philadelphia: Temple University Press.

Conboy, Kenneth. 1995. *Shadow War: The CIA's Secret War in Laos*. Boulder, CO: Paladin Press.

Cooper, Rober, Nicholas Tapp, Gary Yia Lee, and Gretel Schwoer-Kohl. 1991. *The Hmong*. Bangkok, Thailand: Artasia Press.

Cooper, Robert (Ed.). 1998. *The Hmong: A Guide to Traditional Lifestyles*. Singapore: Times Editions.

Dommen Jr., Arthur. 1985. *Laos: Keystone of Indochina*. Boulder, CO: Westview Press.

Fadiman, Anne. 2007. *The Spirit Catches You and You Fall Down*. New York: Farrar, Straus and Giroux.

Gerdner, Linda A. (Author), and Shoua V. Xiong (Contributor). 2016. *Demystifying Hmong Shamanism: Practice and Use*. Bauu Press.

Garrett, W.E. 1974. "No Place to Run: The Hmong of Laos," *National Geographic* 145(1):78–111.

Ganjanakhundee, Supalak. "Laos says No to Gen Vang Pao's Plea." *The Nation*, December 15, 2009. http://www.nationmultimedia.com/2009/12/25/regional/regional_30119180.php.

Hamilton-Merritt, Jane. 1999. *The Tragic Mountains*. Indiana University Press.

Hasting, Deborah. "Suicide Was The Last Resort For Hmong Refugee--Welfare Reform Cut Benefits To Woman's Family." *New York Times*, February 22, 1998. http://community.seattletimes.nwsource.com/archive/?date=19980222&slug=2735914.

Heine, Jeremy. 1995. *From Vietnam, Laos and Cambodia: A Refugee Experience*. Twayne Publisher.

Her, Vincent, and Mary Louise Buley-Meissner (Eds.). 2012. *Hmong and American: From Refugees to Citizens*. Minnesota: Minnesota Historical Society.

Hillmer, Paul. 2010. *A People's History of The Hmong*. Minnesota Historical Society Press.

Kitano, Harry H.L., and Roger Daniels. 2001. *Asian Americans: Emerging Minorities* (third edition). Upper Saddle River, NJ: Prentice Hall.

Labott, Elise. "First on CNN: Obama to Push to Clear Leftover Vietnam-era Bombs." *CNN Politics*, January 25, 2015. http://www.cnn.com/2016/01/24/politics/john-kerry-laos-secret-war/.

Lemoine, Jacques. 2005. "What is the Actual Number of the (H)mong in the World?" *Hmong Studies Journal* 6. http://hmongstudies.org/LemoineHSJ6.pdf.

———. 1972. *Un village Hmong Vert du haut Laos*. Paris: Centre National de la Recherche Scientifique.

Lee, Gary Yia. 1985/1986. *Ethnic Minorities and National Building in Laos: The Hmong in the Lao State*. School of Behavioural Sciences, Macquarie University, North Ryde, Australia. Published in: Peninsule, No.11/12: 215-232.

———. "Minority Policies and the Hmong in Laos." In Martin Stuart-Fox, ed. *Contemporary Laos: Studies in the Politics and Society of the Lao People's Democratic Republic*, 199–219. St. Lucia: Queensland University Press. http://members.ozemail.com.au/~yeulee/History/minority%20policies%20and%20the%20hmong%20in%20laos.html.

Lee, Mai Na M. 1997. "The Thousand-Year Myth: Construction and Characterization of Hmong." *Hmong Studies Journal* 2(1). http://hmongstudies.com/HSJ-v2n1_Lee.pdf.

Lilley, James, and Jeremy Lilley. 2004. *China Hands*. New York: Public Affairs.

Lintereur, Josh. "Hmong Giving Back to Home Country." *The Sheboygan Press*, November 24, 2011. http://pqasb.pqarchiver.com/sheboyganpress/access/2522059071.html?FMT=ABS&date=Nov+24%2C+2011.

Luangphasay, Douangxay. 2012. *Pavaxath Phongsavadan Lao*. Nakhone Si Printing House.

Luong, Minh Phuong, and Wolfgang Nieke. "Minority Status and Schooling of the Hmong in Vietnam." 2013. *Hmong Studies Journal* 14:1–37. http://hmongstudies.org/LuongandNiekeHSJ14.pdf.

Lyfoung, Touxa. 1996. *Touby Lyfoung: An Authentic Account of the Life of a Hmong Man in the Troubled Land of Laos*. Edina, MN: Burgess Publishing.

Lynhiavu, Lyblong. 2015. *The Liver and the Tongue: Memoir of Lyblong Lynhiavu*. Self-published.

McCoy, Alfred. 1972. *The Politic of Heroin in Southeast Asia* (first edition). Harper & Row. http://druglibrary.eu/library/books/McCoy/book/54.htm.

Melo, Frederick Melo. "Hmong Officials say FBI Warning of Homeland Scam." *The Pioneer Press*, October 5, 2015. http://www.twincities.com/localnews/ci_28924882/hmong-officials-say-fbi-warning-homeland-scam.

Morrison, Gayle L. 2013. *Hog's Exit: Jerry Daniels, the Hmong, and the CIA*. Lubbock, TX: Texas Tech University Press.

Mottin, Jean. 1982. *History of the Hmong*. Bangkok: Odeon Book Store.

Moua, Wameng. "Leader in Trouble: 77-year-old General Vang Pao Srrested." *Hmong Today: Twin Cities Daily Planet*, June 20, 2007. http://www.tcdailyplanet.net/leader-trouble-77-year-old-general-vang-pao-arrested/.

———. "The Scholar Hero: The Untold Story of How Dr. Yang Dao Negotiated the Fate of By." *Hmong Today: Twin Cities Daily Planet*, April 13, 2008. http://www.tcdailyplanet.net/scholar-hero-untold-story-how-dr-yang-dao-negotiated-fate/.

Mydans, Seth. "Nomads of Laos: Last Leftovers of Vietnam War." *New York Times*, March 12, 1997. http://www.nytimes.com/1997/03/12/world/nomads-of-laos-last-leftovers-of-vietnam-war.html.

Naotouayang, Khammy. 2014. ວິລະຊົນ ທົ່ງ ຍາໄຊຈູ ແລະ 52 ປີ ຂອງສຽງປືນຈາກທົ່ງໄຫຫີນ *(Hero Thotou Yaxaychou and 52 years of the Sound of Gun in the Plain of Jars)*. Printing House of Lao Writers.

Pfeifer, Mark E., et al. 2012. "Hmong Population and Demographic Trends in the 2010 Census and 2010 American Community." *Hmong Studies Journal* 13(2):1–31. http://hmongstudies.org/PfeiferSullivanKYangWYangHSJ13.2.pdf.

———. 2014. "Hmong Americans in the 2013 American Community Survey." *Hmong Studies Internet Resource Center*, November 2014. http://www.hmongstudiesjournal.org/uploads/4/5/8/7/4587788/2013_acs_hmong_analysis_article_for_website.pdf.

———. 2005. *Annotated Bibliography of Hmong-Related Works 1996-2004*. Saint Paul: Hmong Resource Center of the Hmong Cultural Center.

Quincy, Keith. 2000. *Harvesting Pa Chay's Wheat*. Eastern Washington University Press.

Ranard, Donald A. (Ed.). 2004. *The Hmong: An Introduction to their History and Culture*. Washington, DC: Center for Applied Linguistics.

Robins, Christopher Robbins. 1987. *The Ravens*. New York, NY: Crown Publishers.

Robinson, W Courtland. 1998. *Terms of Refuge*. New York: Zed Books Ltd.

Rosenblatt, Lionel. "How the Hmong Came to be in the U.S." A paper to be published in final form by the Center for Hmong Studies, Concordia University St. Paul.

Sananikone, Oudone (Major General). 1984. The Royal Lao Army and U.S. Army advice and support (Indochina monographs).

Tapp, Nicholas. 1986. *The Hmong of Thailand: Opium People of the Golden Triangle*. Cambridge, MA: Anti-Slavery Society.

Van Staaveren, Jacob. 1993. *Interdiction in Southern Laos, 1960 - 1968. Center for Air Force History (IV)*. Washington, DC: Library of Congress. http://www.afhso.af.mil/shared/media/document/AFD-100927-078.pdf.

Vang, Chia Youyee, Faith Nibbs, and Ma Vang (Eds.). 2016. *Claiming Place: On the Agency of Hmong Women*. Minnesota: University of Minnesota Press.

Vielmetti, Bruce. "Nation's second Hmong-American judge is elected in Milwaukee County." *Milwaukee Journal Sentinel*, April 4, 2017. http://www.jsonline.com/story/news/politics/elections/2017/04/04/nations-second-hmong-american-judge-elected-milwaukee-county/100037470/.

Vilaysack, Mothana. 2011. *Roots of Souphanouvong (ຕາ ສຸພານຸວົງ)*. Self-published.

Vongsavanh, Soutchay. 1981. *RLG Military Operation and Activities in the Laotian Panhandle*. Virginia: Dally Book Service.

Wan, William. "Obama pledges $90 million to help clear remnants of U.S. bombing in Laos." *Washington Post*, September 6, 2016. https://www.washingtonpost.com/world/obama-pledges-90-million-to-help-clear-remnants-of-us-bombing-in-laos/2016/09/06/f7d9db6a-6ee1-11e6-993f-73c693a89820_story.html?utm_term=.696ac0747827.

Warner, Roger. 1996. *Out of Laos: A Story of War and Exodus, Told in Photographs*. Rancho Cordova, CA: Southeast Asian Community Resource Center.

Wilson, Valerie. 2013. "ACS Shows Depth of Native American Poverty and Different Degrees of Economic Well-Being for Asian Ethnic Groups." *Economy Policy Institute*, September 18, 2014. http://www.epi.org/blog/2013-acs-shows-depth-native-american-poverty/.

Yang Dao. 1993. *Hmong at the Turning Point*. Jean L. Blake, ed. Minneapolis: WorldBridge Associates, Ltd.

Yang, Kao Kalia. 2008. *The Latehomecomer: A Hmong Family Memoir*. Minnesota: Coffee House   Press.

Yang, Kou. 2016. *The Hmong and Their Odyssey: A Roots-Searching Journey of an American Professor*. Self-published.

———. "The Deadly, Horrible Mess We Made Still Plagues Indochina." *Modesto Bee*, April 4, 2015. http://www.modbee.com/opinion/opn-columns-blogs/community-columns/article17237951.html.

———. 2013. *Laos and Its Expatriates in the United States*. PublishAmerica.

———. 2013. "The American Experience of the Hmong: A Historical Review." In Mark Pfeifer, Monica Chiu, and Kou Yang, eds. *Diversity within Diaspora:*

Hmong Americans in the Twenty-First Century. University of Hawaii Press. http://www.uhpress.hawaii.edu/p-8939-9780824835972.aspx.

———. 2008. "Hmong American Contemporary Experience." In Ling Huping, *Emerging Voices: The Experiences of Underrepresented Asian Americans*, 410. Rutgers University Press. http://rutgerspress.rutgers.edu/acatalog/Emerging_Voices.html.

———. 2003. "Hmong Americans: A Review of Felt Needs, Problems, and Community Development." *Hmong Studies Journal* 4:1–23. http://hmongstudies.com/YangHSJ4.pdf.

———. 2002 (Winter). "The Passing of a Hmong Pioneer: Nhiavu Lobliayao (Nyiaj Vws Lauj Npliaj Yob), 1915-1999." *Hmong Studies Journal* 3. http://hmongstudies.com/HSJv3_Yang.pdf.

Yang, Xee. "A Hmong: Thriving, A Business In Millions." *Hmong Globe*, February 15, 2016. http://hmongglobe.com/a-hmong-thriving-a%E2%80%A8-business-in-millions/.

Yathotou, Soudala. (n.d.). *A War Hero of the Land of Million Elephants: Tu Ya Xaichu (1916-1961).* Self-published.

Yau, Jennifer. "The Foreign-Born Hmong in the United States." *Migration Policy Institute*, January 1, 2005. http://www.migrationpolicy.org/article/foreign-born-hmong-united-states.

Index

Page references for figures and tables are italicized.

Refugee Camp, 57, 59, 67, 126, 139n1; Nongkhai Refugee Camp, 57–59, 63

Rhino among the Elephants, 122, 144n87. *See also* Touby Lyfoung

Ritruechai, Pranet, Col., 16

roads: *road 6*, 24, 46; *road 7*, 24; *road 13*, 28

Rolling Thunder Program, 22

Rosenblatt, Lionel, ix, x, xii, xiii, xiv, xvii, 62, 63, 65n5, 65n12, *71*

Royal Lao Army, 12–14, 16, 21–27, 29–30, 32, 41n59, 41n60, 48, 50, 56, 67, 117, *127*, 129–131, 134–135

Royal Lao Family, 13

Royal Lao government, 6, 7, 13, 19–20, 24–29, 34–35, 49, 53, 78–79, 119, 122, 136, 146n106

Saen, Thai Col., 58

Sala Phoukhoun, 28

Sam Neua Town, Houaphanh Province, Laos, 120

Sananikone, Oudone, Brig. Gen., 29

Sayaboury Province, Laos, xv, 13, 18, 103, 124–126

Sayavong, Chao, Brig. Gen., 18

Secret War (Laos): Arthur Dommen, Jr., 37 Battalion 2 (Pathet Lao), 37, 116, 117; ceasefire is threatened, 28. *See also* Sala Phoukhoun; Central Intelligence Agency (CIA), 15, 16, 18, 19, 22–23, 31, 47, 49, 55, 58, 60, 73, 75–76; Cold War, 11, 14, 15, 21; Communism, 11; deceased Hmong military leaders, list of, 127–128; Geneva Accords: 1954 Geneva Accord, 7, 11, 20–21; 1962 Geneva Accord, 6, 7, 11, 21, 119; Hmong casualties during the Secret War, 26–27; Hmong colonels in the Royal Lao Army, list of, *127*–128; Hmong colonels in the SGUs aka irregular forces, list of, 127; Korean War, 11; Lao People's Liberation

Army (LPLA), 23, 116; *No Place to Run*, 26–27; North Vietnam, 7, 11, 12, 13, 16, 20, 21, 22, 23, 24, 25, 26, 28, 49, 117; NPCC (National Political Consultative Council), 27–28, 32, 35–36, 60, 77, 79, 126, 136, 146n106; Military Region I (MRI), 7, 13, *14*, 18, 21, 23, 38n5, 130; Military Region II, 13, *14*, 19, 21, 23–26, 28, 29, 31, 32, 33, 38n5, 41n53, 41n61, 46, 48–49, 55, 67, 78, 126–130; Military Region III (MRIII), 13, *14*, 21, 23–24, 26, 38n5, 128; Military Region IV (MRIV), 13, *14*, 21, 23–24, 26, 38n5, 130; Military Region V (MRV), 13, *14*, 21, 38n5, 131; Operation Momentum, 16; Pachay Battalion, 23, 37, 116–118; Pathet Lao (aka Lao Patriotic Front or Neo Lao Hak Xat), ix, 12–13, 17–20, 22–28, 31–32, 35–37, 42n79, 46, 48, 49, 52n5, 53, 55, 78–79, 115–118, 120, 136, 146n106; Pathet Lao Movement, 12, 116; Peace and National Reconciliation Agreement (1973), 28–29, 32, 35, 49, 136, 146n105; PGNU (Provisional Government of National Union), 28–29, 32, 36, ix, 79, 119; regular forces, 24, 127, 128; Royal Lao Army (RLA or FAR), 12–14, 16, 21–27, 29–30, 32, 41n59, 41n60, 48, 50, 56, 67, 117, 127, *127*, 129–131, 134–135; Secret War, xii, 2–3, 5, 7–8, 11–12, 20–24, 26–28, 37, 49–50, 53, 60, 62, 72, 107, 113–114, 129, 153; South Vietnam, ix, xi, xii, 11–12, 14, 20–22, 25–26, 28, 128, 136; 12, 14, 20, 21, 22, 25; Soviet Union, 11; Special Guerilla Units (SGU) or irregular forces, 16–18, 21–24, 26, 29, 32–33, 38n5, 47–48, 51–52, 63, 126–129; *Terms of Refuge*, 26; three factions of the

About the Author

Kou Yang is professor emeritus of Ethnic Studies, California State University, Stanislaus. He is also a former social worker and co-editor of *Diversity in Diaspora: Hmong Americans in the Twenty-First Century* (2013). Additionally, he is the author of *Laos and Its Expatriates in the Unites States* (2013) and 根连万里情依依—*Root Connection from Ten Thousand Miles* (2015), which is published in China and in Chinese.

Lightning Source UK Ltd.
Milton Keynes UK
UKHW021948131119
353477UK00005B/150/P